An understanding of our past is essential to understanding the present and planning intelligently for the future.

American Academy for Park and Recreation Administration
in Cooperation with the National Recreation and Park Association

Building Better Communities

The Story of the
NATIONAL RECREATION ASSOCIATION
(1906-1965)

Compiled and edited by
Charles E. Hartsoe

Associate Editors:
Joseph Bannon, John H. Davis, Tony A. Mobley

With editorial guidance of
Kenneth J. Smithee, Robert F. Toalson, Nathaniel Washington

Supported by a special grant from:
The National Recreation Foundation

SAGAMORE
PUBLISHING
L.L.C.

ISBN-10: 1-57167-532-9
ISBN-13: 978-1-57167-532-3

Publisher: Joseph J. Bannon, Sr.
General manager: Doug Sanders
Editor: Charles E. Hartsoe
Associate editors: Joseph J. Bannon, Sr., John H. Davis, Tony Mobley
Project manager: Andi Hake
Art director: K. Jeffrey Higgerson

Printed in the United States of America

Sagamore Publishing, L.L.C.
804 North Neil Street
Champaign, IL 61820
Phone: 1-217-359-5940
Fax: 1-217-359-5975
www.Sagamorepub.com

Library of Congress Control Number: 2006932717

For

James H. Evans, Susan Lee, Luther Gulick, Robert W. Crawford, Joseph Prendergast, Endicott Davison

and

The dedicated citizen, professional and staff leaders who made the National Recreation Association a great public service organization.

and

Hal Haskell, Earl Groves, Rosemary Evans, Wes Francis, Elly Guggenheimer, Ralph Wilson, Dean Tice, and other citizen and professional leaders who have been committed to building on the success of the NRA to insure a strong and viable public service organization, serving the recreation and park movement in America.

TABLE OF CONTENTS

Appendices

PROLOGUE

The National Recreation Association, organized in 1906 as the Playground Association of America, is the forerunner of the National Recreation and Park Association. From the beginning, the Association has been a non-profit, tax-exempt, civic and service organization.

One of the organizing meetings was held at the White House where President Theodore Roosevelt was elected Honorary President. Its early board members included some of the top social pioneers in the nation. "Building Better Communities" is a tribute to their work and an expression of gratitude for the outstanding dedication and leadership provided in the early years. As a result of their leadership, the Association has been the major institutional influence on the development of public recreation in America.

In 1906 only 41 cities reported having playgrounds, while in 1960 reports were received from 2,968 cities and counties having recreation and park programs. Today over 5,000 local governments have well established recreation and park departments and all states as well as the federal government are extensively involved in this important field.

One of the principal attributes of the National Recreation Association was its ability to recruit and retain a strong base of citizen support. Since 1906, over 200 nationally prominent men and women have served on the NRA board.

Over the years at least three former governors and two former Presidents were directly involved in the work of the National Recreation Association. Much of the success of the NRA can be attributed to the work of public-spirited citizens. In some years the Association had as many as 18,000 men and women, corporations, agencies, and foundations that made financial contributions.

As the National Recreation and Park Association looks to the future, it is both comforting and reassuring to know that it will benefit from the visionary and dedicated leaders of the National Recreation Association.

The recreation and park movement can be proud of the past century of accomplishments and can look forward to improving the quality of life for all citizens in the future.

Ronald D. Lehman

Ronald Lehman
Chairman, Board of Trustees
National Recreation and Park Association

ACKNOWLEDGMENTS

Without the assistance of many people, this story would never have been written. First, I would like to thank the associate editors and those who provided editorial assistance for the project.

A special word of appreciation is due to Richard F. Knapp, co-author of *Play for America*, for his extensive work on the early history of the Playground Association of America and its transformation into the National Recreation Association. Part of his work is used in the early chapters. Special acknowledgment is due to the late George D. Butler whose book, *Pioneers in Public Recreation,* provided background information on the early leaders of the National Recreation Association.

I am grateful for the splendid assistance given by Meredith Bridgers, Information Resources Manager for the National Recreation and Park Association and by David Klassen, Curator for the Social Welfare History Archives at the University of Minnesota. A special word of thanks is also due to Catherine Solomon for her secretarial assistance and to Celina Nickels, NRPA librarian. The staff of the Media and Resource Department of the Virginia Commonwealth University Library were very helpful throughout the project.

The National Recreation Association was very important in the lives of both my wife, Joyce, and I. Willard (Woody) Sutherland, Head of NRA's Personnel Services, recruited both of us for our first jobs working in the Philadelphia Recreation Department under Robert W. Crawford. Bob Crawford was a 1935 graduate of the National Recreation School and was a very strong and loyal supporter of NRA. Bob and his wife, Dorothy, became life-long friends and helped to shape our professional and personal philosophies. They along with Woody Sutherland and other senior leaders provided the spiritual motivation to undertake this project.

I would like to especially express my deep gratitude to Jeff Higgerson for his design and layout work and to his colleague at Johnny Design, Andi Hake, for their tireless efforts in making the project a reality.

I wish to extend my thanks to the National Recreation Foundation for their generous support in making the publication of this book possible. The associate editors join me in requesting that the income from the sale of *Building Better Communities*, be placed in a restricted fund within the American Academy for Park Recreation Administration for use on projects related to the Joseph Lee Memorial Library and Archives. Approval for the use of such restricted funds is to be made by the Executive Committee of the Academy.

Finally, Joyce, my loving wife for the past fifty years, has been a source of immense support not only for this project, but also throughout my career.

Charles E. Hartsoe

EDITORIAL TEAM

and Park Association and the American Academy of Park and Recreation Administration. Mobley is a Professor Emeritus at Indiana University as well as a member of the Joseph Lee Memorial Library and Archives Committee.

Editorial Guidance

Kenneth J. Smithee is a past-president of the NPRA and former Washington Representative of the National Recreation Association. He retired as Director of Maricopa County Recreation and Park Department in Arizona. He served active duty in the U.S. Navy during World War II.

Robert F. Toalson is past-president National Recreation and Park Association and American Academy of Park and Recreation Administration. Toalson retired as Director of the Champaign Park District in Champaign, Illinois. Bob served with the U.S. Marines during the Korean War.

Nathaniel Washington is past-president of the National Recreation and Park Association and former Commissioner of Recreation in Philadelphia, Pennsylvania. Washington also served as Superintendent of the Newark, New Jersey Recreation and Park Department. He served with both the U.S. Army and the U.S. Air Force during the Korean War.

Design and Production

K. Jeffrey Higgerson is the art director for Sports Publishing, LLC, a subsidiary company to Sagamore Publishing. In 2002, Higgerson founded Johnny Design, Inc., a freelance graphic design company. Higgerson holds a bachelor degree in art from Illinois State University, and a graphic design degree from Parkland College.

Andi C. Hake is a marketing and sales manager for Sports Publishing, LLC and does freelance work with Johnny Design, Inc. Prior to working in publishing, Hake worked for the YMCA, a non-profit service organization, for eleven years in many capacities, the longest being, program director.

INTRODUCTION

The Story of the National Recreation Association

The year 2006 marks the 100th anniversary of the creation of the National Recreation Association. The NRA has had a truly remarkable record. It helped establish and gave leadership to the public recreation movement in America. It has been a giant in the expansion of the recreation and park movement. Its predominantly citizen board and its highly trained and committed staff carried out their mission with the fervent belief that their work was improving the quality of life in America's cities and they were expanding opportunities for each citizen to live a more abundant life.

The story of the National Recreation Association which had its beginning during the urbanization of America is told through the writings and articles by board members, staff, and others, as well as, through pictures which give meaning to the story.

It begins with the following overview of NRA's impressive history, written by the late George Nesbitt, Director of Correspondence and Consultation:

> From the beginning the National Recreation Association has been a non-profit, non-political, and non-sectarian civic organization, supported by voluntary contributions. Financially, it began at zero in 1906, operating in office space donated by the Russell Sage Foundation and with a volunteer executive. By dint of hard work and wise planning the Association achieved, by 1916, an annual budget of approximately $74,000. The following figures show the growth of the expenditure budget as time passed: 1921–$121,000; 1926-$342,000; 1938–$249,000; 1946–$364,000; and 1962–$943,000. It should be noted that the 1938 figure shows a reduction. This was during the period of recovery after severe set back in the depression years.
>
> The successive changes in the name of the Association reflect the gradually broadening scope of the Association's work. The name in 1906, when the Association was founded, was The Playground Association of America. In 1911, having become more that an organization primarily interested in playgrounds, the name was changed to Playground and Recreation Association of America. In 1930, further broadening of the Association's interests and services resulted in the change to National Recreation Association.
>
> The executive and board leadership of the Association is of special interest. In more than a half-century since its founding, the Association had only three chief executives. These were: Henry S. Curtis—1906-1908; Howard Braucher—1909-1949, the first paid executive; and Joseph Prendergast, who began his work in 1950.

During the same period of time, the Association had four presidents, namely; Luther Halsey Gulick—1906-1910; Joseph Lee—1910-1937; John Huston Finley—1937-1940; and Howard Braucher—1940-1949. Robert Garrett, then Chairman of the Board, served until 1950 when he was succeeded by Otto Tod Mallery, who served until his death in December 1956. Francis W. H. Adams, after serving for one year, was succeeded by Grant Titsworth in 1958. At his death in 1960, Mr. Titsworth was succeeded by James H. Evans.

Another index reflecting the growth of the Association's field of work is that in 1906 only 41 cities reported having playgrounds, while in 1960, reports were received from 2,968 cities and counties having recreation programs and parks. The main idea in 1906 was to secure more playgrounds for small children where they could play safely, away from the hazards of street traffic. Today the program includes all kinds of recreation activity, indoor and outdoor, for every age, from the smallest child to the senior citizen.

By 1960, the National Recreation Association owned its own headquarters building in New York City, and had a staff of 94 persons, which included staff in eight regional offices. Over 2,000 recreation agencies were affiliated for service and 4,500 individuals were associated for service. There were 14,000 citizens in over 2,700 communities who contributed financially.

With the increasing consolidation of recreation and park departments throughout the county and with the growing interest in outdoor recreation, the 1960's presented NRA with new challenges and with new opportunities. Laurance S. Rockefeller summarized the challenges as follows:

We have entered a new era in this country an era where parks, recreation, and the quality of the environment have become a major item of public concern. With these developments come heavy responsibilities. So it is timely, fitting, and important that we strengthen our ties of organization and mutual cooperation. Our combined strength will be far greater than the sum of the individual components. The stakes are great for our organizations, for our professions, and for the public good.

Following several months of negotiations, the NRA Board of Trustees unanimously approved a merger proposal calling for the consolidation of the National Recreation Association with the American recreation Society, the American Institute of Park Executives and the National Conference on State Parks.

In agreeing to the merger, the NRA Board insisted that the new organization retain the NRA tax-exempt charter, thus ensuring that the new NRPA would remain a non-profit public service organization. The NRA Board also successfully insisted that the top policy board have a preponderance of citizen members. The final formula provided for a top policy board with ⅔ citizens and ⅓ professionals.

The authors of *Play for America* point out that:

> For the National Recreation Association, January 1966 indeed marked the dawn of a new era, albeit an age which had been arising within the field of parks and recreation for at least a generation. How the ideas, people, and services of the Association; its followers; its colleagues; and its related organizations were to fare after the rendezvous is another tale.

Charles E. Hartsoe

Charles E. Hartsoe
August 14, 2006

A Note to Readers

The history of the NRPA spans more than 100 years, and over those years the printed material format, language, program names, and programs themselves have changed.

The original terminology and format have been used, whenever possible, throughout this book to preserve the integrity of the content within the context that it was originally presented.

Chapter One

1906-1916
Promotion
Selling the Idea

Honorary President, Playground and Recreation Association of America, 1906-1919

"This country will not be a good place for any of us to live unless we make it a good place for all of us to live in."

Theodore Roosevelt

America's urban environment in the early 1900s

Background of an Era

Urbanization and problems related to it were among the major phenomena of late nineteenth-century America. By the last decade of the century 29 percent of all Americans lived in 448 urban areas, and 9,700,000 citizens dwelt in the 28 cities with populations of over 100,000. With this increase in urban numbers came such problems as lack of adequate sanitation and housing. Urbanization and congestion disrupted the patterns of relaxation for Americans; the new industrial society did not provide sufficient physical facilities or social organization for recreation of the masses. City governments themselves were weak and incapable as a result of several factors, including corruption and inflexible charters which did not fix clearly the axis of official responsibility. Such conditions caused English observer James Bryce to characterize American city governments in 1888 as "the one conspicuous failure of the United States."

The biggest city in America, and one which exemplified most of the problems of urbanism, then as now, was New York. A brief review of conditions in New York between 1880 and 1900 may make clear some of the many related problems faced by American cities of the era which intensified the need for recreation facilities and programs. New York had the worst tenement problem in America by 1900. Even the city's finest mansions stood side by side, but congestion was far more acute in the slums. One investigating committee found 360 people, including 40 children, living a single tenement building; the death rate for children under five there, whose play yard was 5 feet 10 inches wide and 12 steps below street level, was 325 per 1,000. New York south of Harlem had the greatest density of population in the world; one 32-acre section had 986.4 persons per acre. Many of the tenements housed 26 families in a five- to seven-story building on a lot 25 feet wide by 100 feet deep. By 1900 two-thirds of the New York's 3,400,000 people

Issac and Pat and Tony and Jack formed their friendships on the street or in the playground. Which was better?

No law could ever stop Jack from building fires. The playground could have given him a place where this could do no harm.
No potato ever tasted so good as that roasted and burned in Jack's own fire.

lived in 82,600 tenements. Closely related to the tenement house problem were perils of life in the streets and flourishing crime. With vacant lots gone, the wagon and trolley-filled streets became dangerous playgrounds. Central Park was miles away and inaccessible; only three of forty-eight boys interviewed in a downtown public school in the 1880s had ever been in the park. Public health suffered in the crowded city. Ordinary diseases easily approached epidemic proportions in the slums; and for many, malnutrition was a normal way of life. Police often disrupted harmless street play, and children drifted into gangs of delinquents.

Institutions such as schools and parks seldom adequately relieved these problems. Although a sizable number of youths worked in factories and tenements and evaded ineffective child labor legislation, the schools lacked room even for those who did try to attend. In the school year 1888-1889, 14,085 applicants were turned away for lack of facilities. With crowding on the rise in the next years proper play areas adjacent to the available schools were a luxury. The educational system was hindered by lack of an adequate compulsory attendance law and shared with the park board the common problems of shortages of money and a plethora of politics. The park board was more interested in large landscape parks, such as Central Park, than in recreation spots spread throughout the city. These landscape parks helped fulfill the desire of the upper classes for carriage drives and evening strolls but hardly touched the plight of the teeming slums.

An Organization is Born

Dr. Luther Gulick's chief contribution to the recreation movement was his primary role in establishing the Playground Association of America and his effective leadership of the Association as its first president. Unlike most of the other pioneers in recreation, he devoted only a few years of service to this field, but during this period his influence upon the recreation movement was of great significance. A successful organizer, Dr. Gulick liked to take an idea, develop it, get an organization under way, turn it over to others to carry on, then tackle another problem. Luther Gulick was a founder of the Campfire Girls and also developed the "Spirit, Mind and Body" triangle for the YMCA.

Born in Honolulu on December 14, 1865, the son of missionary parents, Luther Gulick lived as a boy in Spain, Italy, and Japan. His formal education was irregular and superficial, because of the frequent travels of his parents and his periodic severe headaches, so he was essentially a self-educated man. He enrolled as a student in Oberlin College, but soon transferred to Sargent School in Cambridge, Massachusetts, where stayed only six months. After working in the YMCA in Jackson, Michigan, for a

Luther H. Gulick, Md.

brief period, he realized the need for additional education and enrolled in the first class in medicine to be held at New York University's Medical College. The three years of study which won him an M.D. degree were said to be practically the only consistently systematic education he ever had. The fact that, in spite of his meager professional preparation for physical education and recreation Dr. Gulick achieved such a high standing in these fields, indicates that he had exceptional native ability.

Father of the Playground Movement

Joseph Lee, known as the "Father of the Playground Movement", was perhaps the most influential and most beloved of the recreation pioneers. Before the turn of the century he was working effectively to provide playgrounds in under-privileged neighborhoods. As early as 1902 Jacob Riis called Mr. Lee "the practical, common sense champion of

Joseph Lee

the boy and of his rights, in school and in home and in the playground—particularly in the playground, where the boy grows into the man". His book, *Play in Education*, in which his aim was to present a true picture of the child, and in which he demonstrated the major role of play in education, proved to be a recreation classic.

It was said that the whole course of the play movement was changed by Mr. Lee when he sent the Playground Association of America a check for $25,000 (value of $540,000 in today's economy). Certainly, as president of the National Recreation Association for more than twenty-seven years, Joseph Lee together with Howard Braucher, its executive secretary, transformed the infant association into an influential national organization whose leadership in the recreation field cannot be challenged. Mr. Lee's personal gifts and his money-raising ability were important factors that helped assure its continuous support. In addition to his generosity, his gift for writing, his exceptional understanding of recreation and its significance, and his unselfish volunteer leadership enabled him to make a permanent imprint upon the recreation movement in America.

The idea of starting a playground organization had first been suggested by Dr. Luther Halsey Gulick of New York City to Dr. Henry S. Curtis in November 1905; and it became a reality just one year later. Even before this date, steps had been taken toward providing play spaces for America's children, and Joseph Lee—fighting for playgrounds for the slum children of Boston—already had gone a long way toward earning the title, "Godfather of Play." As Clark W. Hetherington was to write in 1931, "Broadly speaking, it is safe to say that previous to 1906 America had no positive philosophy about the social or educational values of play or recreation. There were recreation activities, but no recreation ideals...."

"We do not cease playing

because we are old; we grow old because we cease playing."

Joseph Lee

FIRST SMALL GROUP of organizers included: Beulah Kennard (top left), Dr. George Kober, Commissioner H. B. F. Macfarland, Walter Hatch, Ellen Spencer Mussey, Charles Weller, Myron T. Scudder, Marie Hofer, Mary McDowell, Amelia Hofer, Dr. Luther H. Gulick, Archibald Hill, Seth T. Stewart, Mrs. Samuel Ammon, Sadie American, Dr. Henry S. Curtis (front center), and Dr. Rebecca Stoneroad.

Few individuals exerted a greater influence on the recreation movement than **Henry S. Curtis** during the first two decades of its development. The significant roles he played were as a founder of the Playground Association of America, a practitioner of organized play, a student of the recreation movement in the United States and abroad, a recreation planner, a teacher, and a prolific writer.

Born in Olivet, Michigan, in 1870, he graduated from Olivet College, then from Yale College, and in 1898 he received a Ph. D. degree from Clark University in Worcester, Massachusetts. He was appointed director of child study in the New York City schools and later served as director of school

Henry S. Curtis

playgrounds. In 1906 he became supervisor of playgrounds in Washington, D.C. He helped establish the Playground Association of America and was its first secretary and assistant treasurer. Dr. Curtis traveled extensively to study play and recreation, taught in several educational institutions, and his books were among the first to deal with practical aspects of the subject. For several years he was state director of health and physical education with the Missouri Department of Education, and years later he served as executive secretary of the Parkway Committee that promoted the Huron-Clinton (Michigan) metropolitan park system. Prior to his death on January 8, 1954 he gave much time to writing and lecturing on projects designed to make life for the aging happier and more meaningful.

Playground Association of America

Founding Meeting of Playground Association of America

The Association was founded in Washington, D.C. on April 12, 1906, the initial name being The Playground Association of America. One of the organizing meetings were held in the White House. President Theodore Roosevelt agreed to serve as Honorary President. As soon as the newspapers circulated news of the establishment of the new organization, the Association began to receive mail requests for information about how to meet the local problems involved in starting playgrounds. This was the beginning of the corre-

spondence and consultation services of the Association.

The founders had agreed that the Association should publish a magazine and conduct an annual meeting where people could discuss recreation problems. Accordingly, in April 1907, the first issue of *The Playground*, later known as *Recreation*, was published. In the same year, the first national Recreation Congress was held in Chicago, Illinois. Also, in 1907, the Association issued the first of its many special publications on recreation and undertook its first field service. The time of the first field secretary was contributed by the Russell Sage Foundation since there were no Association funds.

In September 1909 the Association employed its first full-time paid executive. In 1910 it had raised enough money to employ its first field secretary. In this same year the first service of the Association was given to normal schools, colleges and universities. This followed a study of entire field which had resulted in the publication in 1909 of the first edition of *The Normal Course in Play*. The final edition of the book was published in 1929.

Howard Braucher

First Full-time Paid Executive

Howard Braucher, more than any other individual, gave his life to the recreation movement, and its remarkable development during the first half of the twentieth century is an enduring memorial to his genius. Best known as the leading spirit of the National Recreation Association, which he served for forty years, he nevertheless played an important role in starting and guiding many other national agencies. As portrayed on a scroll designed for the board and staff of the Association after his death, "He was a social engineer for national welfare, crusader for creative play and recreation as a public responsibility, promoter of wider opportunities for the right use of leisure by adults, statesman and organizer during World War I of War Camp Community Service, selfless instrument for social progress and farseeing leader and builder of the National Recreation Association." As a recreation pioneer his name leads all the rest.

Other Early Leaders

Jane Addams

The name of **Jane Addams** in the minds of many people is associated with the field of social work, the settlement movement, the elimination of child labor, and the movement for international peace, but she played an important role in the development of playgrounds and recreation. In 1892 she established at Hull House in Chicago what was hailed as a "model playground". It was larger, had a greater variety of equipment, and served a wider range of ages than the earlier sand gardens. Because of its location at Hull House and association with its famous head worker, the playground received nationwide publicity. Miss Addams' first Hull House building contained an art gallery and its program served art, music and drama groups of children and adults.

Miss Addams was one of the first to become aware of the need for recreation in crowded city neighborhoods and of its potential value in the prevention of crime and delinquency. Her writings, especially her book, *The Spirit of Youth and the City Streets,* alerted the American people to the significance of recreation as a basic human need. She was elected second vice-president of the Playground Association of America at its organization meeting and took a vital interest in the new movement. Her conviction that recreation and social work were closely interrelated was clearly revealed in her speech, "Recreation and Social Morality" at the Play Congress in 1907.

Gustavus Town Kirby is another layman much of whose life was devoted to the promotion of recreation, especially athletics and sports. Until his death in 1956 he was a member of every American Olympic Committee since 1895 and was called "the elder statesman of amateur athletics in the United States". His active interest in recreation was demonstrated by his participation in the work of local, national, and international organizations.

Gustavus T. Kirby

Mr. Kirby was elected a member and treasurer of the Board of Directors of the Playground Association of America in 1908, and he held this office continuously until 1946, when he was named treasurer emeritus. He served on the committee which in 1910 submitted a report on the constitution and reorganization of the Association. At its annual meeting in 1911 his notable address on the subject, "The Recreation Movement – Its Possibilities and Limitations" recorded the tremendous impact of the Association on the movement during the five years of its existence.

Robert Garrett's influence upon the recreation movement in Baltimore and the nation can best be appreciated in the light of his many other interests and relationships. A leading financier, art collector and patron, founder and trustee of the Baltimore Museum of Art, for forty years a

Robert Garrett

charter trustee of Princeton University, leader in the State Council of Churches, chairman of the city's Public Improvement Commission, and active supporter of many other institutions, he deserved to be called Baltimore's first citizen. As chairman of the Mayor's Committee on Art Education, he was instrumental in obtaining a generous grant from the Carnegie Corporation, through which art appreciation programs were developed in several agencies, including the Recreation Department. A record holder in track and field at Princeton and Olympic champion in 1908, Mr. Garrett had a life-long interest in sports and the distinction of being the first lay worker to receive the R. Tait Mackenzie Award "for outstanding work in health, physical education, and recreation".

Mr. Garrett's record in Baltimore was matched by his demonstrated loyalty to the National Recreation Association, for he was first elected a member of its Board of Directors in 1910, became third vice-president in 1916, and served as its chairman from 1941 until his retirement in 1950.

Otto T. Mallery, a graduate of Princeton, an economist, and gentleman of means, devoted himself to the advancement of recreation in his home city of Philadelphia, in the United States, and throughout the world. At the time of his untimely death at the age of seventy-five, he was Chairman of

Otto T. Mallery

the Board of Directors of the National Recreation Association, Chairman Emeritus of the Philadelphia Recreation Association, and a member of the Board of the International Recreation Association.

Soon after the Playground Association of America was founded in 1906, Mr. Mallery began to play an active role in it. He served four years on its Council, was elected to its Board in 1912, and was a member the rest of his life, serving as chairman during his last six years. At the Outdoor Recreation Conference in 1924 his paper on city parks and playgrounds, in which he stressed the need to support primary recreation needs, influenced the adoption by the Conference of a resolution favorable to community recreation and the training of recreation leaders.

Mr. Mallery took a special interest in the National Recreation Congress, was helpful in the preparation of Congress programs, seldom failed to attend, and frequently served as chairman at general sessions. Few delegates enjoyed more thoroughly its play sessions and informal group activities. He was a great believer in the role of the layman in the recreation movement and said: "The ultimate strength of the National Recreation Association lies in the devotion and civic spirit of thousands of laymen and women on boards, committees, and foundations, who steadily hold the line and keep advancing it." He was in the very forefront of this group.

NRA Takes Its Services to the People

The career of **Lee F. Hanmer,** the first playground salesman, was devoted almost entirely to the field of recreation, and in his modest and kindly way he played an important part in a wide range of recreation developments. His influence was felt in many national organizations, including the Playground Association of America, and for three decades he gave generously of his time, knowledge, and ability to many agencies in New York City. Scores of cities established playgrounds and created recreation departments as a result of his visits.

Playground Drummer

Lee Hanmer had his introduction to the recreation field following his appointment in October 1907, as the first field secretary of the Playground Association of America, which had been founded the preceding year. While he worked with the Association, his salary was paid by the Russell Sage Foundation. In the pioneering position he was called by such names as "The Playground Drummer" or "A sort of Educational Missionary for Playgrounds". Although he served the Association for only two years, he made a lasting impact on the country and gave the recreation movement a tremendous send-off. The results of his field service were evident in many cities long after he visited them.

Lee F. Hanmer

Mr. Hanmer's report to the Third Recreation Congress, covering his work from September 1908 to May 1909, revealed the variety and scope of his activities. During this period he visited 52 cities in 22 different states—and this was long before the day of the jet and the taxi. He took part in 92 special conferences and public meetings, conducted exhibits at 15 conventions, distributed printed matter at 69 such gatherings, furnished lantern slides for 51 playground meetings, sent out inquiry blanks to 1,213 cities, corresponded with 114 persons about playground positions, read, filed, and recorded data from 6,577 newspaper clippings, and dictated or wrote 3,610 personal letters. Because of his work, he was probably the best-informed person as to the scope and development of the growing movement for play and recreation.

One Day of a P.R.A.A. Field Worker

Wire Received at National Office

"City interested in supervised playgrounds Need assistance Wire name and address Southern representative."

Report of Field Worker

After preliminary correspondence, arrived at Sweetwater, Texas, 15,000 population, 1:30 a.m., April 11th, by automobile from joint meeting at Dallas, Texas, of the Texas Commercial Executives Association and Southern Commercial Secretaries Association, in Company with Monte E. Owen, Manager of Board of City Development, Sweetwater, Texas, after a narrow escape from death by automobile accident.

9:00 a.m.
Appointment with Manager, City Development.

10:00 a.m.
Met with Manager, Board of City Development, City Manager, Superintendent of Schools, and President of City Planning Commission. With this committee, visited city school property and facilities, city park and golf course, all publicly owned properties and vacant areas.

12:00 a.m.
Spoke to civic luncheon club, comprised of all the leading businessmen.

1:30 p.m.
In consultation with City Manager and City Engineer, drafted map of publicly owned recreation areas and those to be acquired, starting from the school grounds already owned and distributed same within a radius of one-quarter mile area for neighborhood playgrounds and one-half mile area for adult athletic fields.

2:30 p.m.
Met with joint meeting of City Planning Commission, School Board, Mayor, City Council, Manager of Board of City Development, and City Manager and outlined proposed basis of recreation areas to be embodied in the general city plan. Also outlined method of procedure for organizing recreation department, financing and administering same. Results: request of this body that the City Commission appoint a committee of three to present a definite plan to the City Commission; secured immediate appointment of this committee.

3:30 p.m.
Met with this committee, which adopted the following plan:

1. To recommend to the City Council at its next meeting a special charter election to provide for a special recreation department, recreation board, and tax budget, patterned after the Fort Worth charter provision for a public recreation board.

2. That the plan for the acquisition and development of recreation property, submitted to the general meeting, be included in the general City Plan, utilizing the school buildings and properties, and all other public properties as community centers.

3. That pending the passage of such charter provision and the availability of fund's therefore after such election, that this committee petition the City Council to set aside, jointly with the School Board, an adequate budget for the first year's work, this budget to be under the control of the recreation board.

4. That this board employ a full-time trained Superintendent of Recreation for the City of Sweetwater and send him to the District Conference to be held at Shreveport, Louisiana, and to the short course National Recreation Training School to be held at New York.

5. That the first year's budget be a moderate one, providing for the operation of four school centers, three as neighborhood playgrounds and one as community-wide athletic and recreation field.

6. Said budget to include grading High School athletic field and other school grounds; layout of all horseshoe courts, fencing against use when not under supervision; beautification, grading, and layout of the three other centers to be used.

5:00 p.m.
Special meeting with committee to select Superintendent of Recreation.

7:00 p.m.
Interview with the man selected as Superintendent of Recreation; arranged for his attendance at District Conference and Recreation Training School.

9:00 p.m.
Meeting with Manager of Board of City Development; Manager of Public Water and Light Corporation and Manager of the Gulf Coast Refining Company to discuss the importance of industrial recreation.

11:00 p.m.
Boarded sleeper for Fort Worth.

From 9:00 a.m. to 11:00 p.m., within the short space of 14 hours, this city was helped to organize and launch a year-round community recreation program. Without the resources of the National Association and the personal help of its representative it could not have been done. Frankly, as you may have supposed, this day's work was unusual, but this is an actual report from NRA files. Some cities require weeks and months, others several years of periodic help and planning. Whatever the help needed on recreation problems, field workers of the Association were ready to respond. The above worker alone last year served 35 cities. Other similar workers served a total of 316 cities during 1929.[1]

(1) This Business of Life. 1929 Report of Playground and Recreation Association of America. pp. 3,4,5

Early Books Written by Board members and Staff

A PHILOSOPHY OF PLAY

BY
LUTHER HALSEY GULICK, M.D.

WITH A FOREWORD
BY
JOSEPH LEE

CHARLES SCRIBNER'S SONS

NEW YORK   BOSTON   CHICAGO

THE
**NORMAL COURSE
IN PLAY**

*Practical Material for Use in the Training
of Playground and Recreation Workers*

PREPARED BY THE
PLAYGROUND AND RECREATION ASSOCIATION
OF AMERICA
UNDER THE DIRECTION OF
JOSEPH LEE, PRESIDENT

REVISED AND ENLARGED

NEW YORK
A.S. BARNES AND COMPANY
1929

PLAY IN EDUCATION

BY
JOSEPH LEE

New York
THE MACMILLAN COMPANY
1915
All rights reserved

PLAY AND EDUCATION
FOR THE OPEN COUNTRY

BY
HENRY S. CURTIS

FORMER SECRETARY AND VICE PRESIDENT OF THE PLAYGROUND
ASSOCIATION OF AMERICA, AND SUPERVISOR OF THE PLAY-
GROUNDS OF WASHINGTON, D.C. LECTURER ON PUBLIC
RECREATION AND OTHER SOCIAL SUBJECTS

GINN AND COMPANY
BOSTON • NEW YORK • CHICAGO • LONDON

PLAYGROUNDS
Their Administration and Operation

NATIONAL RECREATION ASSOCIATION
EDITED BY
GEORGE D. BUTLER

NEW YORK
A.S. BARNES AND COMPANY
INCORPORATED
1936

RECREATION FOR TEACHERS
OR
THE TEACHER'S LEISURE TIME

BY
HENRY S. CURTIS, PH.D.

New York
THE MACMILLAN COMPANY
1918
All rights reserved

**Community Sports
and
Athletics**

Organization-Administration-Program

by National Recreation Association

A.S. Barnes and Company • *Established in 1838*
New York • 1949

EUROPE AT PLAY

*A Study of Recreation and
Leisure Time Activities*

———————————————

By L. H. WEIR

———————————————

NEW YORK
A.S. BARNES AND COMPANY
1937

THE
CHILD AND PLAY

BASED ON THE REPORTS OF THE
WHITE HOUSE CONFERENCE
ON CHILD HEALTH AND
PROTECTION

by
JAMES EDWARD ROGERS

DIRECTOR OF NATIONAL PHYSICAL EDUCATION SERVICE
OF THE
NATIONAL RECREATION ASSOCIATION

THE CENTURY CO.
NEW YORK   LONDON

Promoting the Need for Playgrounds

"We may either smother the divine fire of youth or we may feed it. We may either stand stupidly staring as it sinks into the intermittent blaze of folly, or we may tend it into a lambent flame, with power to make clean and bright our dingy city streets."

Jane Addams

Do you think I can grow up without a playground?

"I and my friends go walking." The answer written by thousands of city schoolgirls when asked to tell what they did out of school hours.

"Recreation is not only for the time. Recreation is forever afterward. Each person has his memory chest."

Howard S. Braucher

What will the street teach them?

"...the individual is more completely revealed in play than in any other way and conversely, play has a greater shaping power over the character and nature of man than any one other activity."

Luther H. Gulick

Even the alley has the clothesline above and the windows on either side. If the ball strikes the clothes or the windows! What shall Jack do?

"What is important in recreation is the seeing eye, the hearing ear, the hand with the touch, the voice that lifts, the face that lights-and, even more, the spirit of good fun that is within."

Howard S. Braucher

Jack lives in a city without a playground. He makes the whole city his playground. He is killed while playing on the railroad track. Who is to blame?

Sadder than death, sadder even than vice, are the figures which show that fifty to sixty per cent of the boys and girls are not even playing the street-but are merely standing about. The boy without a playground is not only father to the man with an empty dinner pail but to the man with an empty life.

Seventh National Recreation Congress

Pennsylvania Railroad

The Direct Line to Richmond
via Washington

has been selected as the

Official Route

to the

Recreation Congress

Richmond, Va.

May 6 to 10, 1913

All Tickets Good for Stop-Over in Washington

———

For full particulars, consult Ticket Agents, or apply to

OLIVER T. BOYD
Division Passenger Agent

Phone "Madison Square 7900."   263 Fifth Ave., New York City

RECREATION CONGRESS

Richmond, Virginia

May 6-10, 1913

AT A RECREATION CONGRESS

Five hundred local committees have been appointed. Enthusiastic workers not only from America but from foreign countries will be present. Will you not come?

PLAYGROUND AND RECREATION
ASSOCIATION OF AMERICA,
1 MADISON AVENUE, NEW YORK CITY

YOU ARE INVITED TO ATTEND THE

RECREATION CONGRESS

Richmond, Virginia

May 6-10, 1913

WILL YOU COME?

Playground and Recreation
Association of America,
1 Madison Avenue, New York City

Editors note: A complete list of National Recreation Congresses from 1907 through 1965 can be found in the appendix.

Messages from Presidents to the Recreation Congress

Greeting from President Taft

The White House
Washington

April 30, 1909

My dear Sir:

I greatly regret that I cannot be with you at your third annual congress at Pittsburgh, from May 10th to 14th of this year, but I write to express my most sincere sympathy in the work which your Association is doing.

I do not know anything which will contribute more to the strength and morality of that generation of boys and girls compelled to remain part of urban populations in this country, than the institution in their cities of playgrounds where their hours of leisure can be occupied by rational and healthful exercise. The advantage is twofold:

In the first place, idleness and confinement in a narrow space in the city, in houses and cellars and unventilated dark rooms, is certain to suggest and bring about pernicious occupation and create bad habits. Gambling, drinking, and other forms of vice are promoted in such a restricted mode of life.

In the second place, an opportunity for hard, earnest, and joyous play improves the health, develops the muscles, expands the lungs, and teaches the moral lessons of attention, self-restraint, courage, and patient effort.

I think every city is under the strongest obligation to its people to furnish to the children, from the time they begin to walk until they reach manhood, places within the city walls large enough and laid out in proper form for the playing of all sorts of games which are known to our boys and girls and are liked by them.

I sincerely hope that your present convention may be a success, and that the work which you have begun may go on until no city in this country is without suitable playgrounds for the children of those who but for such city assistance in this regard would be without them.

Sincerely yours,
(Signed) William H. Taft

Luther Halsey Gulick, Esquire,
President Playground Association of America,
1 Madison Avenue, New York City

April 29th, 1913

Gentlemen:

I sincerely regret that it is impossible for me to come to Richmond and to say how thoroughly I believe in the work you are doing.

It is becoming more and more evident that "life" really is "more than meat." With the enormous increase in material wealth there has not come a corresponding increase in fullness of life. Happiness and possession do not go hand in hand. By work being made increasingly scientific we have reached a sum of production sufficient for comfort. Our task now is to secure a better distribution of comfort, without weakening the springs of individual initiative and responsibility; and also to make the extra hours, over and above the time given to earning a living, productive of more and better life.

Every man and every woman should have the recreation which will enable him or her properly to attain the high purpose for which life is given. Through the whole of life, from childhood to old age, there should be opportunities for the practice of those forms of recreation which renew life, and which make for the joy of living.

Therefore I consider such work as that of our Association, in establishing the best forms of play and in guiding the expressions of recreation among our people, to be an essential factor in our national life.

Faithfully yours,
(Signed) Theodore Roosevelt.

To the Recreation Congress,
Richmond, Virginia.

Gentlemen:

I am very sorry I cannot attend your great meeting, because I have the deepest and sincerest interest in the objects it is seeking to serve. It seems to me of real consequence, morally as well as physically, that the children who are growing up, particularly in our great cities, should have spaces for play and a knowledge of how to play. Amusements they must have, and will have, good or bad, and it is certainly in the interest of the welfare of our communities that they should be assisted to obtain those amusements which are both good and refreshing.

I take genuine pleasure in thus expressing my hope that the Association may meet with the greatest encouragement and with the most complete success.

Cordially and sincerely yours,
(Signed) Woodrow Wilson.

To the Playground and Recreation Association of America.

A Heritage of Physical Fitness

In 1911 the name of the Association was changed to Playground and Recreation Association of America.

By 1912 many cities were asking how they could secure professional leaders to head up the work of new playground and recreation departments. As a result of these inquiries, the Association established a local employment service which has been serving the country ever since.

In an effort to improve the physical condition of boys and girls, the Association developed a series of graded Athletic Badge Tests for boys (1912) and for girls (1915). These tests were used very actively on playgrounds all over the United States during the 1920s and 1930s. The bronze badge awards were earned for meeting minimum standards of fitness. The award was designed specifically for PRAA by **Dr. R. Tait McKenzie,** an internationally renowned sculptor of sports figures. The fitness achievement program was promoted through schools, recreation and park departments, settlement houses, churches, and other community organizations.

R. Tait McKenzie immortalized the Golden Age of Sport in bronze. His work captured dozens of athletes, and it established him as one of America's foremost sport sculptors. Many of his pieces stand as monuments to courage and effort.

His sport sculptures, done primarily in bronze, date from 1900 and include athletic medals for the Big Ten Conference and the Amateur Athletic Union.

McKenzie was born in Almonte, Ontario, Canada, in 1867. After receiving his MD degree from McGill University in 1892, he practiced medicine until 1895. From 1896 to 1938 he taught physical education and served as an administrator in many settings, including McGill University and the University of Pennsylvania. In 1926 he became the cofounder of the American Academy of Physical Education and was elected president of that organization each year until his death in 1938.[2]

Dr. R. Tait McKenzie

(2) Kozar. pp.90, 91

20

THE ATHLETIC BADGE TEST FOR BOYS

The test for boys consisted of three levels and required the following proficiencies:

First Test
    *Pull Up (Chinning) . . . . 4 times
    Standing Board Jump . . . . 5 feet, 9 inches
    60 Yards Dash . . . . 8.3-5 seconds

Second Test
    *Pull Up (Chinning) . . . . 6 times
    Standing Board Jump . . . . 6 feet, 6 inches
    60 Yards Dash . . . . 8 seconds
    or 100 Yards Dash . . . . 14 seconds

Third Test
    *Pull Up (Chinning) . . . . 9 times
    Running High Jump . . . . 4 feet, 4 inches
    220 Yards Run . . . . 28 seconds

THE ATHLETIC BADGE TEST FOR GIRLS

The Playground and Recreation Association of America has adopted provisionally the following as standards which every girl ought to be able to attain:

First Test
    *All-up Indian Club Race . . . . 30 seconds
    Basketball throwing . . . . 2 goals, 2 minutes
    Balancing . . . . 24 feet, 2 trials

Second Test
    *All-up Indian Club Race . . . . 28 seconds
    Basketball throwing . . . . 3 goals, 2 minutes
    Balancing (bean-bag on head) . . . . 24 feet, 2 trials

*When Indian Clubs were not available, the Potato Race may be substituted:
    For First Test 140 yards, 42 seconds.
    For Second Test 140 yards, 39 seconds.

This early effort by PRAA was closely followed by a massive campaign to influence the addition of required physical education to the public school systems.

In 1929, 40,476 boys and girls in 491 cities passed the Association's progressively graded physical fitness tests.[3]

(3) P.M., April 1913, pp. 33 & P.M. May 1913, pp. 57

Raising Funds to Support The Work of PRAA

Playgrounds for a Million Children

Twenty-two million children in the United States are still without year-round playgrounds.

At least one million of these children can be given year-round playgrounds this year.

These playgrounds once established, supported by municipal funds, are, like public schools, likely to go on generation after generation.

It is better for playgrounds, like schools, to be supported by municipal funds.

Each $10,000 given to the Playground and Recreation Association of America means an investment in health, happiness and strengthened powers for the children in America whose need is urgent.

These playgrounds will not be established unless special effort is made.

To secure municipal playgrounds for one million children the help of the Playground and Recreation Association of America is needed.

That a million children may be given year-round playgrounds this year—a man prominent in public life has offered $10,000 on condition that four other men or women give the Playground and Recreation Association of America like amounts, and thus make up a fund of $50,000.

From the New York Times
February 26, 1914

No. _____ NEW YORK. December 24th 1917

COLUMBIA TRUST COMPANY I-III
FIFTH AVE. & 34TH ST.

PAY TO THE ORDER OF ____ Playground and Recreation Association of America $ 50,000
PAYABLE THROUGH NEW YORK CLEARING HOUSE.

Fifty thousand-- DOLLARS

Some Early Advertisements from Playground Magazine

ASK FOR THE BEST Playground apparatus, and the world's play authorities point to Spalding All-Steel.

BECAUSE Spalding All-Steel has for seven years defied weather and the small boy (a formidable combination you'll admit).

AND THESE MEN who have had years of satisfaction with Spalding All-Steel have put down in a little book their expert opinions of apparatus so that you might benefit by their experience.

WRITE US for a copy of the little book, as well as the new catalog of Spalding Apparatus.

This trademark
guarantees perfect satisfaction

A.G. SPALDING & BROS., Inc.
CHICOPEE, MASS.

Junglegym
~The Climbing Structur

"JUNGLEGYM" (Trade Mark Registered)
Climbing Structures are manufactured under patents
of October 23, 1923 and March 25, 1924

JUNGLEGYM TIME IS ALL THE TIME

The playground with a Junglegym is never deserted. Here is the ideal apparatus for constant all-year-round play and exercise. The children to use it must exercise.

Most playgrounds have no supervision in winter — Junglegym does not need supervision or watching.

The experience of all playgrounds that use it is, that there is no quarreling and there are no accidents. No quarreling because there are no fixed positions to acquire and hold, no moving parts to strike and interfere with another child. No accidents because the child climbs up by his own strength and can hold on by his own strength. There are bars all around to grasp with hands, arms and legs. Each person can at any time grasp or hold on to any two or more of sixteen bars.

The Children Love to Play and Exercise on Junglegym

It meets a deep-seated instinct for climbing, and is at all times absolutely safe. The average child gets but little opportunity to stretch out and hang the weight of the body from the arms. Junglegym gives this opportunity and the children who use Junglegym develop a very important set of muscles of the upper body — a muscular development that is fundamental for a real vigorous, healthy life.

Patented Oct. 23, 1923, Mar. 25, 1924.

JUNGLEGYM No. 2   "More fun for children"

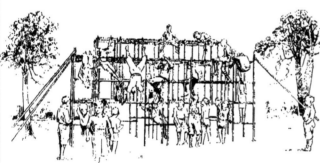

Patented Oct. 23, 1923, Mar. 25, 1924.

JUNGLEGYM No. 1   "More fun for children"
JUNGLEGYM IS THE CLIMBINGEST THING

Patented Oct. 23, 1923, Mar. 25, 1924.

JUNGLEGYM No. 6   "More fun for children"
JUNGLEGYM JUNIOR OF WOOD

Write for Complete Catalog

THE PLAYGROUND EQUIPMENT COMPANY, Inc.
82 DUANE STREET - - - - **NEW YORK, N. Y., U. S. A.**

Editor's note: The material on urbanization in chapter 1 and the background information on the War Camp Community Service in chapter 2 is from *Play For America*, co-authored by Richard F. Knapp and Charles E. Hartsoe. Background information on the early pioneers is from George Butler, *Pioneers in Public Recreation*. Full citations on both sources is contained in the bibliography in the appendix. Photos in chapter 2 are from the May 1918 and February 1919 issues of *Playground Magazine*.

Chapter Two

1916-1919

World War I

Volume XII

Number 2

—NOTICE TO READER—
When you finish reading this magazine, place a one-cent stamp on this notice, mail the magazine, and it will be placed in the hands of our soldiers or sailors destined to proceed overseas.
NO WRAPPING—NO ADDRESS
A.S.BURLESON, Postmaster General

MAY, 1918

The Playground

War Camp Community Service

Surround the Camps with Hospitality

Twenty-five Cents a Copy   Two Dollars a Year

Every town is your home town, and each day's your day. For every mother loves a soldier boy for the sake of the one away. And everywhere that the flag flies, with its red, white and blue, there are hearts like those in the old town, to welcome you.

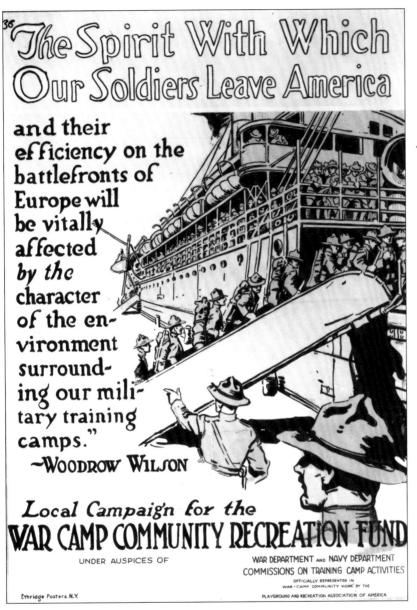

War Camp Community Service

When the United States entered World War I, the PRAA determined to provide recreation for thousands of new recruits in towns near training camps prior to movement overseas.

In 1917, at the request of the War Department, the War Camp Community Service was established. This private war service agency was built upon the Playground and Recreation Association of America and the two organizations had interlocking directorates. The World War I period was one of tremendous expansion by way of the work of War Camp Community Service. The main responsibility of WCCS was to organize the recreation forces of every community in which service men and women might expect to spend off-duty time. No government funds were available for this work. A national campaign for private funds to carry on the war work was conducted. There were intensive training institutes all over the country and special field services were developed to properly and quickly promote such activities as dramatics, music, athletics, and activities for women and girls.

War Camp Community Service gave aid such as information, lodging, and recreation in cities and towns near military bases across the nation. A major goal of WCCS was that local residents befriend servicemen.

A criterion for any activity was whether it helped soldiers feel at home in the community. Volunteers learned soldiers' interests and guided the men to clubs and churches of their choice. A soldier might obtain a bed in town for as little as 25 cents in one of hundreds of WCCS servicemen's clubs, which ranged from a few rented rooms to commodious six-story buildings. Millions of troops used WCCS information booths, went home for dinner with local families, and attended community

Hundreds of soldiers enjoy the Valentine party at the Second Baptist Church. This is one of many churches giving Saturday night socials for the men in uniform.

dances with respectable local girls. Officials of the WCCS provided soldiers on pass with tickets to entertainment of all sorts and opportunities for a variety of recreation. Citizens opened their homes to families visiting Army sons and loaned their cars to soldiers' tour groups. Committees protected transient troops against profiteering by local merchants. In one typical month WCCS events included parties for 208,000 military men; dances for 345,000; on-post entertainments for 223,000; auto rides for 32,000; singing festivals for 1,321,000; rooms for 142,000; and meals for 613,000. The employees of WCCS, of course, depended greatly on local volunteers to staff these services.

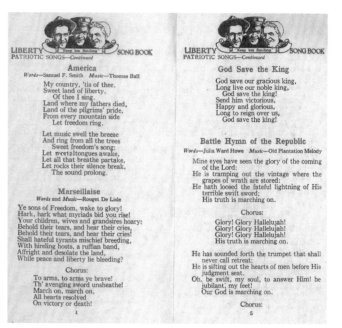

In many cases facilities and good will to support the broad WCCS program for white soldiers away from home already existed and needed merely to be coordinated and supplemented. Suitable facilities were scarce, however, for the first great masses of some 400,000 black American soldiers arriving at training camps late in 1917. Only a few churches offered hospitality to Negro troops in towns such as Petersburg, Virginia, and Chillicothe, Ohio, although thousands of blacks were in camps nearby. Although unequal treatment of blacks was a part of American life, PRAA did not, however, launch a frontal attack on cultural and legal segregation. Instead PRAA pragmatically utilized Negroes as community organizers to set up essentially the same WCCS programs for black troops as those offered to white soldiers. Many of the facilities for the black Americans were of the very best quality. For example, was the cafeteria in the WCCS club at Columbia South Carolina to which federal health officers awarded a mark of 97 for cleanliness, the highest rating then given any hotel or restaurant in the city. At its peak, WCCS operated one hundred clubs for blacks in ninety-seven communities in thirty-one states.

Some Services Provided by WCCS

The War Camp Community Service maintained offices in the Old Federal Building for the convenience of the soldiers and their visitors. An information bureau conducted by the official hostess of the War Board, were listed all available rooms for light housekeeping, rooms for transients, apartments and houses. On an average, forty families, and wives of officers, and enlisted men were placed in permanent locations every week. The number of soldiers who were sent to good homes in Des Moines when off duty was too numerous to keep track of.

Soldiers, sailors and marines from the camps and stations in and around Washington were frequently entertained at the club quarters provided by the W.C.T.U. This was one phase of the War Camp Community Service which was lining up the good club, fraternal, church and home forces of every city and town near camp centers to provide wholesome recreation and home hospitality for the men of the American Army and Navy when they were "on leave" in town.

When the officers and men of the American Army and Navy left their camps and stations and "went to town," they found good clubs, clean entertainment, wholesome recreation and home hospitality open to them through the work being done by the War Camp Community Service. Prominent Army Officers commended this work highly, and declared that it had done much to add to the morale and the efficiency of the American fighting men.

"Welcome the Soldiers." In each camp city the War Camp Community Service tried to help keep the American soldiers "fit to fight" by providing for their comfort, welfare and proper recreation when they were on leave in cities and towns near their camp centers. Of this work President Wilson said: "The spirit with which our soldiers leave America, and their efficiency on the battle fronts of Europe, will be vitally affected by the character of the environment surrounding our military camps." This picture shows soldiers from New York, Brooklyn, Boston and Springfield, Mass., as honored guests in a Washington home.

When Motor Canteens Became Necessary
In the summer of 1918, War Camp Community Service improvised a Motor Canteen Service in Washington, D.C., to help take care of the two hundred thousand extra clerks and executives doing war work there. Through such services it was possible for them to work on a half-hour luncheon schedule.

The "Sign of the Red Circle" Brings Them Here
During the time between a supper of good home-cooked food
served at a War Camp Community Service Canteen in Baltimore,
and the War Camp Community Service dance planned for the
evening, these men pass the time playing billiards in a
War Camp Community Service Club.

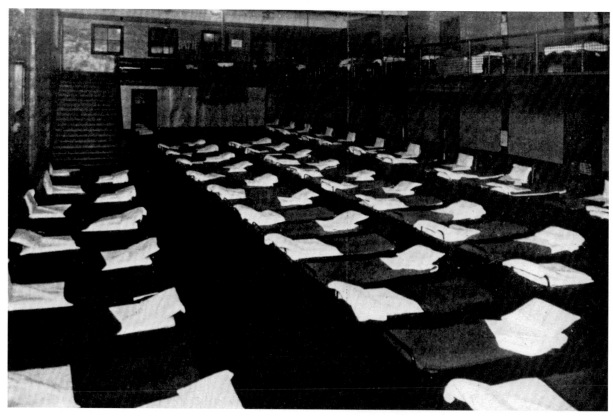

Two hundred beds-clean sheets, pillow slips, showers- fifty cents per night

A Popular Dance at the Colored Club
The clubs for colored soldiers which War Camp Community Service has been establishing throughout the country, have been popular meeting places for the colored troops and the civilians who are doing so much to entertain the soldiers. The Atlanta, Ga., club shown here is meeting a great need.

Where to Go, Eat and Sleep
These were vitally important matters to the soldier or sailor on leave in a strange city and the thousands of information booths similar to the one erected by the Baltimore War Camp community Service, which dot all the camp cities, represent a very practical service.

Scrap Books for Convalescent Soldiers-Guarantees Against Boredom
This group of workers from the Laclede Gas Light Company are making life more pleasant for the convalescent soldiers at the hospitals to whom the hours of waiting are so long, by making scrap books at the War Camp Community Service headquarters in St. Louis.

Celebrating Old Ceremonies in New Surroundings
Eight hundred Jewish soldiers attended a special Passover celebration at Atlanta, Ga. at which religious services were combined with special dinner festivities. The Jewish Welfare Board, which co-operated with War Camp Community Service, entertained three hundred soldiers in the morning; in the evening, five hundred.

U.S. Army Trucks Escort Soldiers to Matinee
In St. Louis, Missouri, as in so many other cities, War Camp Community Service arranged free theatre parties for men in uniform. On this occasion, fourteen hundred soldiers were brought from Camp Scott, twenty-eight miles distant.

Did He Write You a Letter From Here?
"In the City of Norfolk," at the Red Circle Club of War Camp Community Service, over seven hundred letters were written each day. This mail is addressed to homes all over America. Writing materials were always kept on hand in great abundance.

A Community Social in a Social Community
Churches all over the United States cooperated with War Camp Community Service in entertaining soldiers and sailors. These soldiers were guests of All Saints Episcopal Church at Atlanta, Georgia. And there were many uniforms to be seen at the regular church services.

Outdoor Sports in the Northern States
For the Soldiers stationed in camps up North, outdoor carnivals and athletic sports of every description were arranged by War Camp Community Service. These events were always anticipated with a great deal of pleasure.

Origin of the National Recreation Foundation

In 1918 the War Camp Community Service, Inc. joined six other national agencies to create the United War Work Campaign which solicited funds nation-wide to support their war effort programs. The funding campaign took place during the week of November 11 – 18, 1918, as the shooting in Europe suddenly ended. The federated campaign raised 190 million dollars of which $16 million was allocated to the War Camp Community Service. The closing off of war related problems and the reversion of the Playground and Recreation Association of America to serving the peacetime needs of a nation recovering from its war trauma created new challenges which consumed most of the War Camp Community Service funds.

However, a surplus of funds over expenditures in the amount of $1,483,518.00 was identified and placed in an investment portfolio, establishing the beginnings of what has now become the National Recreation Foundation. In the intervening period there was further corporate restructuring.

Recognizing the need for highly qualified administrators to direct the services of a growing number of public and private agencies in recreation, the National Recreation Association (formerly the Playground and Recreation Association) created the National Recreation School in 1926 to provide graduate training for recreation leaders, to train personnel in the field at the local and regional levels, and to provide field workers to assist in the development of local programs. The National Recreation School accepted 45 students each year and the first graduates were in 1927. By 1930 the Board of Trustees of the War Camp Community Service Fund recognized the practicality of transferring the assets of the Fund to its second corporate structure under the National Recreation School, Inc. The certificate of incorporation provided, among other things, that the purposes for which the school was formed were "the development in all communities through public and private agencies and by every appropriate means of play and recreation, higher and more adequate community and neighborhood expression, a better social life and better moral and social conditions, and particularly the training of workers and the carrying on of general educational work for the wise use of leisure and to promote and further any of the above purposes." By that time the fund had grown to $2,703,612.52. By 1935 the effect of the depression and the difficulty of placing trained people in suitable positions together with the emergence of recreation curricula at some universities, resulted in the discontinuance of the graduate school program. The last graduating class was in 1935.

During the 1940s and 1950s the School made certain grants to the National Recreation Association for projects that were consistent with the School's charter. By this time the School was functioning somewhat like a foundation and was hopeful of making grants to other non-profit groups. The School funded the creation of the International Recreation Association (now WLRA) in 1956.

park field. During this same period, since the National Recreation School was no longer functioning as a school, the boards of both the School and the National Recreation Association saw the desirability of formalizing the grant-making functions of the National Recreation School by establishing a separate foundation. At a special meeting of the executive committee of the National Recreation School, Inc., on October 9, 1964, the committee voted to establish a National Recreation Foundation to receive and administer the assets held by the school, subject to final approval of the School's entire Board of Trustees. The approval was granted on January 23, 1965. The National Recreation Foundation was officially incorporated on January 26, 1965 and held its first meeting on February 1, 1965. As of July 1, 1965 the Foundation accepted and received all the assets, securities and funds of the School, book value of $3,503,214.49, the market value of these assets, at that time, was actually $5,441,393.74.

The independent role of the Foundation has been stressed from its inception. The Foundation has recognized the historical role that has existed between itself and the National Recreation Association, a parent organization of NRPA. The Foundation has provided grants to the National Recreation and Park Association for the past forty years and has continually emphasized to NRPA the importance of their establishing a sound financial base so that it would not be necessary for them to seek operational funds from the Foundation.[1]

(1) Minutes National Recreation Foundation Board of Trustees meeting, October 19, 1990.

Editor's note: Since 1965, The National Recreation Foundation has approved approximately 9 million dollars in grants to the National Recreation and Park Association.

Chapter Three

1920-1929
Postwar Period
Prosperity

Heckscher Foundation Building, New York City where the National Recreation School is located.

The Attwell Story

"The Welfare of Any Segment of a Community
Should Be the Concern of All . . ."

Ernest TenEyck Attwell

I.S.

Post World War I

During this postwar period there was a rapid expansion in the number of cities organizing local recreation. Much had been learned through the experience of War Camp Community Service about the need for recreation for young people and adults, and about the techniques needed in supplying it. This period was also marked by important studies, and several new services were created by the Association.

National Physical Education Service

The National Physical Education Service was started as a division of the National Recreation Association. This came about because such a large percentage of young men examined for military service were found to be physically under par. The function of the NPES was to help secure state legislation in the several states, authorizing the employment of State Physical Education Directors and the development of much needed stronger physical programs in the schools. The work of the National Physical Education Service continued until about 1940. Its history was well outlined in the September 1938 issue of the *Journal of Health and Physical Education.*

Largely through its efforts and leadership, legislation was passed in a majority of the states, which then assigned personnel to supervise the statewide programs and to prepare syllabi for use in the schools. The way was thus paved for the employment of thousands of physical education workers and for the establishment of college curricula for the training of these workers. Over the years the National Recreation Association spent one quarter of a million dollars on the National Physical Education Service.[1]

James E. Rogers
Director of National
Physical Education Services

(1) Butler. pp.122, 1965

Bureau of Colored Work

The services of **Ernest Attwell** constituted a major contribution to the growth of the recreation movement in America, in the opinion of his associates who established the E.T. Attwell Memorial Fund in recognition of his thirty years of service with the National Recreation Association. In other tributes he was called one of the truly great men of his generation, a pioneer in the field of providing a more abundant life, an inspiration to workers in the recreation profession, and a man who left an indelible imprint upon hundreds of communities across the country. This praise was well deserved, because without doubt Mr. Attwell accomplished more than any other individual in securing more and better recreation opportunities for minority groups in this country.

Twenty-seven cities continued recreation programs for black citizens begun by War Camp Community Service. Braucher was anxious to see these modest programs succeed and wanted to broaden even further recreation possibilities for Negroes as well as all other Americans.

Ernest T. Attwell

In March, 1919 Mr. Attwell accepted an urgent request to join the staff of the National Recreation Association, which recognized the potential value to the recreation movement of his experience and demonstrated statesmanship in the field of interracial relationships. He was in charge of the Association's Bureau of Colored Work from 1920 until his death on August 5, 1949.

The primary objective of Mr. Attwell's work with the Association was, with the help of its staff, to expand the recreation opportunities, facilities, and leadership available to Negro citizens and to encourage their greater participation in wholesome recreation programs. His services were made available to communities upon request from representative local groups of responsible citizens. Mr. Attwell's success resulted from his understanding of the point of view of people of both races, his rare gift of diplomacy, his skill in resolving controversial issues, his genuine love of people, and his concern for their well being. His advice and services were constantly sought after by both white and colored authorities and agencies in dealing with problems involving community organization and action to meet the recreation needs of the colored population.

Mr. Attwell's work was successful from the beginning; and within six years almost a hundred cities had established recreation facilities for Negroes. The research director of the National Urban League considered the bureau "the one outstanding organization in the field of recreation for Negroes." Attwell was to continue this work until his death nearly three decades later.[2]

A Community Recreation School

For Workers Among Colored People

Atlanta, Georgia

June 26-July 29, 1933

1. Those now employed in a recreation department, educational system or organization functioning in promoting recreation activities, who may not have heretofore attended a training school of this type.

2. Those trained or engaged in physical education or health education work who may wish to broaden their experience.

3. Those who by possession of some special talent or experience would be particularly fitted for service to communities in this field.

For further information write to

E. T. ATTWELL, BUREAU OF COLORED WORK

NATIONAL RECREATION ASSOCIATION

315 FOURTH AVENUE

NEW YORK CITY

Mortgage Burning Ceremony, Sunday, March 19, 1944 Crispus Attucks Center, Lancaster, Pennsylvania Mr. Ernest T. Attwell (Speaking)

Recreation for Everybody—Everywhere

A good recreation program requires good leadership, and toward the end that this may be provided, recreation training courses and conferences are held. The above area conference in St. Louis, Missouri, was one of the last at which Mr. Attwell presided. With him, are members of his staff, were Grace Walker directly behind him, and James Madison, in the front row third from right. Mr. Attwell may be seen at the extreme right, third row back, while young Teneyck Attwell, 2nd, is in the immediate foreground.
(Photos: The Attwell Story)

44

Resolution

*Adopted by the Board of Directors
of the National Recreation Association*

Ernest Teneyck Attwell

That the Executive Committee of the National Recreation Association, noting with profound sorrow the death, on August 5, 1949, of Ernest TenEyck Attwell, adopt the following tribute:

Ernest T. Attwell endeared himself to members of the Board, staff and office force of the National Recreation Association, as few others have done, during his thirty years of service as a member of the national staff.

His gentle, and sometimes sly, humor was tonic to all who knew him well. As one member of the staff said, "Even after a brief visit with `E.T.` one usually comes away with a sense of refreshment of spirit and of renewed faith in the future." He had the rare ability to clear away tensions by creating a good and timely laugh.

Mr. Attwell's work carried him to every quarter of the country. He wanted to see more adequate recreation facilities and a larger number of better-trained leaders in the field of recreation. Because of their relative economic and educational status, he felt that the colored people, even more than the white, needed active help in this field. For this reason, he gave most of his time to the twin objectives of more facilities and a richer program through more and better-trained personnel for the public recreation movement, particularly as it relates to minority groups in America.

"No Room"

One is inclined to believe that patterns, like fashions, appear in cycles or, at least, repeat. Many persons in this and other nations seem to adopt the "no room" attitude when appeal is made for their acceptance of moral and spiritual forces as a guide in their lives and in their relations to others.

A great opportunity was lost by the "innkeeper" who pretended to
have "no room" that first night before Christmas.
Let us pray that we may all find room for the needed moral and spiritual stamina,
without which continuing peace, too, may pass our gates.
With this contemplation we may best enjoy
A Merry Christmas and Happiness for the New Year
Mr. and Mrs. Ernest T. Attwell and E. TenEyck Attwell 2nd
Christmas 1947

He was in constant demand to make studies for communities and neighborhoods and to submit recommendations for their guidance. He was called upon to help groups with their initial, fundamental problems of recreation organization and with the groups not yet under the support of municipal tax funds. He was frequently consulted by local groups for advice on the planning of buildings and, when the Federal Government maintained certain departments authorized to subsidize local groups in supplying a needed recreation facility, he generously and conscientiously helped a number of cities to find their way through the complicated maze of detail and eventually to realize their objectives.

Mr. Attwell was effective in organizing and conducting training institutes and conferences, making use of the other staff members and of persons from local recreation departments in building up his faculty. It is a tribute to the effectiveness of this part of his work that many of the workers found it worthwhile to attend such sessions not only in a single year, but to return in successive years.

He was frequently called in to assist with personnel problems. In fact, his last assignment, from which he had expected to go on his vacation, was in Syracuse, where he had been called to help find a qualified executive to fill an important post.

Associated at Tuskegee Institute with Booker T. Washington during the last fourteen years of the noted educator's life, Mr. Attwell reflected his leader's missionary zeal for the betterment of Negro life through practical education. Much of Mr. Washington's sound social philosophy was a part of Mr. Attwell, who, in all his work, emphasized race cooperation rather than militancy and antagonisms. Mr. Washington taught his students to "put brains and skill into the common occupations of life." Mr. Attwell encouraged men and women to put brains and skill into the profession of public recreation leadership.

To Ernest T. Attwell many leaders owe a debt of gratitude for sound educational guidance given as they prepared for recreation service.

To Ernest T. Attwell many communities will ever be thankful for sympathetic and patient help given as they strove to establish and develop their now successful recreation programs.

To Ernest T. Attwell and his memory the National Recreation Association will be bound for all time in grateful appreciation of thirty years of service well and faithfully performed.[2]

(2) The Attwell Story. National Recreation Association, 1949

Rural Training Institutes

The Association was incorporated under the laws of New York State in 1926. In 1927 a system of Rural Recreation Training Institutes was founded and several staff members of the Association conducted such institutes in all parts of the county. This work was done in close cooperation with the Extensions Service of the United States Department of Agriculture.

In 1927, Mr. William E. Harmon, who had made his own fortune in real estate, became interested both in the problem of having land set aside in real estate sub-divisions for public recreation use and in having land for recreation dedicated in perpetuity for that purpose. Cities meeting certain requirements in having space set aside for perpetual recreation use were eligible for awards meeting the land cost of a Harmon playground. Mr. Harmon worked through the Association in determining award winners.

Girls' and Womens' Activities

In 1928, the position of Katherine F. Barker Memorial Secretary for Women and Girls was created. A special contribution was made to provide the salary of such a field secretary, whose job it would be to encourage communities to give equal opportunity for recreation participation for girls and boys. In the early stages of the movement it had been felt that boys received more recreation attention then girls. This position has been maintained regularly since 1928. It has resulted in a larger number of women recreation employees in the public recreation departments of the United States.

Expanding Park Work

The decade of the 1920s was further marked by energetic efforts on the part of the Association to secure passage of liberal recreation enabling acts in several of the states. This has been a continuing function of the Association through the years.

In 1928, PRAA added a field secretary to enhance recreation for girls and women.

Lebert H. Weir

This period was also marked by important studies, and several new services were created by the Association. Two of the most important studies were the following: 1923-1924: The Camp Study – (*Camping Out – A Manual of Organized camping*, edited by L. H. Weir, 1924); and 1925-1926: The Park Study – (Parks: *A Manual of Municipal and County Parks*, edited by L. H. Weir, 1928).

Lebert Weir, tall, dignified, soft-spoken, and impressive bearing and manner, devoted forty years to service with the National Recreation association. The first field secretary to be employed by Association, he worked every state in the Union and was known and admired by park and recreation workers in every corner of the nation. Director of nation-wide studies, advisor to park and recreation departments of many states and metropolitan cities, lover of nature and the out-of-doors, and student of recreation and parks here

COUNTY PARKS

*County park*s, the latest publication of the National Recreation Association, presents a study of county park development throughout the country, gives a picture of the material and offers a wealth of practical information. Among the subjects discussed are *County Park Development, Legislation, Finance, Establishing the County Park System, Administration, Human Uses of Parks and Economic and Social Effects of County Parks.* In addiction the volume contains a bibliography, a summary of legislation relation to county parks, and a summary of facts concerning county parks development in sixty-six counties. Many illustrations, diagrams and maps add to the interest and usefulness of the book.

Price, $2.00

NATIONAL RECREATION ASSOCIATION
315 Fourth Avenue, New York City

PARKS

A MANUAL OF MUNICIPAL AND COUNTY PARKS

Compiled as a result of a nation-wide study of municipal and county parks conducted by the Playground and Recreation Association of America in co-operation with the American Institute of Park Executives at the request of the National Conference on Outdoor Recreation. The study was made possible through funds granted by the Laura Spelman Rockefeller Memorial.

EDITED BY L. H. WEIR
Director of the Study

Volume One

and abroad, he became widely recognized as the nation's foremost authority on municipal and county parks. An impressive speaker, he did much to give status and stature to the recreation movement in America.

Studies of organized camping and of municipal and county parks carried on by Mr. Weir in the 1920s were more comprehensive than any that had been conducted previously in the field of recreation. Both were made possible through grants made to the National Recreation Association by the Laura Spelman Rockefeller Memorial Fund.

Parks: A Manual of Municipal and County Parks, comprising two volumes containing 1,036 pages, was produced as a result of the park study. The publication, edited by Mr. Weir, was profusely illustrated with photographs and more that 230 plans and diagrams. Its chapters dealt with planning park systems, the design and construction of areas and facilities, types of administration, legislation, staff organization, horticulture, finance, publicity, recreation activities, and a wide range of other park topics. Immediately hailed as a monumental work, it became the authoritative source of information on park subjects.

Weir was appointed director of the Association's Park Recreation Service and for many years served as the chief liaison between park and recreation authorities. His field work, writings, and speeches were a major factor in bringing together the divergent views of many park and recreation leaders and in expediting the expanding concept of recreation as the primary function of parks.[3]

(3) Butler. pp. 109,113,119, 1965

National Recreation School

As a result of the increasing demand for professional leaders to fill the top posts in recreation departments that had been developed in recent years, the National Recreation School was started in 1926. This was a graduate professional school which was limited to forty students each year and which operated from September to May. It provided a one-year course only and the graduates were available for executive positions. There were great reductions in municipal budgets during the depression and it was decided, after operating for ten years, to discontinue the school after 1935 because executive positions could not be guaranteed to the graduates. At that time the Association turned its training facilities toward a new series of one-month institutes which were conducted in many of the large cities of the United States.[4]

NATIONAL RECREATION SCHOOL

CONDUCTED BY

THE PLAYGROUND AND RECREATION OF AMERICA

THE HECKSCHER FOUNDATION BUILDING NEW YORK CITY

Where The National Recreation School Is Located

In 1926 the PRAA established a National Recreation School to train college graduates as municipal recreation executives to fill numerous new positions created by the expansion of public recreation in the decade.

(4) R.M. September 1930

Graduate School Committee

JOHN H. FINLEY, LL.D., *Chairman*

ARTHUR T. NOREN, M.A., *Associate Director*

T. E. RIVERS, B. A., *Secretary*

•

FACULTY AND LECTURERS

R. K. Atkinson, B.A., *Director of Education*, Boys' Club Federation of America.

E. T. Attwell, *Field Director*, Bureau of Colored Work, National Recreation Association.

Lewis R, Barrett, *Superintendent of Recreation*, Newark, NJ.

Mary T. Bliven, *Principal*, Model Kindergarten, Heckscher Foundation.

Ethel Bowers, B.A., *Girls' Work Specialist*, N.R.A.

Erna Bunke, B.A., *Field Secretary*, Play in Institutions, N.R.A.

William Burdick, M.D., *Director*, Playground Athletic League, Inc., Baltimore, Maryland.

George D. Butler, B.A., Research Department, N.R.A.

Dorthy Enderis, *Director of Extension Activities*, Board of Education, Milwaukee, Wisconsin.

Charles H. English, *Executive Secretary*, Playgrounds Association of Philadelphia.

Lee H. Hanmer, Ph.D., *Director*, Recreation Department, Russell Sage Foundation.

Ernst Hermann, *Superintendent*, Playground Commission of Newton, Mass. *Director*, The Sargent School of Physical Education, Boston University School of Education.

Joseph Lee, LL.D., *President,* N.R.A.

Dr. Lois Hayden Meek, Child Development Institute, Columbia University.

Robert K. Murray, B.A., *Social Recreation Institute Worker*, National Recreation School.

Jay B. Nash, Ph.D., *Professor Physical Education and Health*, New York University.

Arthur T. Noren, B.P.E., M.A.

W. W. Pangburn, M.A. *Director*, Publicity Bureau, N.R.S.

George K. Pratt, M.D., New York City Committee for Mental Hygiene, State Charities Aid Association.

James Edward Rogers, *Director*, National Physical Education Service, N.R.A.

Edward Sanders, Ph.D., Department of Education, Colgate University, Hamilton, New York.

Miss Ina Scott, Former *Supervisor of Handcraft*, Westchester County Recreation Commission.

Captain Charles Scully, H. Norman Engleson, American Red Cross, Metropolitan Division.

Charles F. Smith, Ph.D., Columbia University.

Madeline Stevens, *Field Representative*, N.R.A.

William G. Vinal, Ph.D., *Professor of Nature Education*, School of Education, Western Reserve University.

R. S. Wallace, B.A., *Special Field Representative*, N.R.A.

L. H. Weir, *Director*, Park Recreation Service, N.R.S.

Charles Wells, M.A., *Drama Institute Worker*, N.R.S.

Eva Whiting White, B.A., *Director*, Elizabeth Peabody House, Boston, Massachusetts.

Augustus D. Zanzig, *Director*, National Music Service, N.R.S.

Representatives of Boys Clubs, Settlements, Recreation Systems, Park Departments.

Last graduating class of the NRA School, 1935. The school was established in 1926 for professional training.

In the nine years of operation, 295 students completed the curriculum. They were recruited from 118 institutions of higher learning in all parts of the country and had a wide range of interests and training, from music and drama to sports and physical education. Although time was devoted to the technicalities of most, if not all, leisure time pursuits, the main emphasis was on organization for broad approach to full community-wide participation and to the provisions and management of necessary facilities.

The impact of the National Recreation School upon the development of a professional fellowship in recreation can be seen in the following roster of its faculty and graduates who took an active part in the American Recreation Society. In a publication named *The American Recreation Society, Its Early Years*, 1937-1952, issued in 1953, the names of Lewis R. Barrett, Howard S. Braucher, E. Dana Caulkins, George E. Dickie, Dorothy Enderis, DeHart Hubbard, Ernest W. Johnson, Philip LeBoutillier, Mark A. McCloskey, Arthur T. Noren (who was the Society's first secretary), Karl B. Raymond, R.W. Robertson, W. Duncan W. Russell, and Arthur Williams are noted as among its officers and directors.

Distinguished ARS Presidents associated with the National Recreation School

V.K. Brown
Faculty
Director of Recreation,
Chicago Park District

George Hjelte
Faculty General Manager
Recreation and Park
Department,
Los Angeles, California

F.S. Mathewson
Faculty General
Superintendent Union County,
New Jersey
Park Commission

Chas. H. English
Faculty Executive
Secretary Playground and
Recreation Association
of Philadelphia

Robert W. Crawford
NRS Class of 1935
Commissioner Department of
Recreation Philadelphia,
Pennsylvania

Milo Christiansen
NRS Class of 1930
Superintendent Department of
Recreation
Washington, D.C.

Harry H. Stoops
NRS Class of 1933
California State
Recreation Commission

Playground and Recreation Association of America
Statement of Expenditure
For the year ending November 30, 1923

Field Service to Cities Whose Recreation Program Is Supported Largely by Municipal Funds .. $104,775.48

    171 such cities were given personal service in meeting their recreation problems.

Field Service to Cities Whose Recreation Program Is Supported Largely by Volunteer

Contributions $100,720.92

    93 cities were given continuous personal service in meeting their recreation problems through regular district representatives. In addition, a large number of cities were given guidance in their efforts to make their local programs more effective.

Local Employment Service $2,501.82

    151 cities were aided in meeting local personnel needs.

Correspondence and Consultation Service $18,368.70

    Approximately 16,000 requests for information and help were answered through letters, literature and office consultation. Assistance was given to 30 foreign countries.

Bureau of Special Publications $4,845.25

    Through the preparation of handbooks, pamphlets and mimeographed material for use in answering general inquires, the cost of the association's correspondences service is greatly reduced, Proceeds form sale of material help maintain the bureau.

Playground Magazine $19,772.76

    The "tool-kit" of the recreation worker. During 1923 the number of subscribers has increased 48%. A part of the cost of publication is met from receipts from subscriptions and advertising.

Year Book $1,874.81

    The annual stock taking of recreational developments in America which requires correspondence with more than 2,400 communities.

Recreation Congress and Annual Meeting $7,035.70

    Almost 600 delegates, representing 203 cities and 41 states, attended the Tenth Annual Recreation Congress. To encourage democratic control of the Association, members of the Association-approximately 14,000 in number-received notices of the annual meeting and nomination blanks.

Boys' Badges $1,045.00

    Bronze badges are awarded to boys passing the minimum physical efficiency tests issued by the Association. The tests were used last year in 38 states, one territory and two foreign countries. The number of badges awarded increased 42% in 1923.

Girls' Badges $1,200.62

> Forty states, one territory and one foreign country awarded badges to girls passing the physical efficiency tests. The number of badges awarded increased 105% in 1923.

Lantern Slides, Cuts and Photographs $908.48

> Last year 219 individuals and community groups were aided in their local educational work through the use of this material.

Special Study of Summer Camps $10,506.61

> A special gift has made possible a study of summer camps of various types, and the publication of the results of the study, which is to make available in one book the information needed to locate, equip, organize and administer summer camps in accordance with approved standards. Various associations and groups promoting and conduction summer camp work throughout the country nave expressed their appreciation of the value of such a study and suggested the need for it.

National Physical Education Service $33,438.80

> Conducts campaigns for national and state legislation for compulsory physical education. Last year the Service worked with Congress and in a number of individual states. Laws passed in 1923 in five states will affect the physical well-being of 3,000,000 children.

Total $306,994.95

From 1930 Yearbook Published by Playground and Recreation Association of America

---

The Service of the Playground and Recreation Association of America in 1929

---

316 cities in 44 states were given personal service, upon request through periodic visits of field workers.

Special recreation organizers were supplied, upon request to 228 cities.

Helped to find qualified workers for 711 recreation positions.

23,768 requests for literature or information on drama, music, and general recreation problems were handled by the Correspondence and Consultation Service and the Community Drama Service.

Published the monthly magazine, *Playground and Recreation*, the tool kit of the recreation worker.

35 states were helped with specific physical education problems by the National Physical Education Service through field visits, correspondence and consultation service.

212 cities in 32 states were represented by 539 delegates at the National Recreation Congress on "Leadership."

40,476 boys and girls in 491 cities passed the Association's progressively graded physical fitness tests.

33 graduates from 29 colleges were enrolled for the third year's graduate course in community recreation.

More than 7,000 rural leaders were given training at 78 institutes held in 34 states.

Conducted 2 short courses for advanced training of recreation workers.

Administered national contest for boys and girls in building and flying model aircraft.

1,150 people in 610 cities regularly received the recreation bulletins of the Association.

Conducted numerous research projects and published and distributed handbooks, pamphlets and other material.

A Summary of Community Recreation in 1929

Cities reporting play areas under leadership		945
New play areas opened in 1929 for the first time		1,137
Total number of separated play areas reported		13,397
Total number play areas and special facilities reported:		
Outdoor playground	7,681	
Recreation buildings	678	
Indoor recreation centers	2,341	
Athletic fields	1,709	
Baseball diamonds	4,024	
Bathing beaches	409	
Golf courses	299	
Stadiums	81	
Summer camps	115	
Swimming pools	1,010	
Tennis courts	7,960	
Total number of employed recreation workers		22,920
Total number of workers employed full time the year round		2,640
Total number of volunteer leaders		7,411
Total number of persons enrolled in training courses		14,046
Number of cities in which land was donated for recreation use		46
Bonds voted for recreation purposes in 1929		$4,501,127.26
Total expenditures reported for public recreation in 1929		$33,539,805.79

Playground and Community Recreation Statistics For 1929

No. of City	STATE AND CITY	Population	Managing Authority	Paid Workers Exclusive of Caretakers			Volunteer Workers		Expenditures Last Fiscal Year						Source of Financial Support	No. of City
				No. of Men	No. of Women	No. Employed Full Time Year Round	No. of Men	No. of Women	Land, Buildings, Permanent Equipment	Upkeep, Supplies and Incidentals	For Leadership	Other Services	Total	Total		
	ALABAMA															
1	Birmingham	290,000	Park and Recreation Board	20	52	4			7,697.87	39,239.05	19,477.34	39,613.93	59,091.27	106,028.19	M	1
2	Mobile	70,000	Recreation Department	2	15	11		6	3,500.00	3,658.29	14,558.50	240.00	14,798.50	21,956.79	M	2
3	Talladega	8,000	Improvement and Recreational Board	1	1					150.00	575.00		575.00	725.00	P	3
	ARIZONA															
4	Bisbee	20,000	Warren Mining School District	1							600.00		600.00	600.00	M	4
5	Douglas	14,000	Playground Committee	2	2					340.00	660.00		660.00	1,000.00	M	5
6	Phoenix	48,000	Parks Department										2,657.00	2,657.00	M	6
7	Tucson	26,733	Playground Commission and School Board	1					13,600.00		220.00		220.00	13,820.00	M	7
8	Yuma	8,000	Swimming Pool Commission	1	1					600.00	1,350.00	850.00	2,200.00	2,800.00	M	8
	ARKANSAS															
9	Camden	7,500	Parent Teacher Association		1					150.00	225.00		225.00	375.00	P	9
10	Crossett	3,000	Community Club	2		1				1,500.00			3,000.00	4,500.00	P	10
11	El Dorado	30,000	Playground and Recreation Association	1	1	1	25	6		975.00	3,600.00	900.00	4,500.00	5,475.00	P	11
12	Fort Smith	40,000	Parks and Playgrounds Commission	4	4				15,000.00	200.00	1,200.00	100.00	1,300.00	16,500.00	M	12
13	Little Rock	108,000	Playground Association	3	7					1,147.50	1,877.50		1,877.50	3,025.00	P	13
14	Stuttgart	7,000	Harmon Playground Committee and Board of Education	1	2		25		800.00		4,375.00		4,375.00	5,175.00	M&P	14
15	Texarkana	32,425	Playground and Recreation Association	2	12					49.25	478.75	152.00	630.75	680.00	P	15
	CALIFORNIA															
16	Alameda	42,000	Recreation Department and Municipal Golf Commission	1	6	7								129,774.00	M	16
17	Alhambra	35,000	Playground Commission and City	5	6					1,700.00	3,825.00	8,415.00	12,240.00	13,940.00	M	17
18	Anaheim	13,000	Recreation Department	2	2	1			1,963.65	2,514.89	1,913.04	3,428.39	5,341.43	9,819.97	M	18
19	Arcadia	6,000	School Board	1					5,000.00	750.00	350.00		350.00	6,100.00	M	19
20	Berkeley	85,500	Recreation Department and Board of Education	30	15				21,077.96	12,776.62	33,775.00	6,900.00	40,675.00	74,529.58	M	20
21	Burbank	25,000	Playground and Recreation Commission	7	4					1,093.22	4,007.50	310.00	4,317.50	5,410.72	M	21
22	Chico	15,000	Park and Playground Commission												M	22
23	Colton	8,500	Parent Teacher Association / City of Colton	1 / 4	1 / 1			2		3,475.93	230.00		230.00 / 3,933.87	230.00 / 7,409.80	P / M	23 / a
24	Colusa	2,750	City of Colusa											901.50	M	24
25	El Cajon	1,200	Board of City Trustees	1							373.00	237.00	610.00	610.00	M	25
26	Fresno	80,000	Playground and Recreation Department	14	15	2			1,870.00	7,269.00			28,930.00	38,069.00	M	26
27	Fullerton	12,500	Playground Commission	2	3					300.00			960.00	1,260.00	M	27
28	Glendale	80,000	Recreation Department	33	47	3								48,186.00	M	28
29	Grass Valley	4,500	Chamber of Commerce	1	1		3			500.00	1,400.00	300.00	1,700.00	2,200.00	P	29
30	Inglewood	30,000	Advisory Recreation Board	4	2				2,525.00	400.00	4,140.00	15.00	4,155.00	7,080.00	M&P	30
31	Long Beach	160,000	Playground and Recreation Commission / Park Board	126	80	25	194	454		15,000.00	106,000.00		106,000.00	121,000.00 / 77,000.00	M / M	31 / a
32	Los Angeles	1,441,730	Department of Playground and Recreation / School District / Department of Parks	140 / 116	105 / 177	90 / 1			347,954.89 / 4,190.00 / 1,548.80	209,164.75 / 105,050.00 / 29,085.98	278,113.51	187,159.14 / 120,656.67	465,272.65 / 105,050.00 / 120,656.67	1,022,392.29 / 109,240.00 / 151,291.45	M / M / M	32 / a / b
33	Los Angeles County[2]	2,200,000	Department of Recreation, Camps and Playgrounds	5	4	4			191,245.00					355,285.00	C	33
34	Merced	8,000	Rotary Club		1					150.00	360.00		360.00	510.00	C	34
35	Monrovia	14,000	Public Welfare Commission and School Board	1	1		1	1						4,543.42	M	35
36	Oakland	400,000	Recreation Department	74	77	98			81,680.00	86,245.21	77,992.15	164,237.36		245,917.36	M	36
37	Oxnard	8,000	Community Service	4	1	1				1,500.00	5,000.00	1,200.00	6,200.00	7,700.00	M&P	37
38	Pasadena	85,000	Playground Community Service / City and Park Department	16 / 4	31 / 1	4 / 5	55	275	60,678.02	3,919.96 / 24,924.66	24,779.14 / 12,450.00	95,439.27	24,779.14 / 107,889.27	28,699.10 / 193,491.35	M / a	38
39	Pomona	25,000	Park Department	4			1	2	6,968.35	204.50	1,920.00	4,298.35	6,218.35	13,391.20	M	39
40	Red Bluff	5,000	City of Red Bluff		1					178.52	480.00		480.00	658.52	M	40
41	Redlands	18,000	Park Department	2						2,799.75			2,328.50	5,128.50	M	41
42	Richmond	30,000	Park and Playground Commission	7	1	1					6,216.00		6,216.00	44,824.78	M	42
43	Riverside	30,000	Parks and Trees Department / P. T. A. Playground Commission	2	2					15.00	480.00		480.00	495.00	P / M	43 / a
44	Sacramento	109,000	Recreation Department	23	13	5			7,446.53	16,978.92	16,486.61	48,568.61	65,055.22	89,480.67	M	44
45	San Bernardino	40,000	Parent Teacher Recreation Committee	4	3					235.00	1,365.00		1,365.00	1,600.00	M&P	45
46	San Diego	163,000	Department of Playground and Recreation / Park Board	10 / 6	11	19	5	8	15,268.00	10,432.37 / 2,500.00	16,950.00	12,560.00	29,510.00	55,210.37 / 15,488.00	M / a	46
47	San Francisco	756,188	Playground Commission / Board of Park Commissioners	61 / 1	68 / 1	99			199,328.12	148,057.70	98,612.13	151,847.98	250,460.11	597,845.93 / 159,753.00	M / M	47
48	San Leandro	17,000	Recreation Department	3	3	1	1		200.00	1,044.43	3,152.00	652.00	3,804.00	5,048.43	M	48
49	San Marino	4,000	Playground Commission	1	2						1,600.00		1,600.00	1,600.00	M	49
50	Santa Ana	35,000	Board of Education and City Council	9	10				60.71	259.56	2,334.25	480.00	2,814.25	3,134.52	M	50
51	Santa Barbara	40,000	Recreation Commission	8	3									13,630.00	M	51
52	Santa Barbara County[3]	75,000	County Board of Forestry						4,971.49	444.64			4,196.75	9,612.88	C	52
53	Santa Cruz	16,500	City of Santa Cruz													53
54	Santa Monica	50,000	Community Service and Board of Education	17	21				7,343.74	3,000.00	9,652.50		9,652.50	19,996.24	M&P	54
55	Selma	4,000	Park Commission							150.00		1,000.00	1,000.00	1,050.00	M	55
56	Stockton	55,000	Recreation Department	18	10	8	12	6		15,325.73	11,699.00	10,537.00	22,236.00	37,561.73	M	56

RECREATION STATISTICS FOR 1929
the table

No. of City	Playgrounds Under Leadership: Year Round	Summer Only	School Year Only	Other Seasons Only	Total	Total Yearly or Seasonal Attendance	Recreation Buildings: Number	Total Yearly or Seasonal Attendance	Indoor Community Centers: Number	Total Yearly or Seasonal Attendance	Athletic Fields, Number	Baseball Diamonds, Number	Bathing Beaches: Number	Total Yearly or Seasonal Participation	Golf Courses 9-Hole: Number	Total Yearly or Seasonal Participation	Golf Courses 18-Hole: Number	Total Yearly or Seasonal Participation	Swimming Pool Indoor: Number	Total Yearly or Seasonal Participation	Swimming Pool Outdoor: Number	Total Yearly or Seasonal Participation	Tennis Courts: Number	Total Yearly or Seasonal Participation	Source of Information	Total No. of Different Play Areas	No. of City
1	3	41			44	338,534	2	25,245	3	13,860	1	12			1	14,974	1	59,310			3	44,162	40		R. S. Marshall and F. G. Swaim	45	1
2	8	4	10		22	275,117	2	8,460	11			5									1	16,570	5	48,000	Mrs. Carl A. Klinge	13	2
3	1	1			2	10,000						2													Judson Snead	2	3
4		2			2																				G. E. Brown		4
5		1			1	300						2											1	750	H. Glenn Penny		5
6												4									2	78,547	2		D. A. Matthews	6	6
7		1			1	7,680															1	7,680			Mrs. R. W. Bilby	1	7
8																					1				Ike Leposky		8
9		1			1	4,500						1	1										1		F. W. Whiteside		9
10		2	2		4				2			2	2										1		I. M. Barnes		10
11	3				3	25,386						1	1										2	5,167	Charles E. Osborne	4	11
12		5			5	17,500																			W. H. Vaughn		12
13		4			4	51,000						2	2						1	6,000			7	20,000	Mrs. Al. W. Kinsolving	6	13
14	2	1	1		4	3,200			2			2	1										4	1,500	L. D. Griffin	5	14
15		3			3	21,000						3	1										1		Ruth G. Bratton	3	15
16	4				4	554,491	1					4	4			1									E. J. Probst		16
17		6			6	35,098	1	1,100												1			11		Mrs. M. E. Carroll		17
18	1				1	105,384						1	1							1			4		J. W. Price		18
19					1							1	1							1			2		Drummond J. McCunn		19
20	17		6		23	572,607	5	101,241	2	14,463	4	5					2						18		Charles W. Davis	24	20
21		3			3	4,067														1			2		Lola B. Steiner		21
22													1			1				2			2		George P. Morse		22
23		1			1	4,800						1	2							1			3		Mrs. R. H. Mathews	1	23
a																			1			1			E. N. Hubbs		a
24													1							1			2		B. L. McCue		24
25																			1					Charles F. Richardson		25
26	12	4			16	711,385	5		5			4	9										20	33,774	Raymond L. Quigley	13	26
27		4			4															1					Roy B. Leach		27
28		9	17	28	54				5			2	5							1			16		Marion G. Sibley		28
29	1				1	8,000	1	8,000				1	1	1						1			2		W. E. Dick		29
30	1	5			6	116,000	1	3,500	6	40,000	6	7					1	3,500	1	500			8		Virgil Dahl		30
31	49	17			66	7,672,000	6		27		16	16	1				1						26		Charles H. Hunt		31
a															1		1								Charles H. Hunt		a
32	37				37	6,399,352	47					29	5	10000000					1	37,803	7	364,941	46		George Hjelte	48	32
a	85		112		197	4,241,840			197		41	28											92		C. L. Glenn	197	a
b													2		1		2						18		J. J. Hassett	24	b
33	2				2	16,200			1	80,000			4	1,500,000							2	30,000	2	2,000	F. E. Wadsworth	12	33
34	1				1																				C. H. Wright		34
35		1		1	2	12,000						1								1	31,421			3		C. L. Daniels and A. R. Clifton		35
36	53		16		69	2,256,545	3	160,617	11			8					1	61,433					47		R. W. Robertson	79	36
37	2	3			5	50,000	1	30,000	1			2	1												F. J. Hokin	5	37
38	12	1	8		21	534,681			1	1,885		7	5							2	43,690			58		Cecil F. Martin		38
a							4					4	5				1	67,832			2	140,000	16	120,000	G. L. Skutt		a
39	2				2								1								1	60,000	2		C. B. Wall	7	39
40				1	1	5,101						1							1						Enville C. Spaulding		4
41									1																W. T. Ferguson		41
42		3	6		9	201,600	3	6,000					3						1	140,292			5	18,200	John A. Miller		42
43																			3				3		R. C. Hendricks		43
a		1			1	6,765																			Gustavus Schneider		a
44	6			5	11	28,000	4					15	1		2	59,586					1	66,799	14		George Sim		44
45		3																							Mrs. V. B. Sands	3	45
46	11	5			16	553,503			6				5	1									14		W. A. Kearns		46
a																							8		J. G. Morley		a
47	42				42	3,781,233	20		1				11				1				2	41,115	44		Veda B. Young	43	47
a												2	17	2			2	400,000	1	120,000					B. P. Lamb		a
48	1	3			4	166,250	1						3						1	9,000				9,000	Edward V. Henley	6	48
49		1			1							1	2										4		M. O. C. Hull		49
50		7			7	24,720						2	2						1				10		L. W. Archer	4	50
51		2	6		8								2												W. H. Orion		51
52												1	2	200,000											Frank F. Dunne	14	52
53													1												S. A. Evans		53
54	4		8		12	269,880	4					6	6										7		R. E. Munsey	12	54
55																			1						E. P. Todd	1	55
56	3	8	6	2	19	247,326	2	4,117	4	11,912		7	1	45,000	1	36,000			1	6,000	1	25,000	9	30,500	B. E. Swenson	12	56

In 1908 the first of a long line of Yearbooks was published. For many years the Yearbook was issued annually. It was discontinued in the early 1960s due to the increased research activity by the federal government.

(5)1930Yearbook Published by Playground and Recreation Association of America

Chapter Four

1930-1939
Depression
and Recovery

The Great Depression created enforced leisure for millions of unemployed Americans.

The well-known picture at the top of the page showing four-year-olds enthusiastically singing "America" was taken on a San Francisco playground in 1922. Below is the same quartet—all high school students now—recently rediscovered and re-photographed in their original pose. (Photo courtesy *The Parents' Magazine* photo by Haas-Schreiner)

Leadership through the Depression Period

Depressed economic conditions in the early 1930s made a great difference in the lives of most people in the United States. There was less money to spend and in many cases there was much more time to spend because so many people were out of work. This meant that recreation was more important than ever and that recreation activities needed to be promoted which would enable people to enjoy their leisure time with the least possible expenditure of money. Because of the expanding scope of the work during this period the name was changed in 1930 to National Recreation Association, dropping the word playground. A number of special services were developed to promote participation in music, arts and crafts, nature, gardening, and other inexpensive activities. A special service on play in children's institutions was inaugurated and a special field service on school recreation.

Delegates representing two hundred and twenty-one cities in the United States, Canada, England and Bermuda were present

The PAA fostered both supervised municipal playgrounds and a stronger financial base for its work by seeking businessmen as board members. Three such directors joined Howard Braucher for a walk at Atlantic City: (left to right) Gustavus T. Kirby, Otto T. Mallery, Braucher, and Walter May.

Since the unemployment emergency, the use of public bathing beaches has increased by 130 percent.
(Courtesy Playground and Recreation Department, Los Angeles.)

Unemployment, 1929-1933

The Wall Street crash did not immediately throw millions out of work. It came late in the year, and employers hoped it was only temporary. Only as recession deepened and pessimism engulfed the nation did unemployment begin to rise steeply. By 1933, when joblessness hit its peak, the situation was truly frightening.

Average Annual Unemployment for Workers 14 years and Older

Year	Number	Percent
1929	1,550,000	3.2
1930	4,340,000	8.7
1931	8,020,000	15.9
1932	12,060,000	23.6
1933	12,830,000	24.9

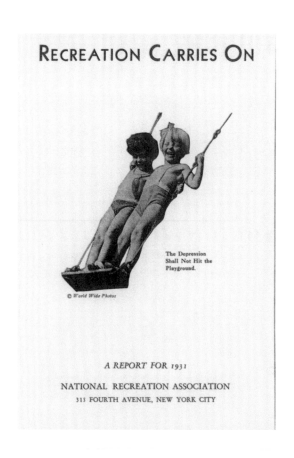

RECREATION CARRIES ON

The Depression Shall Not Hit the Playground.

© World Wide Photos

A REPORT FOR 1931

NATIONAL RECREATION ASSOCIATION
315 FOURTH AVENUE, NEW YORK CITY

Dr. L. P. Jacks Tour

The national educational effort in the field of recreation included in 1931 and 1932 arrangements for a nation-wide lecture tour of the United States by the late **Dr. L. P. Jacks** of Oxford, England. A noted scholar and philosopher, the addresses of Dr. Jacks proved to be of tremendous help, particularly in those days of depression. Dr. Jacks himself was a plain, simple man who liked to do things with his own hands. He had built his own brick house. He had made the bricks in a special kiln and had designed the house in such a way as to include the kiln as a part of the structure. Dr. Jacks wore woolen suits which had been woven from the wool by his wife. He inspired many people to try new, inexpensive and rewarding ways of using their free time.

A man is no longer master of his own time, as his forefathers were. On every side artful operators have studied his weak points and capitalized his leisure.

Lawrence P. Jacks, LL.D.

Expansion of the Performing Arts

A community symphony orchestra of 75 men and women of all ages from 18 to 70 and of a large variety of the common vocations or jobs of life played one evening at the National Recreation Congress. They played *Finlandia* by Sibelius, the Overture to *The Barber of Seville* by Rossini and the *Andante Cantabile* from a String Quartet by Tschaikowsky, and they played this fine substantial music so well that many of the recreation executives who heard them wanted to know how to establish such orchestras in their own cities or towns.

This orchestra came to the Congress from Irvington, New Jersey, through their own generosity in giving up working time to do so, and through the generosity of the Board of Commissioners who voted a special appropriation to take the members of the orchestra to Atlantic City. Many people other than the delegates to the Congress enjoyed the concert which the orchestra gave for through the courtesy of the Columbia Broadcasting System a nationwide broadcast was made possible. Preceding the broadcast, Mrs. Thomas A. Edison spoke over the radio on *The Musical Amateur* and Dr. John H. Finley discussed *Recreation for Moderns*.

Twenty-eight stations broadcast the story of recreational music as described by Mrs. Thomas A. Edison and Dr. John H. Finley.

The NRA dealt with increased free time in various ways. Lee sent British professor L.P. Jacks on a long lecture tour to stimulate education for leisure. Editor John H. Finley, long a proponent of constructive leisure became president upon Lee's death in 1937. Finley (right), a contact with President Roosevelt, introduced Mrs. Roosevelt at the Recreation Congress of 1934.

25th Anniversary Board Meeting Held In White House

Having reached its 25th birthday in 1931, the Association held its Silver Anniversary meeting in Washington, D.C. At the invitation of President Herbert Hoover one of the meetings was held in the Cabinet Room of the White House. In welcoming the group, President Hoover said, "I have followed the work of the Association for many years. It has taken a most significant and magnificent part in the whole recreational development of the country. Its work today is of increasing importance because of the growing congestion of the cities on one hand, and the increasing leisure of people on the other."

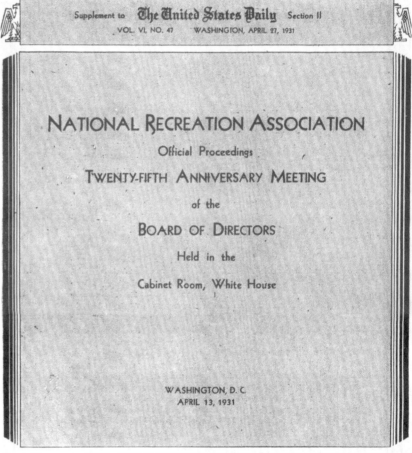

PRESIDENT HOOVER'S ADDRESS

I AM GLAD TO welcome the directors of the National Recreation Association at the White House on this occasion. The Association was organized at the White House 25 years ago, and it is a most fitting place for your twenty-fifth anniversary meeting.

I have followed the work of the Association for many years. It has taken a most significant and a magnificent part in the whole recreational development of the country. Its work today is of increasing importance because of the growing congestion of the cities on one hand, and the increasing leisure of people on the other. The whole recreational movement is one not only vital to public health, but it is vital to public welfare. The growing congestion of the cities presents constantly new problems of physical and moral and mental training of children, on one hand, and the growing leisure by shortened hours of labor presents increasing problems in provision of opportunity for proper use of increasing leisure for adults. Many less problems in government arise which concern people while they

© Underwood & Underwood.
The President

are at work than while they are at leisure. They do not often go to jail for activities when they are on their jobs. Most of our problems arise when the people are off the job. Every progress in constructive recreation for leisure time not o n l y improves health, but also morals.

The Federal Government during the period of the Association's activities and to a considerable degree due to the efforts of t h e Association, has developed in itself a great number of recreational activities. I assume that the growth of social aspects of government will increase the interest of the Government in recreational questions, and we need the assistance of the Association in directing these policies. If there is anything that we can do to cooperate with the Association in any direction you will find a most hearty welcome to the views of the Association in every section of the Government.

I wish to express to you the most profound admiration that I hold for the work of the Association and to extend to you my best wishes for its further development.

—HERBERT HOOVER

"Mr. President, we appreciate your interest in our movement," said Joseph Lee, president of the National Recreation Association. "We are grateful not for ourselves but for the children and those who have been children in this country."

Supplement to

The United States Daily

Stenographic Record of the Twenty-fifth Anniversary Meeting, Board of Directors, National Recreation Association, White House, Washington, D. C., April 13, 1931

VOL. VI. NO. 47. WASHINGTON, APRIL 27, 1931 SECTION II

Addresses of Cabinet Members and Government Representatives

Hon. Charles Francis Adams

© Underwood & Underwood.

Hon. Ray Lyman Wilbur

© Underwood & Underwood.

From
Hon. Charles Francis Adams
Secretary of the Navy

I AM very glad to take part in this. I am very glad to say thank you on behalf of the Navy. We have been walking along the same path, arm in arm, for a good while. The Navy has exactly your problem. In our hands are a very large number of youths who have got to be protected from the sort of things which wrecked the sailor man of the past. We have got to turn those boys out better citizens when we get through with them, and we found, as you know, and as everybody else has found, that recreation and athletic sports were good occupations when those boys were on shore and a very essential part of what we could do for them.

Athletic sports also give them good qualities on shipboard in the organization which they have to meet—good fellowship, team play, the right spirit, quickness and alertness—everything that they need. And athletics, with the other recreations which we can find for them on shore, and good contacts with good citizens and ladies on shore, protect them, keep their moral quality as it should be.

I want to say to you also that it pays. That isn't your first consideration, nor is it ours, but it is a fact. Our men are more efficient, they stay with us better, they come back and reenlist. They are better men, more efficient, and you are saved labor turnover, and the actual dollars and cents aspect for us, as for you, means that these things pay richly in other than moral ways.

Now, what have you done for us? Let us take an example. Our fleet had to go to New York a year or sc ago. That meant that some 45,000 men would be turned loose in the streets of that city, almost a calamity if nothing were done for them. There were plenty of friendly institutions—the Red Cross, Army and Navy Clubs, Y. M. C. A., Citizens Committees—but somebody had to put those organizations together and give them direction, and you did that. You spent time. You got these agencies together. You got a headquarters. You provided a program of what was to be done. You saw that that program was carried out. You provided an infinite number of tickets to every sort of entertainment in New York where the boys could safely go—ball games, theaters. You even provided tickets for good, safe beds, and that is a pretty useful function. You provided a banquet to which our officers could come and make good contacts with the citizens of New York. You provided an opportunity to dance, a ball for the youngsters, and they appreciate that sort of thing. It is easy enough to provide the room and music, but you provided girls to dance with and the matrons to look after them. It was a real service which we very much appreciate, and that illustrates very well what you did during the war.

Perhaps it is the best testimony of the skill with which you did your job that our officers hadn't the need of troubling their heads with it. They found that you had provided everything of that sort that could be provided and that it was well done, and, as a matter of fact, I think they discharged their minds of it. At any rate, it appears that our historical section doesn't know in detail much of what you did, but that does not mean that we didn't appreciate it. It means that it was done as well as it could be done, and it certainly means that we appreciate it.

Wherever our ships are over this country, particularly where we haven't regular headquarters, you help us and provide just this sort of thing—good recreation, good associates, the things which will protect our boys and overcome the difficulties inherent to the young, and all that we very much appreciate. And as we look forward to the future, we hope that we may continue to go on arm in arm with you gentlemen doing what we can for the welfare of youth.

\+ + +

From
Hon. Ray Lyman Wilbur
Secretary of the Interior

SOME time ago when I was in active work in the University, one of the boys got into a good deal of difficulty and the question came up of sending him away from the institution. His father came to see me and told me this story. He said: "This boy has always been something of a problem. The first day he went to school, his mother insisted that I had never done anything for him since he was born and I could at least take him to school that first day. So we walked along together, with the boy holding my hand, down the street toward the school house. Just as we came in sight of the school house, he turned to me and said, 'Daddy, when does vacation begin?' "

A good deal of our attitude toward recreation has been based on just that kind of thinking. We thought of recreation in the way that that boy thought of a vacation, as something distinct from ordinary life, as no real part of the world itself but the play part, which was insignificant. That has been more or less in our tradition in this country all the way through. But now, as the President has said, we find recreation has become a function of the National Government and of many of its branches, of the State Government, of the municipal government; it is a function associated definitely with education all the way through; it has been brought into our religious organizations not only in this land but in others, so that it has a spread such as we have never dreamed of in the past. In fact, it has become a function of life, and, like other functions in a complicated organization such as we have, it requires organization and planning. If allowed to drift, it does not accomplish its full purpose.

I look on this organization of yours as very important since it does have that need of visualizing organization not only for the governmental side but for all sides of our civilization.

The increasing importance of recreation need not be dwelt upon, but we need to dwell upon the importance of thinking ahead in recreation, planning for it, deciding what ought to be done.

The modern American city is a colossal joke on humanity. It never thought of the real basis of humanity from the biology side, or of the future, in so far as the children were concerned. That has been a pure afterthought. We have gone to work and done a lot of these things we call civilization without any regard for those who are going to carry them on, and now we have to elbow in and get in in various ways something for the children that was forced out by the processes through which we let our civilization go. And it is important to know just how that should be done and what shall be the processes of financing those changes because there must be changes. Either we must build up a great city, throw all the children out of it, make it a magnificent, big office building where the work is done, and live away from it and get methods of transportation to it, or we must clean out certain areas where the children can get a fair chance. At the present time we are killing too many of them with our method of transportation, we are destroying the opportunities for too many of them so far as nutrition and food and fresh air are concerned, and it isn't just good common sense. So that I hope you will help steer us so hat we can steer ourselves as we go ahead in the organization of our civilization—steer ourselves into waters that are better for children.

\+ + +

From
Hon. F. Trubee Davison
Assistant Secretary of War

I AM here in a dual capacity, as a director of the National Recreation Association and a representative of the War Department. On behalf of the War Department I want to make a statement regarding the work during the War of the National Recreation Association, at that time known as the Playground and Recreation Association of America.

Early in 1917 when the United States became an active participant in the World War, the War Department organized the War Department Commission on Training Camp Activities for the purpose of maintaining the highest possible morale in the army. A similar body was created later by the Navy Department and these two commissions promoted a cooperative and coordinated program. On May 5, 1917, the War Department Commission on Training Camp Activities passed the following vote:

"The Commission on Training Camp Activities asks the Playground and Recreation Association of America to be responsible for the work of stimulating and aiding communities in the neighborhood of training camps to develop and organize their association and recreational resources in such a way as to be of the greatest possible value to the officers and soldiers in the camps."

In response to this request the Association drew upon its national recreational resources and contacts and organized this war service under the name of War Camp Community Service. Early in May, 1917, the first worker was sent to organize the recreational resources in Chattanooga, Tenn., and others were rapidly recruited and assigned to other communities.

On the basis of needs and resources discovered in the earlier communities in which the work was started, plans were developed. The service steadily and rapidly enlarged until 755 communities in 47 States and two Territories were being served by War Camp Community Service, under the direction of 3,059 staff workers selected and given intensive training by the national organization. These workers multiplied themselves many times and the number of service men reached and the breath of activities promoted were made possible only by the tremendous amount of local volunteer service given. In one month local community service committees reported volunteer service from a total of 566,748 individuals throughout the country.

Perhaps one of the most widely known and best patronized phases of the War Camp Community Service program was the club service for soldiers, sailors and marines. Buildings appropriate for club use were rented, many temporary clubhouse facilities were erected, and existing club facilities were temporarily loaned for this purpose. War Camp Community Service during the war operated a total of 528 clubs, including clubs for officers and Negro service men. The clubs varied from a few rented rooms to six-story buildings. They were equipped with reading, writing and lounging rooms, shower baths, swimming pools, dormitories, cafeterias, and about every other facility that could be desired. All the clubs had checking facilities, stationery was furnished free of charge and beds could be secured by men in uniform at an average price of 35 cents per night. There were 100 clubs operated for Negro service men with Negro secretaries in charge. During the ten-month period ending October 31, 1919, more than 350,000 men per week used club facilities, 35,000 men used dormitory facilities weekly, and canteen services were provided each week for more than 126,000 men.

War Camp Community Service provided Information and Travelers' Aid Service in practically all cities which were used extensively by service men investigating the resources of the strange communities to which they were sent. This service was used extensively, also, in helping relatives of soldiers coming to the communities to visit the men before leaving for France. It was helpful in investigating and listing rooming-house accommodations for relatives and also for service men themselves at those times when dormitory accommodations proved inadequate. War Camp Community Service also provided, where necessary, additional comfort stations, rest rooms and drinking fountains for the men and their relatives.

Local War Community Service organized

Hon. F. Trubee Davison

—Photo by Keystone View Co., Inc.

Joseph Lee, LL.D.
Since 1910 President of the National Recreation Association

—Blank & Stoller, Inc.

The Board of Directors With President Hoover at the White House

Reading from left to right the above are: Otto T. Mallery, president, Philadelphia Playgrounds Association; Mrs. Charles D. Lanier, Greenwich, Conn.; F. S. Titsworth, attorney, New York City; Gustavus T. Kirby, president, Public Schools Athletic League, New York City; Joseph Lee, Boston, president of the Association; President Hoover; H. S. Braucher, secretary of the Association; Carl E. Milliken, former Governor of Maine; Mrs. Arthur G. Cummer, Jacksonville, Fla.; Austin E. Griffiths, former Justice of the Superior Court, Seattle, Wash.; Mrs. Edward W. Biddle, Carlisle, Pa.; J. C. Walsh, publisher, New York City; William C. Butterworth, president, Chamber of Commerce of the United States. Others who were present at the White House were: F. Trubee Davison, Locust Valley, N. Y., Assistant Secretary of War for Aeronautics; Dr. John H. Finley, associate editor of The New York Times; Robert Garrett, banker, Baltimore, Md.; and Frederick M. Warburg, banker, New York City.

our population need to be on the farms now—the whole manner of living of a considerable fraction of the people is being changed and there is particular need for thought as to life and recreation values.

4. The building up of towns and cities has meant less space per family indoor and less open space, sunshine outdoors.

5. There has been a rapid growth in apartment houses, which, too, means a change in habits and surroundings of life.

6. Steam heat, bath tubs, limousines, speed boats, electric ice boxes, and many other things formerly regarded as luxuries have lessened the extent to which the modern family "roughs it." Boys and girls often crave the opportunity to camp out without any modern luxuries.

7. Daylight saving in our cities has made it easier for workers to take time for recreation.

8. Luncheon clubs—Rotary, Kiwanis, Lions—give an opportunity for comradeship and recreation.

9. There has been a great revival of interest in contact with nature, in exposing the body to the sunlight, in getting out to the woods and the streams, in going to the bathing beach.

10. The purchase of summer homes by the well-to-do has made many of the water-fronts and old swimming holes no longer open to the public for swimming, fishing and skating.

11. City and regional planning each year command greater interest.

12. The building of more or less model

towns such as Radburn, Longview, demonstrates what planning can contribute to city-life values.

13. The donation of land and buildings for recreation has become an important factor in increasing recreation opportunity.

14. The growing alliance between play and education will ultimately have far-reaching effects.

15. The automobile has changed recreation habits. The aeroplane is making airports necessary for pleasure as well as for commerce. The radio changes the home recreation habits.

16. The modern mechanization of life creates a greater need for a recreation which develops the individual and makes him really care about people.

17. Because of the tremendous power which is now being put into men's hands not only mechanically but also in the way of control over the destinies of their fellow men, there is greater need of sportsmanship, need for recognition of the principle of trusteeship.

18. Because all modern operations are so complicated and depend for their success upon the cooperation of so many individuals, there is also need for men and women who have satisfaction in cooperation, who through recreation have learned the meaning of team play.

In my boyhood we were taught and we sang with zest the song "Work for the Night Is Coming," which urged us to work through the morning hours and mid springing flowers, to work even through the sunny noon, and then on through the afternoon till "the last beam fadeth, fadeth to shine no more." The only sad line was that which spoke of the coming of night "when man works no more." But now, even on the farm, there is not work enough to go around and there is on the other hand a dissipation of the free time that was once given to systematic productive labor. The economists of the world are giving their attention to the first of these problems. The second is not less important even though it has to do with the leisure periods.

In an English labor paper I once saw the estimate which shocked me when I first read it; that we sleep, on the average, 21 solid years of our lives, assuming that we live to seventy. The workingman spends 18 solid years doing his share (if he has a chance) of the world's work. He spends 3 years in eating, 1½ years in sick, and 2½ in washing, shaving and dressing. But he has after that something like 25 solid years of free time in which to make the most of himself as a man and to help his fellow men.

Arnold Bennett, who died a few days ago, once wrote a little book on how to live on 24 hours a day and mentioned especially the free time that one had to cultivate one's immortal soul. They are fortunate who find that opportunity in their hours of necessary labor. For millions it must be found (if they find it at all) in their free time—their hours of leisure.

I began 30 years ago preaching the gos-

pel of educating for the best use of leisure time. I thought that I was a voice crying in the wilderness, but I discovered after I had reached my own conclusion that Aristotle had reached the same conclusion somewhat more than 2,000 years ago. Only he went farther than I did. He said that it was the chief end of education. Invention is doing its part in reducing men's hours of labor. It remains for us to make the most of the hours of leisure, to prepare the new generations for their new freedom, the use of which "determines all." And for this trained leadership is needed. A new profession is at last being developed to give guidance in the application of this Aristotelian principle—the creative and recreative use of leisure.

"Leisure," said Aristotle, "is the principle which determines all." Our word school comes from the Greek word for leisure. The recreation leader is a person who has gained such a knowledge of the activities which men and women like to follow in their leisure and has so mastered the skills involved that he is able to show the child the delightful paths before him that he may learn for himself which paths are his paths, which paths bring him satisfaction. Then the play leader is ready to help the boy to develop the skill necessary for the complete enjoyment, for more or less complete self-expression at the chosen activity.

Such leadership in games, in handcraft, in dancing, in singing, in swimming, in story acting, in learning about nature, in caring for pets—all such leadership is for freeing the child rather than for shutting him in. It is only by discipline in learning the rules of the game that complete freedom in the game can come. The play leader is not a policeman, not a nurse, not a supervisor, but one who leads, who points the way, who shows how joy is to be found by mastering the game. Interference from others is prevented—likewise attempting feats that are impossible. The path of childhood is made safe but not too safe for real and high adventure.

In each activity leadership is different. At certain ages it is different. With adults often leadership means providing an attractive time and place and letting the group itself do the rest without interference from any other groups.

Leadership in music is different from leadership in drama. The contagious enthusiasm of the nature study life is again something different. In all recreation activities the need is not for driving, directing, supervising, but for leading—the come hither spirit, the lighting of the way.

The Boston sandpits 1885-1887, worked out play leadership. Always the play movement in America has stood for play leadership—has been an educational movement. Twenty-five years ago in 1906 there were but a few play leaders—we do not even know how many, but we do know they were found in only 41 cities and in some of those cities only in July and August. Today 2,640 persons serve as play leaders and recreation workers—on full time.

Many colleges give undergraduate courses in recreation and the National

Recreation Association has a Graduate School which develops about 40 students each year for positions as recreation executives.

The recreation movement has created something which did not exist before—except perhaps that certain Indian tribes had their Delight Makers—a group of people to help children be children in the fullest sense of the word, to get the most of joyful, healthful childhood activity and to grow into the fullest and richest possible manhood and womanhood.

Of course there is much of knowledge and experience that goes into the planning of gymnasiums, swimming pools, athletic fields, parks, bathing beaches, skating ponds if they were to be satisfactory. Recreation leaders study to make themselves Masters of Arts of Recreational Living. We cannot know yet all that will come out of this new profession.

A mere statement of what is included in local year-round recreation program shows the sweep of the movement in which this new profession is engaged.

I. Community Recreation provides for all age groups:
Small children.
Boys.
Girls.
Young Women.
Young Men.
Adult Women.
Adult Men.

Dr. John H. Finley

—Wide World Photo.

Frederick M. Warburg

Carl E. Milliken	Mrs. Arthur G. Cummer	William Butterworth

—Community Service Photo.   —Blank & Stoller, Inc.

Officers and Directors of the National Recreation Association

Officers

Joseph Lee, President.
John H. Finley, First Vice President.
John G. Winant, Second Vice President.
Robert Garrett, Third Vice President.
Gustavus T. Kirby, Treasurer.
Howard S. Braucher, Secretary.

Directors

Mrs. Edward W. Biddle, Carlisle, Pa.
William Butterworth, Moline Ill.
Clarence M. Clark, Philadelphia, Pa.
Henry L. Corbett, Portland, Oreg.
Mrs. Arthur G. Cummer, Jacksonville, Fla.
F. Trubee Davison, Locust Valley, L. I., N. Y.

John H. Finley, New York, N. Y.
Mrs. Thomas A. Edison, West Orange, N. J.
Hugh Frayne, New York, N. Y.
Robert Garrett, Baltimore, Md.
Mrs. Charles A. Goodwin, Hartford, Conn.
Austin E. Griffiths, Seattle, Wash.
William Hale Harkness, New York, N. Y.
Charles Hayden, New York, N. Y.
Mrs. Charles V. Hickox, Michigan City, Ind.
Mrs. Francis de Lacy Hyde, Plainfield N. J.
Gustavus T. Kirby, New York, N. Y.
H. McK. Landon, Indianapolis, Ind.
Mrs. Charles D. Lanier, Greenwich, Conn.

Robert Lassiter, Charlotte, N. C.
Joseph Lee, Boston, Mass.
Edward E. Loomis, New York, N. Y.
J. H. McCurdy, Springfield, Mass.
Otto T. Mallery, Philadelphia, Pa.
Walter A. May, Pittsburgh, Pa.
Carl E. Milliken, Augusta, Me.
Miss Ellen Scripps, La Jolla, Calif.
Harold H. Swift, Chicago, Ill.
Frederick S. Titsworth, New York, N. Y.
Mrs. James W. Wadsworth Jr., Washington, D. C.
J. C. Walsh, New York, N. Y.
John G. Winant, Concord, N. H.
Mrs. William H. Woodin Jr., Plainfield, N. J.
Frederick M. Warburg, New York, N. Y.

Honorary Members

David Alexander, Akron, Ohio.
Ray Stannard Baker, Amherst, Mass.
Mrs. George D. Barron, Rye, N. Y.
A. T. Bell, Atlantic City, N. J.
Mrs. Edward C. Bench, Englewood, N. J.
Union N. Bethell, Montclair, N. J.
Nathan D. Bill, Springfield, Mass.
George F. Booth, Worcester, Mass.
Miss Anna H. Borden, Fall River, Mass.
John R. Brinley, Morristown, N. J.
Richard Evelyn Byrd, Winchester, Va.
Frederick P. Cabot, Boston, Mass.
G. Herbert Carter, Huntington, N. Y.
Mrs. Julian C. Chase, Tarrytown, N. Y.
Mrs. George Edwards Clement, Peterborough, N. H.
Mrs. Walter S. Comly, Port Chester N. Y.
Charles M. Cox, Boston, Mass.
Winthrop M. Crane Jr., Dalton, Mass.
Z. Marshall Crane, Dalton, Mass.
Julian W. Curtiss, Greenwich, Conn.
Henry L. deForest, Plainfield, N. J.
Mrs. John W. Donaldson, Irvington-on-Hudson, N. Y.
Clyde Doyle, Long Beach, Calif.
Mrs. S. S. Drury, Concord, N. H.
Mrs. A. Felix du Pont, Wilmington, Del.
Mrs. Coleman du Pont, Wilmington, Del.
Mrs. E. P. Earle, Montclair, N. J.
Mrs. D E. F. Easton, San Francisco, Calif.
Mrs. Paul FitzSimons, Newport R. I.
Mrs. Irving Fisher, New Haven, Conn.
Mrs. Ralph E. Forbes, Milton, Mass
Robert A. Gardner, Chicago, Ill.
Charles C. George, Omaha, Neb.
Charles W. Gilkey, Chicago, Ill.
Thomas K. Glenn, Atlanta, Ga.
Mrs. Charles C. Glover Jr., Washington, D. C.
C. M. Goethe, Sacramento, Calif.
Rex B. Goodcell, Los Angeles, Calif.

Charles W. Gordon, St. Paul, Minn.
William Green, Washington, D. C.
Franklin T. Griffith, Portland, Oreg.
E. K. Hall, Hanover, N. H.
Mrs. Norman Harrower, Fitchburg, Mass.
Mrs. S. H. Hartshorn, Short Hills, N. J.
Miss Ellen R. Hathaway, New Bedford, Mass.
Mrs. F. R. Hazard, Syracuse, N. Y.
Miss Dorothy Heroy, Stamford, Conn.
Mrs. William G. Hibbard, Winnetka, Ill.
Mrs. Francis L. Higginson, Boston, Mass.
Mrs. Albert W. Holmes, New Bedford, Mass.
Mrs. Howard R. Ives, Portland, Me.
H. H. Jacobs, Milwaukee, Wis.
Mrs. Ernest Kanzler, Detroit, Mich.
Miss Helen Keller, Forest Hills, N. Y.
John Harvey Kellogg, Battle Creek, Mich.
Mrs. William Kent, Kentfield, Calif.
C. S. Weston, Scranton, Pa.
Willard V. King, New York, N. Y.
Tully C. Knoles, Stockton, Calif.
A. H. Lance, Kenosha, Wis.
William Lawrence, Boston, Mass.
Philip LeBoutillier, New York, N. Y.
Miss Alice Lee, San Diego, Calif.
Lucius N. Littauer, New Rochelle, N. Y.
Seth Low, New York, N. Y.
Mrs. Louis C. Madeira, Philadelphia, Pa.
Samuel Mather, Cleveland, Ohio.
Henry L. Mayer, San Francisco, Calif.
John W. McClure, Memphis, Tenn.
Mrs. F. O. McColloch, Los Angeles, Calif.
Mrs. Medill McCormick, Chicago, Ill.
Sumner T. McKnight, Minneapolis, Minn.
Charles G. Middleton, Louisville, Ky.
Charles M. Miller, Mt. Vernon, N. Y.
Mrs. Ogden L. Mills, New York, N. Y.

John F. Moors, Boston, Mass.
Charles Nagel, St. Louis, Mo.
Roy Benton Naylor, Wheeling, W. Va.
F. Gordon Osler, Toronto, Canada.
Mary Parsons, Lenox, Mass.
Arthur Pound, Slingerlands, N. Y.
Herbert L. Pratt, New York, N. Y.
William Cooper Procter, Cincinnati, Ohio.
Frederick H. Rike, Dayton, Ohio.
Mrs. R. Sanford Riley, Worcester, Mass.
Mrs. Theodore Douglas Robinson, Mohawk, N. Y.
Mrs Willoughby Rodman, Los Angeles, Calif.
Hon. Franklin D. Roosevelt, Governor of New York State.
Hon. Theodore Roosevelt, Governor General of Porto Rico.
David H. Ross, Conshohocken, Pa.
Mrs. Henry H. Sanger, Detroit, Mich.
Charles Meigs Schenck, Denver, Colo.
Benjamin Jay Shove, Syracuse, N. Y.
John D. Spencer, Salt Lake City, Utah.
M. Lyle Spencer, Seattle, Wash.
Alfred J. Sporborg, Albany, N. Y.
A. A. Sprague, Chicago, Ill.
Robert Gordon Sproul, Berkeley, Calif.
Mrs. A. J. Stallings, New Orleans, La.
Florence M. Sterling, Houston, Texas.
Mrs. S. Emlen Stokes, Moorestown, N. J.
Lorado Taft, Chicago, Ill.
Benjamin Thaw, Pittsburg, Pa.
W. E. Upjohn, Kalamazoo, Mich.
Henry van Dyke, D. D., LL.D., D. C. L., Oxon, Princeton, N. J.
W. L. Ward, Port Chester, N. Y.
Ridley Watts, Morristown, N. J.
Dwight C. Wheeler, Bridgeport, Conn.
Mrs. Thomas G. Winter, Minneapolis, Minn.
Stephen S. Wise, Ph.D., LL.D., New York, N. Y.
Henry Young, Newark, N. J.

Index to Contents

First International Recreation Congress

(Held in conjunction with the 1932 Olympic Games)

CONGRESS FEATURES

International play night and social dancing. All delegates participating. Monday night, July 25.

A special tea for all delegates given by the Directorial Staff of the Department of Playground and Recreation, City of Los Angeles.

Four afternoons free for tours of Los Angeles and vicinity to see parks, playgrounds, beaches, community activities and facilities, as well as other points of interest, including moving picture studios, and estates, the famous California orange belt, and camps, also for golf and swimming at municipal courses and beaches.

An international exhibit showing recreation around the world.

Olympic Games open the day after the Congress closes.

CONGRESS FEATURES

A picturesque water pageant in the new Olympic Pool put on by 600 children from the Los Angeles Playground and Recreation Department. Audience of 10,000 being planned for. Saturday night, July 23.

A music demonstration in the beautiful municipal Greek theatre including massed bands, community symphony orchestra, civic chorus of 1000 voices, Negro spirituals, and group singing by the 5000 spectators. Sunday night, July 24.

An international Play Day at the Rose Bowl, Pasadena, depicting the traditional games and sports of various nations. Staged by foreign groups. Wednesday night, July 27.

An old-fashioned Spanish Barbecue at Pasadena's nationally known Brookside Park. Wednesday night, July 27.

Dr. Karl Ritter von Halt, attorney, banker and sportsman of Germany, will discuss the subject of Family Play.

G.D. Sondhi, latest member of the advisory Committee, is connected with the Indian Educational Service at Lahore.

GENERAL SESSIONS

Count de Baillet Latour, president of the International Olympic Committee, Belgium
Response (to Address of Welcome) for Visiting Delegates.

Sir Harold Bowden, Chairman and Managing Director of the Raleigh Cycle Co., England
Use and Abuse of Leisure.

Noel Curtis-Bennett, C.V.O., Honorary Treasurer, The National Playing Fields Association, England
Contribution of Sport and Recreation to British Life and Character.

Walter F. Dexter, President of Whittier College, Whittier, California
Recreation and Citizenship.

J. Sigfrid Edstrom, Managing Director, Swedish General Electric Company, Sweden
Recreation in the Scandanavian Countries.

Dr. Joseph Gruss, President of the Czechoslavak Olympic Committee, Czechoslavak
Sokols in Czechoslovakia.

Gustavus T. Kirby, Treasurer of the National Recreation Association, New York City

Dr. Seiichi Kishi, President, Japan Amateur Athletic Association, Japan
Recreation in Japan.

Dr. Rufus von Kleinsmid, President, University of Southern California, Los Angeles, California.
Possibilities of Recreation in Promoting International Good Will.

Dr. Theodor Lewald, President, German National Commission for Physical Training, Germany
How Does Germany Justify the Large Public Expenditure for Sport Facilities?

Alderman E. S. Marks, Australia
Recreation in Australia and Games Played There.

Dr. Robert Millikan, Director, Norman Bridge Laboratory of Physics and Chairman, Executive Council, California Institute of Technology, Pasadena, California
The New World of Leisure as Viewed by a Scientist.

Dr. F. M. de Molnar, International Commissioner, Hungarian Boys Scouts Association, Hungary
Contribution of Scouting to Recreation in Europe.

OCTOBER 1935

A Message To the Recreation Congress

You know how heartily I believe in the adequate provision of opportunities for recreation, and how through the years I have cared for the work of the National Recreation Association. I rejoice in the growing public interest in this subject as evidenced by the fine facilities now being provided by the government—federal, state, loca—for the enjoyment of the people.

Of even greater importance in my opinion is the definite recognition that the field of recreation is a fruitful one for those desiring to render notable public service. I earnestly hope that in each of our local communities men and women interested in the public welfare will give increasing thought and time to this great democratic method of providing recreation for all the people untrammeled by any motive except that of living fully and richly.

Please express to the recreation leaders gathered together at Chicago and to all those serving in the recreation movement the appreciation of the federal government for their cooperation and loyal service in carrying forward recreation projects of the various emergency agencies.

I believe the exchange of information and ideas among the leaders at the National Recreation Congress will result in carrying forward the recreation movement with the same high enthusiasm which has always characterized your group.

Franklin D. Roosevelt

Professional Organization Formed

By the mid-1930s municipal executives had already formed several local and state organizations of recreation administrators, such as the Public Recreation Association of New Jersey which had grown in four years from a group begun in a single county. There were also such groups as a regional Eastern Association of Recreation Workers and an organization alumni group of the National Recreation School.

The recreation executives met in May 1937 at the annual congress and provisionally organized their new society. They elected V. K. Brown of Chicago as chairman of a national committee of sixteen of their peers charged with developing plans for permanent organization at the congress the following year. The group, which was later to be the American Recreation Society (ARS), was officially independent of, but still connected with the NRA.

V. K. Brown was elected the first president of the Society of Recreation Workers of America, later the American Recreation Society, because of the part he played in getting it established. Ten years later he again served as its president. The park workers of America also recognized his leadership qualities and elected him president of the American Institute of Park Executives—the first "recreation" leader to receive this distinction.

Virgil K. Brown

Joseph Lee

Joseph Lee

In June 1910—twenty-five years ago—Joseph Lee accepted election as president of the Playground Association of America. For all but four years of the Association's history Joseph Lee has been its president and its leader.

Play and recreation in 1910 were no new interest to him. Before the Association was organized Joseph Lee had worked many years in this field. As a boy he had known what play meant in his own life and the life of his family. He had read and studied Froebel's books. He was interested in progressive education before there was any such thing. Not only had Joseph Lee paid for apparatus and equipment and the salaries of the play leaders for the Boston Columbus Avenue Playground in the early days. For years he had carefully observed the play of children of all ages. With a lively memory of his own play days he had recorded what he had observed.

At the time Joseph Lee graduated from Harvard every man was expected to go into business or enter a profession but he did not need to make money and he was not interested in doing so. In England a man could enter public service with entire self-respect. In America a man could go to live in the slums, but to devote the major part of one's time to play and recreation and to think of this not in terms of the poor alone but of every one, was then hard to understand. Courage was required forty years ago to devote oneself to play.

Joseph Lee was a courageous pioneer with vision to see a great need and with readiness to leave beaten paths. While Joseph Lee worked in Boston and New England others were working in other cities and many persons and many influences were united in the organization that later became the National Recreation Association. Many of these persons were professional workers, but Joseph Lee as a layman, a public-spirited citizen, an educator, a thinker, with many many fields open to him, has not only for the twenty-fine years of his presidency but before, dedicated himself specially to the recreation movement. Year in and year out, in good seasons and in bad, in war and in peace, without thought for himself, Joseph Lee gave himself and his influence to the national recreation movement. No task was too little, or too big, or too demanding. No job, even that of money raising, was too disagreeable.

Fortunately Joseph Lee was in position to contribute his time to pay his own expenses as he made trips in behalf of the movement, and of course with his interest went his own financial support. But most of all the Association and the movement are indebted to him for his philosophy, his understanding of fundamental principles, his readiness always to think in terms of quality rather than quantity, to stand resolutely for what he thought really mattered. His presidency these twenty-five years has been no casual attendance at occasional meetings, but a vital continuous leadership.

Few could know the extent to which his humor, his keen mind, his knowledge of human nature, his wise administrative judgments have helped mould the national movement day by day for a generation. There is a spirit and a tradition which he has had a large part in building up. The movement of course is the result of the work of many thousands of workers in more than a thousand communities throughout the county. Its strength has been in its cooperative spirit. What has happened—has happened, however, under Joseph Lee's leadership.

The end of the twenty-five period of consecutive service is a fitting time in behalf of the thousands who serve with him to record what his leadership has meant, the affection it has inspired.

—HOWARD BRAUCHER.

THE WHITE HOUSE
WASHINGTON

May 26, 1938

Dear Dr. Finley:

I am heartily in accord with the idea of setting aside a special time to pay trib-ute to the life and work of Joseph Lee. His simplicity, his humor, his philosophy, his integrity, his courage endeared him to all who came to know him and work with him-and these were legion.

He saw that for children, play was the serious business of life; that for youth recreation was an important school for citizenship; and that for adults leisure right-ly used meant the difference between mere existence and fruitful living. The genius of Joseph Lee lay not alone in seeing these things. He used what he was and what he had to forge the machinery necessary to make them real in American life.

Today in the far flung communities of a great nation children are happier, youth is better served, and men and women have a chance to live more richly because of the life and work of Joseph Lee. No greater tribute could be paid than to have a share in helping to strengthen and build further this vital part of our community and of our national life.

Very sincerely yours,

(Signed) Franklin D. Roosevelt

Dr. John H. Finley,
President,
National Recreation Association,
315 Fourth Avenue,
New York, NY

Resolution Adopted by the Board of Directors of the National Recreation Association

From June 7, 1910 until July 28, 1937, the day of his death, for a period of more than twenty-seven years, Joseph Lee served as President and leader in the National Recreation Association.

Previously, on April 12, 1906, when the Association was formed—as the Playground Association of America—Joseph Lee had been elected Third Vice President. Later, on May 14, 1909, he was elected First Vice President and served in that capacity until he was elected President.

Though Joseph Lee had in 1910 been active in the play movement for a score of years and was then known to many as the "father of the playground movement," he was reluctant to accept the presidency for he never desired the position for himself.

Joseph Lee, once he had accepted the position, dedicated himself and all his great gifts as leader, thinker, philosopher, educator, scholar, man of vision, statesman, speaker, writer, practical man of affairs, to the movement. He chose the Association as his major medium through which to make his contribution to his times. His book *Play in Education* was used extensively throughout the world and was an outstanding contribution to the movement. He gave generously of his own means and worked steadily in raising money from his friends for the Association.

The Board members had extra satisfaction in their meetings because they were associated with him in his inspired leadership. The staff members did better work because they felt he understood the difficulties they faced and the significance of their achievements. Local recreation leaders thought of the whole movement on a higher plane because they knew that quietly and without seeking anything for himself Joseph Lee was devoting his ability to the problems of the movement.

The members of the Board of Directors are profoundly grateful that for so many years they were privileged to follow such a leader. Though the national recreation movement is clearly larger than any one man or any group of men yet in part the National Recreation Association is a living monument to the life and work of Joseph Lee.

Warmly human himself, he imparted warmth and depth and richness of life to those about him. No one exceeded him in gifts of friendship. The world became Warmly human himself, he imparted warmth and depth and richness of life to those about him. No one exceeded him in gifts of friendship. The world became a more friendly place when he came into the room.

Made by a Playground Boy. Model airplane intrigues Joseph Lee, who exhibits the craft project to Mrs. Thomas Alva Edison and Howard Braucher.

The Service of the
National Recreation Movement in 1939

733 cities in **47** states were given personal service through the visits of field workers.

1,197 local leaders were given special training in recreation skills, methods, program, and the philosophy of the recreation movement at seven four-week institutes. Nature recreation, arts and crafts, music, drama, social recreation and games, organization and administration, and recreation for girls and women were stressed.

38 cities were given personal field service by the Bureau of Colored Work. Some time was given to training, and a conference of colored workers was held in Raleigh, North Carolina.

33 cities were visited by the Katherine F. Barker Memorial Secretary on Recreation for Girls and Women. The secretary also gave courses at the four major institutes, **2,076** women recreation leaders were enrolled in the training sessions conducted.

48 institutions for children and the aged in **5** states were visited by the Field Secretary on Play in Institutions.

13,338 boys and girls in **379** cities received badges, emblems, or certificates for passing the Association's athletic and swimming badge tests.

5,445 individuals attended the **92** institutes conducted by the Rural Recreation Service in cooperation with the Extension Service of the United States Department of Agriculture.

42 states received personal service from the representative of the National Physical Education Service, who visited **74** cities. Through correspondence, consultation, and the monthly News Letter, **47** states and the District of Columbia were served.

6,654 different communities in the United States and in **35** foreign countries received help and advice on recreation problems through the Correspondence and Consultation Bureau. Approximately **32,000** letters were handled by the Bureau. **5,213** individuals called at the office for personal consultation.

1,324 delegates from **353** cities in **37** states and **8** representatives from Canada attended the Twenty-Fourth National Recreation Congress held at Boston, Massachusetts, October 9-13, 1939.

1,655 cities and towns, **46** of them in foreign countries, received *Recreation*, the monthly magazine of the movement—an increase of **103** over 1938.

2,294 individuals in **944** communities received the bulletins issued by the Association. Books, booklets, pamphlets, and leaflets were published on various subjects in the recreation field.[1]

(1) R.M. June 1940

An Album of the Early Years of Public Recreation

Six of the boys in this picture are in the air with both feet off the ground. Nearly every boy is alert to dodge the ball. A boy at the left has leaped out of sympathy for the boy on the other side at whom the ball was throuwn. (Photo from *Playground* No. 2, Newark, N.J.)

Nine of the girls in this picture are in the air with both feet off the ground. Nearly every girl is alert to dodge the ball.
(Photo from *Playground* No. 2, Newark, N.J.)

Imagine life as a child during the depression

"...the individual is more completely revealed in play than in any other way
and conversely, play has a greater shaping power over the character
and nature of man than any one other activity."

Luther H. Gulick

A Toy Symphony in San Francisco

Stories are always fascinating to the children of Oak Park,
Illinois. The setting adds to the charm.

NRA Mourns Loss of an Important Leader

For **John Huston Finley** every hour of life was adventure, adventure of the spirit, adventure in imagination.

John H. Finley belonged to the National Recreation Association before it was formed. The purpose to which it was devoted was his purpose—that children might have their rightful heritage of play, that all might have a permanently satisfying use of leisure.

Dr. John H. Finley, *President NRA; Editor, New York Times*

Dr. Finley liked to read of the new Jerusalem and of the children playing in the streets thereof. But, he asked, why not give children in our cities a real chance to play here and now. If the heaven of men's dreams is to have music and dancing and poetry—why not let joy express itself now. He wanted even the blind to see and feel the beauty of the world.

From 1913 to 1940 a member of the Board of Directors, from 1922 to 1937 First Vice-President, from 1937 President, Dr. Finley gave himself whole-heartedly to the movement that was so much a part of his own life. He spoke for it, presided with rare charm at the Recreation Congresses, raised money for the Association, placed his prestige and his great influence back of the entire recreation movement. There was no other quite like him. Not soon shall we see his equal. We record with deep gratitude a little of what his life and work meant to the National Recreation

Association and to us personally. We shall ever think of him with affection.[2]

Dr. Finley was a great walker and, shunning hat and overcoat, he was a familiar figure on the sidewalks of New York. On one occasion he walked the seventy-one miles from New York City to Hanover, New

(2) From the Minutes of the Board of Directors of the National Recreation Association, March 13, 1940.

Hampshire, part of the way over the mountains, in nineteen consecutive hours, to attend the installation of a new president of Dartmouth College, Each year, to the very end, he celebrated his birthday by walking around the perimeter of Manhattan Island, a distance of some fifty miles. In honor of its famous walker, the City of New York erected on the East Side Drive wrought-iron signposts with the silhouette of Dr. Finley on one of his walks. To add zest to his walks, he carried a pedometer and kept track of the distance covered, while pretending that he was traveling in a foreign country. At the end of each day he checked his progress on a map and read about the place where he imagined he was spending the night.

A Well Deserved Award

Stephen Schwartz wished to become an apothecary, but arthritis dashed his ambition. For three years he walked at a snail's pace from his home in Brooklyn to the subway and then several blocks to the workroom, defying rain and slush. Such optimism so impressed Dr. John H. Finley that he declared, "I have a medal I give to my friends who walk a thousand miles a year, and I think Schwartz deserves one for the effort he makes in getting to his work—and here it is." The medal bears a relief of a pedestrian with a stride that shows no sign of rheumatism and is inscribed "A la Sainte Terre." Dr. Finley himself later presented this medal to Stephen Schwartz at the Sheltered Workroom.

July 1930 Stephen Schwartz Receives His Medal.

Editors note: John Finley had been President of City College of New York, Commissioner of the Education for the State of New York and later Editor of the *New York Times*.

Chapter Five

1940-1946
World War II

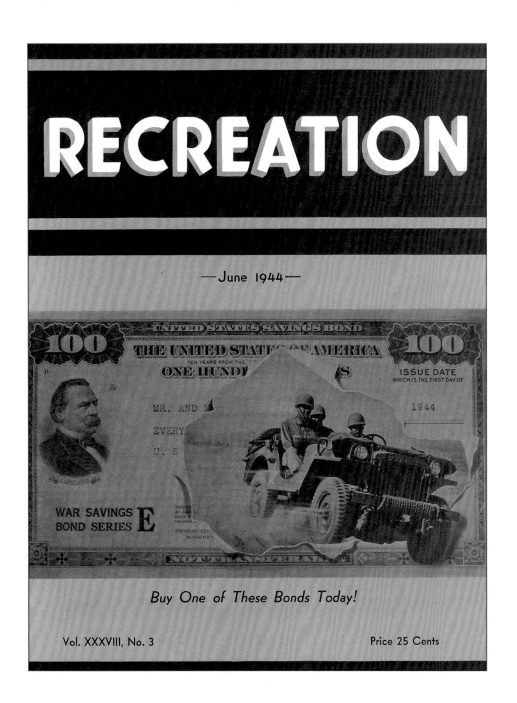

RECREATION

—June 1944—

WAR SAVINGS BOND SERIES **E**

Buy One of These Bonds Today!

Vol. XXXVIII, No. 3   Price 25 Cents

A Message from John G. Winant

The ambassador to the Court of St. James' stresses the wartime importance of the national recreation movement in the United States

The time that I have spent in England makes me feel more than ever the importance of the work being done by the National Recreation Association. In this war period it seems to me that what our national movement is doing now is essential in our war effort because it contributes to morale and the health and well-being of the community.

I am much concerned that in the period following the war the Association should be as strong as possible to help with the problems of living, including recreation, which must receive attention then.

I wish every contributor to the Association could see as I have seen what it means to have a going concern in the field of recreation available in a time of emergency like this.

(signed) John G. Winant

First Vice-President

National Recreation Association

March 1943

John G. Winant

1940-1946 – World War II

During the period of World War II, the Association maintained a heavy program of defense recreation services to industry. It also maintained a heavy program of war recreation service to the armed forces and to governmental and non-governmental agencies. Among these services were personnel, publications, training and special field services. The defense aspects of the wartime work of the Association were financed by emergency war service funds raised privately to help a designated group of voluntary agencies in financing their respective defense services.

RECREATION FOR WAR WORKERS...

This booklet, designed to serve as a guide for workers in charge of recreation in war plants, is a particularly timely publication. It attempts to suggest in very simple terms the ways in which recreation can help workers in war plants get the most out of their leisure time and find personal satisfactions in spite of their heavy responsibilities and demanding jobs.

Because community recreation workers have so definite a responsibility for providing facilities and activities, suggestions are offered in the booklet which will be of interest to municipal recreation departments and private groups providing recreation.

The chapter headings cover such subjects as Special Problems in Wartime Industrial Recreation: Activities; Planning and Starting the Program; the Community and the War Worker; Organization and Administration of the Plant Program.

Appendices offer constitutions and by-laws of employees activities associations and athletic associations, a form for an industrial recreation interest survey, a number of sample programs, and similar information.

Order your copies at 35 cents each
from the
National Recreation Association
315 Fourth Avenue   **New York 10, N. Y**

"How many stamps did we sell?"
Two young box office clerks count their receipts after a performance at the Children's Theater, sponsored by the Recreation Department in Memphis, Tennessee.

Preventing   12/03/1944
War Delinquency

A series of articles by Lois Sager, special writer for the Dallas, Texas, *Morning News.*

There are suggestions here for the many groups which are working to discover the basic cause of juvenile delinquency and to provide a solution to a problem causing deep concern.

Order a copy, at 15 cents,
from the
National Recreation Association
315 Fourth Avenue
New York 10, N. Y.

The War Recreation Congress

The whole recreation movement is alert to its opportunities for services in the war. The call for a War Recreation Congress at Cincinnati has met with eager response. Leaders in all phases of war recreation service have welcomed a chance to discuss together practical problems facing those responsible for providing recreational services for all the people in wartime.

Although only a short time has elapsed since the advance notice of the War Recreation Congress was sent out, 500 persons have said they are coming, and more cards are arriving daily. Inquiries from many sources are asking for further information.

Planning for the War Recreation Congress has become a cooperative undertaking in which many have generously shared.

The topics chosen for group discussion are listed below. Developments in the war may make changes desirable. The Congress Committee is in close touch with government and military leaders and will adjust war recreation plans to meet new conditions.

Topics for Group Discussion

How are Recreation Departments effectively adapting their services for the War effort?

Recreation service in special emergencies: Air raids, Evacuation, Epidemics, Black Outs

Helping families of war industry workers to adjust to community life

What special problems do girls and women face because of the war?

- First session-keeping teen age girls normal in wartime
- Second session-women in industry

Recreation services for industrial workers

- First session-In the community
- Second session-special problems of industrial recreation leaders

War problems of members of local recreation boards (two sessions)

Problems of defense recreation committees in camp communities

Locally financed and operated recreation programs for men in uniform

Wartime Recreation in towns under 8,000 population

Wartime Recreation Problems in cites Under 30,000 Population

What are the Effective Ways of Telling the Story of Available Recreation Services to All Engaged in war Service?

In What Ways Should Training Programs for Recreation Leaders Be Adapted to Serve War Needs?

Boys' and Girls' and Other Clubs in Wartime. Recreation for War Workers' in Housing Projects Building and maintaining Financial Support for Recreation in wartime

Public and Private Agencies Working Together in Meeting Recreation Needs

How Can Churches Help to Meet War Recreation Needs of the People?

Special Recreation Problems of Colored Groups in wartime

Long Range Planning for Recreation–National and Local

Wartime Problems and Use of Municipal and County Parks

How Can Music Be More Effectively Used in Winning the War?

During 1941 the community recreation movement was concerned not only with the provision of recreation for civilians–for children on playgrounds, for adults at recreation centers, and for community groups everywhere–but also with the pressing need for recreation for service men in training camps near many cities, and for the rapidly growing army of defense workers. For "our community recreation facilities are dedicated to our country in wartime. They belong to *all* the people and are for use by all the people."

Adjustment in Sports Programs to Serve Wartime Needs.

Effect of War on Employed Recreation Personnel

Plays, Pageantry, Patriotic Demonstrations as an Aid to Our War Effort

Meeting Normal Needs of Children in Wartime

What Are the Problems of Relationship Between Local Recreation Departments and National Emergency Agencies?

Recruiting, Training, and use of Volunteers for War Recreation Service

Supplies and Equipment for War Recreation Service–Priorities–Shortages and Substitutes

Home and Family Recreation in Wartime

War Recreation Problems in Rural Communities

First Session-Villages and Small Towns

Second Session-Open Country

In What Ways Can Organized Camping More Effectively Contribute to Winning the War?

At the five general sessions of the War Recreation Congress authoritative leaders from the Federal Government, the armed forces, industry, labor, and related fields will speak.

Further details of the War Recreation Congress will be announced in future issues of *Recreation*.

Community Centers Aid the War Effort

"Your social centers are war service stations and information centers," reads the Social Center Directory issued by the Department of Municipal Recreation and Adult Education of Milwaukee, Wisconsin, in listing the addresses and telephone numbers of the city's twenty-one school centers. And the emphasis being laid by the Department on the place of the social center in the war effort is indicated in the announcement made in the directory of special classes designed to help in winning the war.

The announcement reads as follows:

HELP WIN THE WAR ON THE HOME FRONT

CONSERVE MATERIALS *Cloth, Wood Are Needed to Win the War*
Sew clothes for your children and your family.
Remodel old coats and dresses into attractive, modern garments.
Reknit old sweaters into socks, caps, and mittens.
Learn to be a "handy man" with hammer and nails.

GIVE SERVICE *Keep Yourself and Your Family Well and Strong*
EAT the right kind of food—Attend a Red Cross Nutrition Course to learn how to buy the best and the most food with your dollar.
EXERCISE regularly—Join a gymnasium group, a class in boxing, dancing, wrestling; play basketball, volleyball; join a hiking club.
RELAX from the strain and worry of the day—Enjoy an evening of social recreation with friends and neighbors.
AVOID ILLNESS—Learn to check colds and illness at the start. Join a Red Cross course in Home Care of the Sick.

GIVE SERVICE *Social Centers are War Service Stations*
Red Cross Knitting and Sewing—Scrap Collecting—Bond and Stamp Sales—Air Raid Warden Meetings—Information on War Regulations.

CARE FOR OUR CHILDREN *They Are the Citizens of the New World We Are Fighting for*
The Social Centers conduct classes, clubs, and play activities for your sons and daughters after school and evenings.

CHERISH CITIZENSHIP IN THE UNITED STATES OF AMERICA
Continue your study at a social center class. Be intelligent about public affairs. Take part in the life of your community through the social center activities.

Special Classes

At one of the centers a Layman's Aviation Class for Men and Women, which started October 28, 1942, is being conducted once a week from 7:30 to 9:30 P. M. The course, which consists of eight lessons, is taught by a government trained, licensed pilot. The content of the course is indicated in the questions asked in the announcement: "Do you know what keeps a plane in the air?" "Do you know how a pilot operates his plane?" "Can you recognize the different types of planes?" "Do you know about traffic laws of the air?"

At the same center the Red Cross is offering a course in nutrition under the leadership of expert dieticians.

Last summer, cities all over the country adapted their playground programs to meet wartime needs. Many of these same communities are doubtless expanding and changing their indoor community center programs to aid the war effort. We want to know how you are serving in the emergency. Won't you send us this information?

Miss Katherine Montgomery Donaldson devoted over twenty-five years of her life to recreation; and was a member of the first Recreation School conducted by the National Recreation Association in 1925.

During the early stages of World War II, trained recreation workers were wanted by the War Department to plan and execute a well-rounded recreation program for enlisted personnel on the military bases. Miss Donaldson was a member of one of the small original groups of Army hostesses assigned to Camp Lee, Virginia.

During wartime and the early occupation, she was with the Red Cross in a supervisory capacity–in New Guinea, the Philippines, and Japan. She also served for a time with the United States Navy at Samar and Cavite. She was the first woman Supervisor of Recreation for the American Red Cross, Far Eastern Theater of Operations, procuring and organizing the establishments used as Red Cross Clubs. Since July 1947, when Special Services took over operation of Service Clubs from the Red Cross, she assisted in the administration of sixty-two installations on the three main Japanese islands.

Katherine Montgomery Donaldson

Americans' Wartime Service

Some 16 million Americans served in uniform, 12 million of them draftees from an under-26 pool of 30 million men. Many won exemptions by having "essential" jobs. About 37,000 men received conscientious objector status on religious grounds and did alternative service. From a prewar strength of 55,000, the merchant marine swelled to 215,000 men; deaths were higher here than in any other branch of service: about 9,300, or 1 in 26. more than 250,000 women served in women's branches, and 70,000 as military nurses. In all, 18.1 percent of American families had at least one member in the armed forces.

Recreation Activities
by Number of Cities Reporting, 1941 (1)

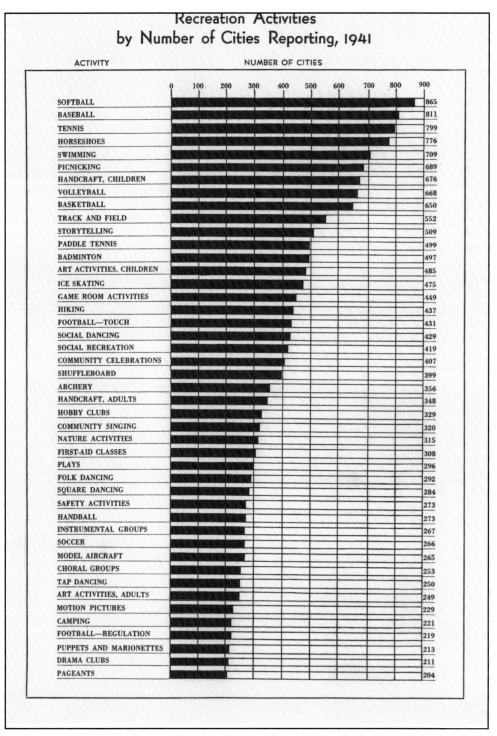

Recreation Activities
by Number of Cities Reporting, 1941

ACTIVITY	NUMBER OF CITIES
SOFTBALL	865
BASEBALL	811
TENNIS	799
HORSESHOES	776
SWIMMING	709
PICNICKING	689
HANDCRAFT, CHILDREN	676
VOLLEYBALL	668
BASKETBALL	650
TRACK AND FIELD	552
STORYTELLING	509
PADDLE TENNIS	499
BADMINTON	497
ART ACTIVITIES, CHILDREN	485
ICE SKATING	475
GAME ROOM ACTIVITIES	449
HIKING	437
FOOTBALL—TOUCH	431
SOCIAL DANCING	429
SOCIAL RECREATION	419
COMMUNITY CELEBRATIONS	407
SHUFFLEBOARD	399
ARCHERY	356
HANDCRAFT, ADULTS	348
HOBBY CLUBS	329
COMMUNITY SINGING	320
NATURE ACTIVITIES	315
FIRST-AID CLASSES	308
PLAYS	296
FOLK DANCING	292
SQUARE DANCING	284
SAFETY ACTIVITIES	273
HANDBALL	273
INSTRUMENTAL GROUPS	267
SOCCER	266
MODEL AIRCRAFT	265
CHORAL GROUPS	253
TAP DANCING	250
ART ACTIVITIES, ADULTS	249
MOTION PICTURES	229
CAMPING	221
FOOTBALL—REGULATION	219
PUPPETS AND MARIONETTES	213
DRAMA CLUBS	211
PAGEANTS	204

(1) R. M. June 1942, pp. 122

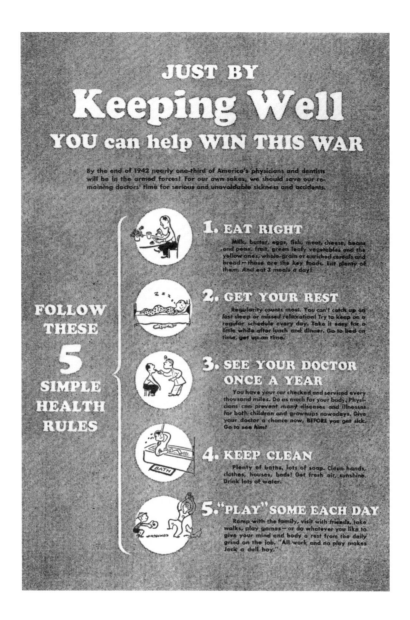

The poster reproduced here, which measures 13 x 20 inches and is printed in an attractive shade of blue, may be secured free on request from Wilbur Nelson, Director of the Keep Well Crusade, in care of the Institute of Life Insurance, 60 East 42nd St., New York City.

"Each individual can contribute to his own health protection and improvement by adopting a few simple ways of healthful living. Each of us must accept this responsibility and stick to it with a firm purpose. The total of individual responsibility for personal health accepted by millions of American men and women will make an incalculable contribution to victory." – *Thomas Parren,* M.D., Surgeon General, U. S. Public Health Service.[2]

(2) R.M. January 1943, pp.581

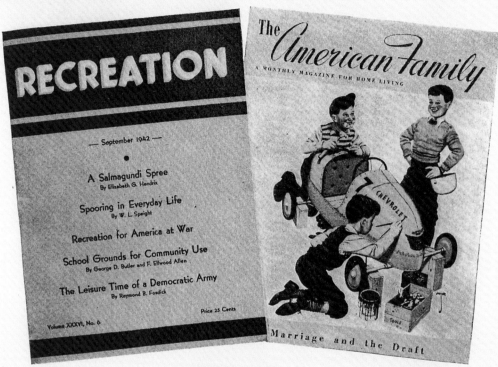
(3) R.M. November 1942, pp.477

(3)

What Is It We Defend?

The world we have known is all changed. We do not know what a day will bring forth. Gone are Czechoslovakia, Austria, almost Poland. Partitioned is Finland. Suspended are Norway, Denmark, Holland, Belgium as we have known them. Prostrate are China, France. The British Empire fights on. Defense in the United States come first.

What is it we defend? What is the America we know? How runs The American Way of Life?

America is liberty, freedom, the pursuit of happiness.

America is also discipline, courage, the pioneer spirit, aspiration.

America is romance, adventure, sport, music, culture, life for all here and now.

We cannot defend America well without keeping strong that which we defend. America is life, real life for all from the cradle to the grave. Through recreation we build much that is above the mere cellar foundations of existence. In our cities and in our open country blossoms a civilization of abundant living which has been the dream of men always everywhere. Leisure is no longer an empty word.

All this we will defend. All this is worth defending. But surely this dream land that we have made real land-we will not give up just because we are going to defend it. We will keep our park lands and waters, our music, our beauty, our sports, the laughter of little children, a measure of rhythm and lightheartedness even as we step out ready to defend to the full all we have, all that we have with God's help builded.

Rhythm and smiles are a part of gallant defense and help keep away the tenseness that weakens defense. The hunger of all men and women for spiritual comradeship is greater at the present moment because of all that is happening in the world at large.

Keep the home fires, the heart fires burning. Keep the morale high. Here's no place to think of cheapness, of pinching pennies, of cutting taxes. Recreation, the song in the heart, must be strengthened, not weakened when we prepare to defend our shores.

The flag of our dreams as to what America is and can be and will be must not be lowered.

Always we must hold firmly that this part of the world with all its share of sorrow must still everbe kept a land of high courage.

(Signed) Howard S. Braucher

(4)

(4) R. M. August 1940

A MESSAGE FROM THE NRA FIRST VICE PRESIDENT

A Message to the Children on the Playgrounds of America

From

Honorable John G. Winant

Ambassador to the Court of St. James; Former Chairman Social Security Board; Three times Governor of New Hampshire; First Vice-President, National Recreation Association

London, W. I.
June 27, 1944

Today your fathers and brothers fight bravely on the far-flung battlefronts of the world.

I like to think, as I know many of them do, of the playgrounds, athletic fields, swimming pools and beautiful parks in communities all over America. In their mind's eye they see your smiling face and know your carefree life. They remember it was good to live in that kind of country. They are determined that you and all of America's children shall continue to have that kind of life.

On the playgrounds of America this summer your happiness will lighten the load of your fathers and brothers. They will know you are living the kind of life for which they are fighting and that you too will become the kind of men and women that will keep America a much beloved land, but because you have good fun, don't think that those who are fighting around the world to protect America don't also know that you are doing your share in helping at home.

Sincerely,

John G. Winant

(5)

(5) R.M. August 1944, pp. 225

94

"The war now has to be fought—it has become a necessity in order that freedom may not be lost on earth. Victory for freedom we must have, and it can only come through the ways we know, now that war is here. But I beg you, when you are being forced by the ways of war to do the things which contradict all that you have been taught in the years of peace, that you will not allow civilization to die in you... Today your country thinks of you as soldiers—it may need you as soldiers. But that is a temporary need. There will be another and more permanent need—the need for you to help rebuild your country worn with war, whose civilization is shaken and half destroyed... When war is done with us, we shall sorely need those men in whom the light of civilization still burns. Be those men!"

Pearl Buck in *Men of Tomorrow*

Album of Recreation Activities During World War II

"Night Life" for teen age boys and girls
(Photo by Soverance Studio, Watertown, New York)

Dancing to the music of Johnny Gannon and his high school orchestra
at the popular Club Victory

Volleyball, like badminton, may be played in the back yard or in a gymnasium. A "team" sport, it is good fun for either adults or children, requires only a net and ball, is an excellent conditioner.

A bicycle was once a schoolboy's vehicle, but today gas-rationed citizens every-where are adopting it for pleasure and necessity. It is easy to manipulate, uses no fuel, helps keeps its users healthy.

Rope skipping is probably the simplest com-bination of fun and exercise yet invented. A rope be bought for a dime, used anywhere and any time. Although long associated with moppets skipping is no sissy pastime, is used by even prizefighters as a means of toughening legs.

Many school children take part in the vacant lot projects dotting all districts of Chicago. Here is a group at 80th and Ingleside Avenue, with whole families helping in food production.

At the close of the Victory Garden season in Chicago, neighborhood festivals were arranged in all parts of the city, with school children taking part in the festival in their particular district. The faces of these boys and girls at the exhibit held in the Rutherford-Sayre Park neighborhood mirror their enormous pride and satisfaction in their achievements!

Like many another city, Houston, Texas, went on a wartime schedule in 1942. How the Recreation Department adjusted its program to meet new needs is described here in extracts from the annual report.

Walking the broomstick at one of those affairs without-men which the ladies have learned to like.

A crowd of neighborhood "gypsies" turns out for an evening of fun around a huge community pot of stew at Milroy Park.

The barbecue oven at the Playhouse provides a sheltered fire on a rainy afternoon. Husbands in the Army, boy friends in the Navy, but they can still have fun!

The shuffleboard courts are especially popular with war workers and older men who are retired.

Wartime activities played an important part in the program of the Houston, Texas, Recreation Department during 1942.

With the cooperation of the Federation of Women's Clubs, the American Red Cross, and individual volunteer instructors, war classes and production groups were begun in all park clubhouses late in 1941. These groups, including the Red Cross first aid, home nursing, nutrition, knitting and sewing, continued throughout the year, with new ones being formed as others finished. Consumer education and canteen classes were added later in the year. A by-product has been the old-time neighborliness they have fostered. Victory dinners and luncheons were a practical application of the principles taught in the nutrition classes.

The large dances for servicemen held in the city auditorium last year had to be abandoned for several practical reasons early in 1942. Civic clubs were encouraged to continue their dances, picnics, and other entertainments for servicemen. The Sunday afternoon open house at the Recreation Clubhouse was continued, and monthly dances were held at the Playhouse. More than forty service clubs, social clubs, and other organizations have extended their services through cooperation with the Department and its War Activities Committee in these affairs.

Wartime trends in recreation

In spite of the lack of trained personnel and adequate equipment, and in the face of tremendous difficulties, every effort has been made to provide the civilian populations of our cities with the recreation activities necessary to relieve wartime tensions and strains. Such programs as that promoted by the Minneapolis Park Department are doing much to help keep life normal for children and adults.

(Photos courtesy Lancaster, Pennsylvania, Recreation Association)

(Photos by Walter Dahlberg Courtesy Minneapolis Board of Park Commissioners)

For three days last June Oklahoma City held its Eleventh Annual Recreation Festival. Many citizens subscribed to the slogan of the city's Park Department—"Save your money, and build your health by going to your neighborhood park or playground for your recreation." (Milwaukee Journal Photo)

Another important development has been the provision of recreation for war workers and their families. A worker from the Los Angeles Playground and Recreation Department organized play activities for these children and other residents of the Romano Gardens Housing Project.

Members of the New Century Community Center in Oakland give a performance of "The King's Crown."

The Slopes of Elmwood

Let's All Sing Together!

Two sailor lads and their friends tune up with "Anchors Aweigh" at one of Omaha's mammoth community sings. More than 15,000 people turned out the night this picture was taken.

Courtesy Omaha World-Herald

"Come to the slopes of Elmwood
Where a tenor or bass is king!
Where sopranos and contraltos
Tilt up their chins and sing!
Where butchers, bakers
and common folk Sing to
the star–studded skies."

"Where banker, merchant,
and landlord
Are no better than us other 'guys.'
So, come to the slopes of Elmwood
Each Sunday night and sing.
Sweethearts, mothers, sisters, brothers,
Long may your voices ring."

Advertisements From Recreation Magazine

but it is Matériel of War nevertheless

Many a devastating bomb has been dropped into Naziland; Many a grenade has been speeded to its target—by arms that learned their skill and accuracy while handling a basketball. For this great wintertime American sport is one of the best sources of the agilities, skills, coordination and endurance that make our fighting men champions at war as they are at play. While engaged as far as our facilities permit in the production of fighting equipment, the Wilson name is still being stamped on basketballs and other basketball equipment of the finest quality. Wilson Sporting Goods Co., Chicago, New York and other leading cities.

Wilson BASKETBALL EQUIPMENT

It's WILSON Today in Sports Equipment

TUNE IN ARCH WARD'S WEEKLY SPORTS PREVIEW Every Wednesday night 10:15 P.M.—E.W.T. Over Mutual Sponsored by *Wilson*

IN AMERICA'S FUTURE

★

Play with the best—as you work for Victory

GENUINE AUTOGRAPHED LOUISVILLE SLUGGER BASEBALL BATS LOUISVILLE SLUGGER SOFTBALL BATS, LOUISVILLE POWER-BILT, LOUISVILLE GRAND-SLAM and LOUISVILLE LO-SKORE GOLF CLUBS

HILLERICH & BRADSBY CO

LOUISVILLE, KENTUCKY.

Agility

The Most Valuable Physical Asset and Best Protection of Our Fighting Sons

THE MOST valuable "Human Machine" in any mechanized army today is the boy who can do a maximum of damage to the enemy with a minimum of damage to himself.

The agile boy who can flop to the ground — then leap to his feet and charge ahead, all in a flash —

The boy whose agility makes him just a fraction of a second faster at ducking into a fox hole, or a trench, under a sudden machine gun burst or a bomb —

The boy whose skill and agility give him a split second advantage with a bayonet thrust, a knife slash or a hand grenade —

The boy who sees, decides and acts just a shade faster — on land, on sea, or in the air —

These are the boys who are the best fighters — who are able to take care of themselves anywhere — and whose chances of coming back intact are 100% better than those who do not have these skills and agilities.

Actual physical fitness records of this war prove that the boys whose basic military training and basic calisthenics are supplemented by baseball, tennis, boxing, football, basketball, track, judo, etc., develop skills and agilities that make them the best fighting men in the world.

Could anything be more important than the equipment that is necessary to give them this priceless training?

* * * * *

So far as the materials made available to us, and facilities not engaged in war production permit, we will continue to supply equipment for the sports that help to make American fighting men the most efficient "Human Fighting Machines" in the war.

Wilson Sporting Goods Co. and Wilson Athletic Goods Mfg. Co., Inc., Chicago New York and other leading cities

Wilson SPORTS EQUIPMENT

IT'S WILSON TODAY IN SPORTS EQUIPMENT

THE NEW COACH... On the Home Front

An important war job for the wives and mothers of America

UNTIL NOW, no American mother, as she tucked her little boy into his crib, has had to face the frightening thought that some day he would *have* to be a soldier. Our mothers have been spared that fear.

Now, with America determined to *fight* for the things we hold dear, we cannot neglect these *human machines* upon which we depend for victory.

America's fighters must be *made* and *kept* physically fit for a winning fight against enemies who have lived and trained for war since childhood.

And this is where the patriotic women of America —women made of just as sturdy stuff as any women in the world, can do another important job for victory, and for postwar progress.

We need a Coach in every home where a boy is approaching military age. A coach, with a mother's love, to inspire this youth. To keep him playing your rugged American sports, which develop the *strength*, the *skills* and *agilities* that will assure him a better chance to win—and to come home from the war with a sound mind in a sound body.

We need a Coach in every home

where there are *war-workers* and *civilian workers* the Home Front. A Coach with a mother's inte est—a wife's love—to keep these indispensable m exercising—playing their golf, tennis, badminton, so ball, volley ball; doing their calisthenics, taking wal gardening, etc. They, too, must be kept strong for t job ahead of us during the war and *after* the war.

We need a Coach in every home where there a growing daughters—a Mother-Coach. She must s that they develop the health and vitality — throu regular exercise — that America's women must ha to meet the problems of the war and the postwar ag

This is extra war work that the patriotic women America are being asked to assume — a new job f them, but a job *they* will love because it's for the on they love.

On *our* part, and we speak f the whole Sporting Goods Indu try, we shall continue to voice t importance of America's compe tive sports to the physical fitne of our fighters, workers and pe ple. And we shall continue to su ply all the sports equipment th *available materials permit.*

Wilson Sporting Goods Co., and Wilson Athletic Goods Mfg. Co., Inc. Chicago, New York and other leading cities

Wilson SPORTS EQUIPMENT

IT'S WILSON TODAY IN SPORTS EQUIPMENT

AFTER THIS WAR ... An Ever READY America!

By L. B. ICELY, President

BUT for the grace of God, and the protecting breadth of our oceans, *we* might have been another France, another Poland, or another Greece.

With this fearful lesson on the value of preparedness still fresh in mind, let us here and now *resolve*, as a nation, that *never again* shall America be caught physically unprepared and untrained.

Our national purpose in this war is to help establish world-wide peace and freedom.

But—let us resolve that *from this war on*, America shall be *a physically fit, ever ready people*.

First—let us see that our returning fighters are *kept* in good condition, through participation in organized sports and vigorous games, to form the nucleus of the new, *physically fit* America.

DECEMBER 1943

Through compulsory Physical Training in our schools, colleges and universities, let us train *all* of America's youth, from the beginning, to be robust, strong and adept in the skills and agilities that football, basketball, baseball, tennis, boxing, and other American competitive sports develop.

Let us broaden the application of Industrial Recreation so that *all* the millions of young men and women who work in our great industrial plants may have access to organized sports and games that will keep *them* healthy and vigorous.

Let there be more golf clubs, more tennis and badminton courts, more play fields and gymnasiums, and organized participation in them by more business executives and office workers.

Let there be more help for that part of the youth of America whose only play-grounds are the sand lots of our cities and towns.

As a vital factor in our Postwar planning let us establish new and higher physical standards *for all of America*.

Let us resolve that not only our industrial and economic machinery, but our millions of Human Machines shall be physically equal to the challenge of our job leaders in world restoration and progress after the war.

Wilson Sporting Goods Co. *and* Wilson Athletic Goods Mfg. Co., Inc., Chicago New York and other leading cities

Wilson
SPORTS EQUIPMENT
It's Wilson Today in Sports Equipment

521

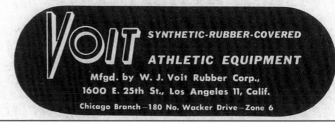

Chapter Six

1947
Postwar Period

Prosperity

Canadian Delegates
National Recreation Congress
January 28th to February 1st 1946
Madison Hotel   Atlantic City N.J.

*"To live
and to live
gloriously...
as much of the time
as possible
that is the thing..."*

Howard Braucher

A Long-time leader Dies

Howard Braucher, leader in the recreation movement, early developed an interest in social problems and a devotion of the cause of helping all people to find rich and satisfying uses of their leisure time. While a student, he worked at the Church of the Covenant and the Madison Square Church House, and after graduation from Cornell and subsequent work at Union Theological Seminary, Teachers College, and the New York School of Philanthropy, in 1905 he became Secretary of the Associated Charities of Portland, Maine.

Howard Braucher
1881-1949

Later, concerned, as were Jane Addams, Joseph Lee, Jacob Riis and other social leaders, about the lack of play space for children in slum areas, in 1909 **Howard Braucher** accepted the call to become the first paid secretary of the Playground Association of America, on the condition that the Association become the spearhead of a nationwide movement to bring broad recreation opportunities to all the people, regardless of age, sex, race or religious faith. This was his text then and his guiding principle throughout the years. It was soon reflected in the change of the name of the Association in 1911 to the Playground and Recreation Association of America, later in 1930, changed to the National Recreation Association, its present name. He realized that only as all forces that affect human living made their own contributions to the recreational life of the people could the full measure of success be achieved. He saw recreation permeating all phases of life work, worship, education and leisure. In 1941 he was elected president of the National Recreation Association, in which capacity he served until his death.

It is impossible to estimate the influence which the regular, continuous service of the Association, given on request, has had on the growth of community recreation programs throughout the country. Hardly a locality interested in recreation has not used, at some time or other, one or more of the services of the Association—its field representatives, correspondence bureau, district conferences, National Graduate Recreation School, local training institutes, and the many other special services made available through the years. Publications of the Association, now reaching the proportions of a substantial recreation library and tool kit, were started early during Howard Braucher's service. Under his leadership the services of the Association were extended to include active cooperation with the various federal and state agencies which are concerned in any way with recreation.

No one was more aware of the value of and need for cooperative effort among the various service organizations. He was one of the leaders in establishing the National Information Bureau in 1918, which provides potential supporters of national social agencies with a central source of information on the essential facts about national agencies appealing to the public for financial support, and he served as a member of its board of directors for twenty-two years.

Under his leadership, the foremost national social work agencies organized in 1922 the National Social Work Council (now the National Social Welfare

Assembly), to provide a forum for clearance of ideas and a channel for cooperative thinking and planning and he served as its chairman until 1940.

In the spring of 1932, the President's Organization on Unemployment Relief requested Howard Braucher to bring together representatives of a number of organizations promoting recreation opportunities for youth and adults for the purpose of drafting a program of recreation for the enforced free time of the unemployed. This group was later expanded and organized as the National Education-Recreation Council, to provide in the recreation and informal education fields the same facilities as those provide in the national Social Work Council for the social work field.

Howard Braucher was an active member of the Advisory Committee of the National Youth Administration, the Conference Committee on Urban Problems of the United States Chamber of Commerce, the Department of Christian Social relations of the Federal Council of the Churches of Christ in America, and the New York City Committee on the use of Leisure Time. He was a trustee and member of the committee which helped to establish the National Health and Welfare Retirement Association in 1945.

Always aware of the importance of strong leadership, he felt this required a deep professional consciousness and spirit, so that he was happy to help with the organization of the Society of Recreation Workers of America in 1938 (now the American Recreation Society) and to serve ex officio on its Executive Committee and Administrative Council.

His death on May 22, 1949, brought to a close a career which has immeasurably enriched recreational living for the people of America.

Services Available Through The National Recreation Association

District Field Service to Local Communities

Fifteen (15) district field workers are each charged with the responsibility for helping a definite group of cities maintain and extend their gains and enlarge their programs. Another worker helps with special emergencies arising in various areas. Many cities have in writing asked the Association to render this service.

Exchange of Recreation Information Between State Government Bureaus Active in the Recreation Field

Four workers (three full-time and one part-time) are giving field service to the various bureaus in state governments which are providing recreation as a part of their total program. The state bureaus include state park departments, conservation departments, forestry services, departments of education, extension departments of state universities, and state planning boards. Information on what is being done in one state bureau is carried to the corresponding state bureaus in other states and there is clearing of information between the bureaus within the states. Many governors and state leaders are asking for information as to what is being done in the recreation field by the other state governments. This service enables the Association to pass on such information to the various governors and others as the requests come in to the National Recreation Association.

Special Field Service for Colored Citizens

A field worker on recreation for colored citizens is provided for the more than 150 cities which have programs available for Negroes. These cities look to the

Association for help in extending their programs and achieving substantial progress. A second worker helps with special emergencies in postwar planning. A special field worker is assigned to recreation for colored girls and women. Many additional cities are served through correspondence and consultation at headquarters.

Recreation Personnel Service

The Recreation Personnel Service helps cities and private agencies and state government and federal government bureaus obtain trained recreation workers and assists recreation workers in finding positions suited to their capacities.

Apprentice Fellowships

Budget provision is made to train four apprentice fellows for one year. These apprentices secure their training in local recreation systems. The income from the Henry Strong Denison Fund Provides for part of this service.

Recreation Areas and Facilities Service

A specialist in recreation areas and facilities is provided, a trained landscape architect with successful experience in the recreation field, continuously studying the vast developments in the design, construction and maintenance of recreation facilities and clearing this information among all cities, making it possible for local funds to be expended most wisely and economically, so that expansion of facilities my bring the greatest return in recreation opportunities to the people who depend upon local public facilities for their recreation.

Recreation Buildings Service

An effort is made to bring together the best plans for community recreation buildings both for rural areas and for city areas, and to advise with local archi-tects as to the successes and failures in the planning of recreation buildings.

Service to Industry

This special service is designed to help the problems of management and labor in connection with recreation for industrial employees.

Library and Information Service

The Library and Information Service attempts to secure and bring together and maintain a national reservoir of the accumulated experience and thinking of the recreation movement in the United States and foreign countries. It has been felt that there ought to be a center where all experience may be registered for possible later use. This material has value not only for local recreation departments, for state government bureaus active in the recreation field, but also for church and school leaders, parent associations, women's clubs, rural groups, American Legion groups service club groups and many national organizations which provide recreation as a part of their program. Experiences are gathered from a great many communities, large and small, and from rural districts as well, so as to be available for use by the Correspondence and Consultation Bureau.

Special Publications

Whenever the National Recreation Association receives a large number of requests for information on a given subject, it has been found to be more economical to prepare a piece of printed literature that can be used to answer inquires on this subjects. There is a very considerable demand for the circulation of material as to what is being done in the various communities. The Association also publishes booklets and even books. New programs, new developments, successful experiences are thus circulated for the benefit of recreation systems, summer playground leaders, park superintendents, recreation workers in industrial plants and institutions and all those concerned with the promotion of recreation.

Bulletin service

The association sends bulletins and special material at regular intervals to local and state recreation and park workers, to industrial workers, to workers in institutions to clear information more quickly than can be done through a magazine. A very attractive Playground Summer notebook is sent to the smaller communities maintaining only summer playgrounds because so many of these summer workers change each year and there has been demand for special material to be placed in their hands each week of the summer season.

Katherine F. Barker Memorial
Field Service for Women and Girls

An experienced field worker helps localities with the special problems arising from the recreation needs of women and girls. There has been a tendency to neglect this part of the recreation program in localities. The cost of this work is covered by a special contribution.

Correspondence and Consultation Service

This service is used extensively by small towns, rural areas and cities. Each year some 6,000 communities in the forty-eight states and the District of Columbia write to the Correspondence and Consultation Bureau. Many foreign countries also use this service. The 30,000 requests are answered sometimes by suggesting a printed publication, sometimes by special research and sometimes by personal consultation. During the course of the year 5,000 persons come to the office for such help. The requests come from public and private agencies community groups,

and individuals. Thus far there is no record of any request for service that the Association has not ultimately been able to render, though some of the requests have made necessary considerable research.

Recreation Magazine

An essential item of equipment for each professional and volunteer worker is the monthly magazine, *Recreation*, which in its twelve issues annually provides up-to-date practical information on nearly all phases of recreation.

Recreation Congress

The Recreation Congress is a mobilization of the recreation forces in America, which provides information, inspiration and a national clearing of experience between volunteer and professional leaders form many agencies.

Educational Service to Local
Communities through Newspapers,
Magazines, Conventions and Public Addresses

Continuous newspapers and magazine publicity, radio broadcasts, circulation of motion pictures and lantern slides—all these have helped materially to build up favorable sentiment toward play and recreation which is reflected in a more responsive attitude toward local developments. This service has proved its basic educational value. Occasional addresses are also given before influential national, state and local meetings.

Research

Certain of the inquiries received by the National Recreation Association require a very considerable amount of investigation before adequate answers can be given. Various studies of important problems affecting national and local recreation service are steadily being made. Many of the studies have to be rechecked every few years. There have been studies of recreation administration, standards for areas and facilities, personnel standards for areas and facilities, personnel standards and related problems, volunteer service in the national recreation movement. Material has been assembled on games, social recreation, and seasonal activities. Programs have been prepared for church, industrial and other special groups in cities and rural districts. There have been studies of source material and compilation of bibliographies. There have been studies of recreation, recreation in day care centers for children, recreation for disabled veterans, community buildings as war memorials. A number of these research problems have involved the cooperation of recreation executives and of laymen.

Institutes for Recreation Workers

The training institutes are offered to help make as effective as possible the present recreation service being carried on and to provide opportunity for widening the knowledge and improving the skill of the recreation leaders. Sessions are open to volunteer and paid workers in municipal recreation departments and all community agencies.

National Bureau for the Advancement of Music

The Bureau was taken over by the Association in January 1943. In addition to personal conferences, answering inquiries by mail, the Bureau has the executive responsibility for National Music Week—a cooperative undertaking involving many national, state and local organizations. Music Week is carried on in 3,000 communities.

Drama Service

Special service is given to drama workers through correspondence and consultation, and also through special work in the field. Local drama institutes are held.

Arts and Crafts Service

An effort is made to interpret the place of arts and crafts in a community recreation program through local institutes. Local workers are trained in the technique of leadership in arts and crafts, are given the history of crafts, and are shown the use of selected arts and crafts, activities in demonstration of program building and group leadership.

Nature Activities, Camping and Garden Service

This service has been given not only to local recreation workers but also to state workers. Many who help in this field are volunteers. Nature activities for children, for youth, for adults are all covered; also questions relating to camping, local museums, trees and forests, birds, flowers, wild animals, playground beautification. Attempt has been made to help leaders in community gardening. Information has been brought together to help individual and groups interested in starting garden programs for young and old alike.

Rural Recreation Institutes

Part of the time there have been as many as five persons in the field, working very closely in cooperation with the Extension Division of the United States Department of Agriculture in conduction rural recreation institutes. At the present time one such worker is available. Through these institutes some 78,628 volunteer rural recreation leaders have received special training.

Social Recreation and Game Service

Effort has been made to train employed recreation leaders and volunteers in social recreation and games. This has been done partly through institutes and partly through consultation at headquarters.

Park Service

Because of the special experience which one of the field workers gained in making a two–year study of recreation under park auspices, an attempt has been made to have this worker available to give assistance from time to time on special recreation problems affecting park departments.

General Recreation Surveys

Workers specially trained have helped communities in drafting long time plans for recreation programs suited to the individual areas. Most of these services have been worked out because of the very specific request which come to the National Recreation Association. The Association has endeavored to find out what people want and has planned its work to try to meet the people's wants.[1]

A Tribute To Mrs. Thomas A. Edison

Mrs. Thomas A. Edison, a pioneer in recreation

Mrs. Thomas A. Edison died August 24, 1947, at the Presbyterian Hospital, New York City, at the age of 82. She had been active in the National Recreation Association up to within a short time before her death, even attending a Board meeting of the Association as late as May 1947. For thirty-four years Mrs. Edison had been one of the most devoted workers in the National Recreation Association. She gave generously of herself and of her time. Not only was she one of the larger contributors, she also did much in raising money. Because of her interest in rural people she paid the salary and traveling expenses of a rural recreation worker to train thousands of rural volunteers. She had a deep interest in music, nature activities and in gardens.

During all of the thirty-four years that Mrs. Edison was a member of the Board of Directors of the Association she had very definite ideas about policies and made a substantial contribution in helping in their formulation. She was particularly enthusiastic when boys and girls shared in the actual construction of their own playgrounds. She campaigned for a number of years for the use of abandoned canals for recreation for canoeing, boating, swimming and skating. Many are enjoying opportunities for recreation on waterways because of her leadership.[2]

(1) R. M. February 1947, pp. 621-624
(2) R.M. November 1947, pp. 361

114

Mrs. Edison opened up her own home for recreation gatherings in behalf of the National Recreation Association and persuaded her husband to share in the activities. Thomas A. Edison spoke with pride of the part which his wife had had as a pioneer in helping to develop the recreation movement. She attended a number of the Recreation Congress gatherings. Through her addresses at the Congress she was known to a great many of the recreation workers throughout the country.

Mrs. Edison was very happy when her son, Charles A. Edison, later to be Governor of New Jersey, gave nearly two years of his life as a young man to serving as a volunteer recreation leader.

Mrs. Edison's father, Lewis Miller, was founder of the Chautauqua Institute, and Mrs. Edison remained active in its leadership.

The Thomas A. Edison estate at Ft. Meyers, Florida, was deeded to the City of Ft. Meyers to be administered for the benefit of the people. The estate consists of fourteen acres of land and several buildings located on the Caloosahatchee River.

Through the years the local municipal recreation departments of the country received many communications from Mrs. Edison. She took very great pride in seeing the constant growth of the recreation movement. Much of what exists today has come because of the devoted work of Mrs. Thomas A. Edison and other volunteer leaders like her throughout the entire country.

—Howard Braucher

Mrs. Herbert Hoover

In the death of **Mrs. Herbert Hoover** on January 7, 1944, the national recreation movement lost one of its devoted friends. For twenty years Mrs. Hoover had been a supporter and contributor to the National Recreation Association. She was particularly interested in the work for women and girls. She had herself led an active outdoor life. On trips with her father she had developed a fondness for the joys and hardships of strenuous outdoor living. She knew what it was to tramp cross-country. She had lived with her husband in remote mining camps and was well acquainted with all that is involved in camping out.

For several years Mrs. Herbert Hoover was president of the Girls Scouts, was a leader in that organization for many years.

Mrs. Hoover was ready to help in building the national recreation movement. She understood its

Mrs. Herbert Hoover

possibilities as only a few individuals do. No one could meet her and talk with her about the problems of the work without being deeply impressed by her simple, direct ways, her sincerity, her effectiveness, her statesmanship, and her readiness at all times to give her best. Mrs. Herbert Hoover made a notable contribution to her generation and to those who are to come after her.

—Howard Braucher

(3)

(3) R.M. March 1944, pp. 673

Some of the Citizen Leaders Who Supported the National Recreation Association

John G. Winant

Ella Strong Denison

John G. Winant had been a member of the Board of Directors of the National Recreation Association since 1926, a Vice-President since 1928, and First Vice-President since 1937. He was present at meetings as often as his travels and his crowded life would permit. He addressed the National Recreation Congress gatherings on three occasions and shared helpfully in the planning of the Associations work even when his official duties kept him away for long periods of time. His belief in the recreation movement was profound. To him it was a matter of primary importance not only to the United States, but also to the world.

Governor Winant fostered a movement to bring greater recreational opportunities, including music, to the people in rural parts of the state. Music festivals were held in which various racial groups sang their native songs, attired in homemade national costumes. Hymn festivals of combined congregations were held in rural areas. He promoted traveling libraries. He improved the recreational welfare of children in orphanages and other institutions. He encouraged New Hampshire folk to revive the old-time arts of pottery, glass making and cabinetwork for which their ancestors were famous. The common people of the state looked upon him as a great and good friend.

On March 13, 1940, the recreation movement lost one of its early friends and one of its pioneer workers in the death of **Mrs. Ella Strong Denison** of Denver, Colorado, and San Diego, California. Mrs. Denison was interested in the local recreation movement in Denver, Colorado. She attended the Richmond, Virginia, Recreation Congress in 1913. She was elected a member of the Denver School Board in 1921.

In memory of her son, Dr. Henry Strong Denison, who studied at Cornell University, Mrs. Denison established a $50,000 Trust Fund, the income from which is used to meet the cost of apprentice fellows gaining experience and training in the recreation field.

Mrs. Denison was for years a regular contributor to the Association and one who took a personal interest in its work, visiting the office of the Association to talk about recreation problems. Mrs. Denison believed particularly in making government work in recreation effective.

Mrs. Ella Strong Denison's daughter, Mrs. John D. Jameson, is a member of the Board of Directors the National Recreation Association.[4]

(4) R.M. May 1940, pp. 118

J.P. Morgan

For twenty years **J.P. Morgan** contributed to the National Recreation Association. In his death the Association has lost another loyal friend. His father before him was a contributor. The first contribution of $1,000 came through a cable from J.P. Morgan, Sr., from England. Mr. Morgan's secretary, Mr. King, reported to me that Mr. Morgan had been deeply impressed by a leaflet "More Playgrounds or more Jails," and wanted to share in the national movement for more adequate playground and recreation centers for the children of America. It was characteristic of the senior Mr. Morgan that instead of waiting until he should return to the United States, he should have cabled asking that the contribution be made.

For a number of years, as First Vice-President of the Association, Henry P. Davison of J.P. Morgan and Company gave outstanding help not only in advising about current recreation problems but also in writing and telephoning to his friends and building up a very substantial financial support. After the death of Henry P. Davison, the writing to the individuals whose support his father had enlisted was taken over by F. Trubee Davison and continued by him for the last twenty years. Harry P. Davison, son of Henry P. Davison, as well as F. Trubee Davison has served as a member of the Board of Directors of the National Recreation Association. Harry P. Davison has been a member of J.P. Morgan and Company. Other partners in the House of Morgan have also been contributors to the Association through the years.

The national recreation movement owes much to the moral and financial support it has received from the House of Morgan.[5]

—Howard Braucher

Charles Hayden

On January 8, 1937 **Charles Hayden** of New York City died. When his will was read it was learned that the greater part of his estate, estimated at about $50,000,000 had been left to establish a foundation for boys and young men to be known as the Charles Hayden foundation.

Charles Hayden for ten years served as a member of the Board of Directors. Mr. Hayden's first service to the Association was in 1917 when he helped on the finance committee for War Camp community Service. Mr. Hayden always gave generously himself. In later years as sponsor for the Association in New York City, he helped to increase the number of friends giving and the size of contributions. He was generous in allowing the use of his name and connections in the service of the Association. With all of his business interest, Charles Hayden found time to think about and work for recreation, education and leisure-time activities.[6]

William Butterworth

William Butterworth did not wait to be called upon for service. He himself took the initiative in a creative way. "As President of the United States Chamber of commerce I want to send letters to each local chamber about the setting aside of land for playgrounds and parks in the new real estate developments. I want to ask certain questions about recreation planning. Unless you see some objections I shall send out these letters." That was his characteristic way. And again he took the leadership in arranging for certain publications relating to recreation planning.[7]

(5) R.M. May 1943, pp. 105; (6) R.M. April 1937, pp. 6; (7) R.M. July 1936, pp. 187

As he came to new York from time to time he would come in with his list of problems he wanted to take up—always wholehearted, enthusiastic, so very human and kindly that all of us who met him had more power for going on with our work. He was like a father in his spirit with members of the staff. One could talk over any kind of problem with him and be so sure of his interest and of the wisdom that came from a long experience of life. Incidentally as one talked with William Butterworth one would catch glimpses of many things he was doing in different fields-doing them all quietly, simply. William Butterworth sought nothing for himself. He gave many addresses on recreation and many of his articles appeared in various magazines. He was always ready to help, but he cared nothing for recognition for himself.

Clarence M. Clark

Clarence M. Clark gladly accepted responsibility for the money-raising efforts for the Association in Philadelphia, not hesitating to ask others to contribute because he was giving generously himself. He helped in calling upon other public-spirited citizens to talk about the work. He refused on certain occasions to take on other responsibilities because as he stated, "I am afraid that would interfere with my work for the National Recreation Association which must come first."

The field of sport and its values he knew from active participation. He had been one the nation's leading tennis players.[8]

Gaylord Donnelley, Jr. was Chairman of the Executive Committee of R.R. Donnelley & Son. He was recruited at a very young age—actually in his twenties—to be a sponsor in Chicago of the National Recreation Association. In those days this was just a matter of sending out letters, receiving replies, and mailing them unopened to New York headquarters, where they were acknowledged. He later became a member of the NRA Board and served as a Board member for several years.

Gaylord Donnelley, Jr.

Hon. F. Trubee Davison

Mr. Davison was both a sponsor and member of the Board of NRA for over twenty years. He served as assistant secretary of War for Aviation in the Coolidge and Hoover administrations and later served as president of the American Museum of Natural History. His son Endicott became a member of the NRA Board. Following the merger of NRA to form the NRPA, Endicott became chairman of the NRPA Board of Trustees.

Brig. Gen. Theodore Roosevelt

Brig. Gen. Theodore Roosevelt, son the late President, died suddenly on July 12, 1944, on a battlefield in Normandy.

For many years he had been a devoted friend of the National Recreation Association and an honorary member, and ever an ardent believer in the playground and recreation

(8) R.M. August 1937, pp. 275

center movement in the localities of the United States. He gave encouragement to the Association workers, wrote for the *Recreation* magazine, spoke at a Recreation Congress. At the time of the President's Outdoor Recreation Conference he was the real executive leader, and the Association worked closely with him, contributing the full time of a worker for many months to help in making the Conference a success. He was active in the work of the Boy Scouts of America.

Brig. Gen. Theodore Roosevelt thought of his own father, President Theodore Roosevelt, as a real recreation leader, recognizing the unusual opportunity he and the members of his family had had for recreation in their own home. His father had been Honorary President of the National Recreation Association for a great many years, and one of the first organization meetings of the society was held in the White House with his father present. In giving support to the Association he was carrying on his father's interest as well as his own. Many supporters are now of the second generation.

Brig. Gen. Theodore Roosevelt believed deeply in the principle of decentralization of government—that the roots of a strong recreation movement should be in each locality and that particular attention should always be given to the home.

In his own family and in his own personal life Brig. Gen Theodore Roosevelt practiced what he preached and carried the spirit of recreation and good fun into all that he did. He was deeply concerned to serve the generation in which he lived. In his death the recreation movement has lost a very real and understanding friend.[9]

John H. Goss

On the morning of October 16, 1944, the national recreation movement suffered a severe loss in the death of **John H. Goss** of Waterbury, Connecticut, age seventy-two, retired president of the Scovill Manufacturing Company. Mr. Goss had been the sponsor of the Association in Waterbury and the surrounding area for sixteen years and had been an honorary member of the Association. His belief in the national movement and his readiness to give leadership to it had helped greatly for many years. Mr. Goss himself in his college days had been a varsity baseball pitcher, a quarter-miler on the track team, and he knew from personal experience the value of recreation.[10]

As President and later Chairman of the Board of the Standard Oil Company in New York, **Herbert Lee Pratt's** statements in behalf of recreation carried great weight. On one occasion Mr. Pratt wrote: "One has but to drive through our cities and countryside to see the wonderful development of parks and playgrounds which have been laid out during the past three years... I repeat again that I believe much, if not

Herbert Lee Pratt

all, of the incentive which brought about those developments, was furnished by the Playground and Recreation Association, which was followed by the National Recreation Association..."[11]

(9) R.M. August 1944, pp. 229
(10) R.M. January 1945, pp. 548
(11) R.M. March 1945, pp. 640

In the death of **Alfred E. Smith** on October 4, 1944, the national recreation movement lost a loyal friend.

Al Smith
(Photo courtesy Pach Brother, New York)

Many years ago, before Al Smith gained a world reputation, he was asked if he would join the staff of the National Recreation Association. He sat back in his chair and looked out of the window and talked about how much he cared for boys and how much he enjoyed working for them. He spoke of how much music could mean in the lives of the boys even in the most crowed city districts, and wished that something could be done to make sure that there were a very much larger number of music teachers who would give lessons at a fee not exceeding fifty cents a lesson.

Though he did not feel free to devote himself to the national recreation movement as a staff member, he was always ready to throw his influence to help when called upon. At one time a bill was before the New York State Legislature to amend the act giving local communities home rule in establishing recreation systems. Al Smith was so deeply interested that he, as a Governor, sent three separate messages regarding this bill, and it was his help that brought about its passage.

One of the close associates of Al Smith in days at Albany was Belle Linder Moskowitz, who had been so successful a member of the National Recreation Association staff, working on commercial recreation problems. Another close friend was Robert Moses. Al Smith gave wholehearted backing to Robert Moses in building up various parks in New York State and particularly in the development of the internationally famed Jones Beach. Jones Beach is a monument not only to Robert Moses but also to Al Smith.[12]

Program Training Staff in the 1940s

The National Recreation Association is "at your service" with a staff prepared by training and experience to help recreation leaders—professional and volunteer—increase their efficiency and enrich their program. Some of these men and women give leadership training courses in social recreation, arts and crafts, nature, creative recreation, rural recreation and recreation for women and girls.

Helen Dauncey

Miss Dauncey's institutes are designed primarily for leaders of activities for women and girls, but they have proven time and again to be of service to the whole community.

Mrs. Livingston and **Mrs. Ehlers** each after her own fashion and each, therefore, with her own special emphases, present three courses—an institute in recreation activities for men and women who have recently become recreation workers; a co-recreation institute, an advanced course for professional workers and mature volunteers; a playground leaders institute which offers suggestions for the commu-

Anne Livingston

Ruth Garber Ehlers

(12) R.M. November 1944, pp. 393
Editors note: Albert E. Smith served as governor of New York State for four terms. He was the first Roman Catholic to run for the U.S. Presidency in 1928.

nity use of playgrounds. Games, activity programs, skills, practical suggestions on ways to increase program interest for all ages in the community are the matter of these courses.

Grace Walker

Grace Walker stresses creative recreation, those aspects of the well rounded program too often neglected because of lack of trained leaders. In her institutes she has demonstrated again and again that the techniques of the drama, dance, choral speaking are not outside the use of the average leader, can be used in any program for its greater richness by anyone with a general recreation background.

Jane Farwell's first concern is with rural groups. Her courses are filled with the things she has learned and experienced and—out of that knowledge and background—created, which add more color and joy to living in the county. She works with and through rural organizations whose leaders are interested in broadening their recreation programs.

Jane Farwell

Frank Staples has taken arts and crafts for his province. He goes to a community armed with truckloads of materials and a head full of ways to use them. He conducts two courses—one for beginning, one for more advanced crafters. Both are

Frank Staples

designed to teach teachers varied and richer craft techniques.

Reynold Carlson offers training for outdoor recreation leadership. Nature is his field—nature and the activities indoors and out that are allied to nature or spring form it. Field trips and nature study courses; camping, overnight or day; museums and zoos and parks; nature crafts and nature games and gardening make up the burden of his teaching.

Reynold Carlson

Federal Inter-Agency Committee on Recreation

The growing interest on the part of Federal agencies in recreation and the increasing number of such agencies that provided some kind of recreation service resulted in the recognized need for volunteer coordination and cooperation among them. In November 1946, several Federal agencies formed the Federal Inter-Agency Committee on Recreation with the help of the National Recreation Association, which offered

George E. Dickie

to provide it with executive leadership. The following year **George E. Dickie** was assigned as the Committee's executive secretary in Washington, D.C., where office facilities were furnished in the Department of the Interior.[13]

(13) Butler. 1965

Born in 1884, Mr. Dickie earned a law degree at the University of California in 1906. While a college student he worked as a part-time playground director under church auspices in Alameda; early in his business career he supervised a boys' club in Oakland, and during the summers of 1907 and 1908 he was employed as playground instructor by the Oakland Club, a progressive woman's organization. The Club's Parks and Playgrounds Committee succeeded in having a recreation commission appointed in 1908 and Mr. Dickie was named its superintendent. In 1917 he joined the staff of the National Recreation Association, where he held top-ranking positions for thirteen years, and served as executive secretary of the Federal Inter-Agency Committee on Recreation until retired 1960.

The primary function of the Committee was to serve as a clearinghouse for an exchange of information on policies, plans and activities of the member agencies and for a consideration of common problems. It attempted to determine the responsibility of the Federal government in the field of recreation, to discover unmet needs, and to develop plans for achieving cooperative action to meet them. It also fostered the organization of state inter-agency recreation groups to serve a similar function on the state level.

In achieving its purpose, the Committee issued a number of publications under Mr. Dickie's direction. Among them were *The Role of the Federal Government in the Field of Recreation*—a summary of the development and current status of Federal recreation services; *Summary of Basic Federal Legislation Relating to Recreation; Selected Recreation Publications of Federal Agencies; Fees and Charges for Federal Recreation Facilities and Services;* and *The Conservation and Development of Outdoor Recreation resources*, prepared for the President's Water Resources Policy Commission. The demise of the committee, after the Bureau of Outdoor Recreation was established in the Department of the Interior, occurred only two years after Mr. Dickie retired in 1960.

Chapter Seven

1950s and Golden Anniversary

NATIONAL RECREATION ASSOCIATION

EIGHT WEST EIGHTH STREET

Welcome

New Executive Director

As we go to press, we are happy to announce the appointment of **Joseph Prendergast**, New York lawyer and official of the State Charities Aid Association of New York, as executive director of the National Recreation Association. Mr. Prendergast will shortly take over his new post, a leading position in the national recreation movement. He assumes the executive responsibilities formerly held by the late Howard Braucher.

A former assistant to the United States Attorney General and, before that, associated with the New York law firm of Sullivan and Cromwell, Mr. Prendergast entered social work in 1946, following his discharge from the Army as Major. He studied at Columbia University's New York School of Social Work where he majored in community organization, receiving a Master of Science degree in 1947. Mr. Prendergast has been with the State Charities Aid since then—first as assistant and later as executive secretary of its Welfare Legislation Information Bureau. During the same period he has been a member of the faculty of Columbia University where he gave a course in social legislation.

As executive director of the National Recreation Association, Mr. Prendergast will head an organization which, for more than forty years, has played a leading role in the development of community and municipal recreation. The Association, through its headquarters and field staffs, each year serves several thousand communities throughout the country, government units as well as many individuals, industrial firms, churches and other groups interested in recreation. The Association is supported by voluntary contributions.

Mr. Prendergast, a native of Chicago, attended the Evanston, Illinois public high school, Phillips Exeter Academy and graduated from Princeton University, class of 1927. While at Princeton he was star halfback and the only student in its history to have been elected president of his class in each of his

Joseph Prendergast

four undergraduate years. He studied law at Balliol College, Oxford, and as a member of the Inner Temple qualified for admission as barrister-at-law.

Associated first with Sullivan and Cromwell, and later with the legal firm of Osborn, Fleming and Whittlesey, also of New York, Mr. Prendergast was with the United States Department of Justice during the years between 1934 and 1942. He filled a variety of posts in the department, as assistant to United States Attorney in the Southern District of New York, as special assistant to the Attorney General, as assistant to Mr. Justice Stanley Reed, chairman at the time of the President's Committee on Civil Service War Policies Unit of the War Division, Department of Justice.

He enlisted in the Army in 1942, serving overseas with the 12th Armored Division, was wounded, captured and escaped in Germany in 1945. He is now a Major in the Armored Reserve Corps.

Joseph Prendergast is a man of vision and great sincerity of purpose. He brings to National Recreation Association those qualities of mind and spirit, and of leadership, so essential in furthering the growth and development of its vital work in the field of human service.

The Past is Prologue to the Future

This year, 1956, marks the Fiftieth Anniversary of the founding of the National Recreation Association. During this half-century there have been far-reaching changes in the American way of life. There have been two Worlds Wars and a major depression. The population has more than doubled and the standard of living has risen enormously during this time. We talk today of atoms and jets and automation. In these early days of the Association, conversation was about the horseless carriage and the wonders of the transcontinental telephone.

On April 12, 1906, a group of leading educators, civic leaders, and social workers met in Washington to discuss the problem of how children could be assured a reasonable chance for happy, healthy, and constructive lives in the unplanned and congested American cities of the times.

These far-sighted thinkers were very much alert to the new trends of the twentieth century. They were conscious that something had to be done about the American cities in which growing slum-infested areas were filled to overflowing with immigrants from abroad and emigrants from the surrounding rural areas. They were not alone, because this was the period in American history when civic leaders were becoming active in campaigns for better communities; when the term "muckracker" was prominent as a description of the crusading journalists who were exposing corruption it city government; when "reform" was in the mouth and on the lips of a new generation moving into places of leadership.

So powerful was the appeal for the playground movement in 1906 that within a year, many prominent national leaders became identified with the program. President Theodore Roosevelt spoke to the organizing group at a meeting in the White House

and later in the year agreed to serve as honorary president of the new organization. By the end of the first year Jacob Riis was serving as honorary vice-president and Joseph Lee and Jane Addams were among its influential supporters. Within a year the Russell Sage Foundation was providing the services of a field consultant employed full-time to assist local communities. Within eighteen months of its formation, the Association helped to establish more community recreation programs than had been established in the previous eighteen years.

From the very first, the new association drew support from, and in turn served, every segment of American life. There was an eagerness on the part of educators and social workers from all over the country for the kind of leadership and service the new organization was established to give. But the support came from more than professional leaders in these two professions. It came also from lawyers, religious leaders, bankers, industrialists, and thoughtful citizens from all walks of life.

In the past fifty years, the concept of recreation has broadened to keep pace with the changing times. Founded as the Playground Association of America, the name was changed in 1911 to the Playground and

Recreation Association, and in 1931 to the National Recreation Association. It is noteworthy that within the last few months the National Recreation Association has produced a motion picture on hospital recreation, a booklet on family recreation, and, by special request, has consulted with the United States Air Force on a manual about recreation for the dependents of airmen.

From the very first, the National Recreation Association has worked in many ways to advance the causes of the physical education program in the public schools. It has provided training in recreation leadership to nearly a million volunteer and paid leaders in communities throughout the country. It has helped to create a public understanding of recreation as the finest, most creative use of non-working time for adults, and free-time for children, and has encouraged the use of this time in every kind of wholesome indoor-and-outdoor recreation, including music, drama, arts and crafts, cultural, social, and athletic activities. It has encouraged recreation for the individual, for the family, and for groups of people wherever they tend to come together—whether it be in churches, clubs, on the job, in the city or in rural areas.

In all of its years of service it has sought to help every organization in any way concerned with recreation. At the national level, the Association has been a resource of encouragement and information for youth serving agencies, civic and service clubs, government recreation agencies, and similar organizations. At the local level, its many services have been expanded to include individuals of all ages, groups and public and private agencies of all kinds.

It is especially in the area of community recreation, however, that the National Recreation Association takes pride in its accomplishments of the past fifty years. The enthusiastic sponsors of the playground movement in 1906 called for every community in the country to accept the responsibility for estab-

lishing public playgrounds under leadership. Today more than three thousand communities have many thousands of playgrounds staffed with professional leaders. More than one thousand two hundred cities have recreation departments headed by a full-time recreation executive. There are more than a million acres of public park and recreation properties owned and operated by cities and regional governmental park and recreation agencies.

These significant advantages in planned recreation for better living have been encouraged and nurtured by the National Recreation Association. The unique relation of the Association to the recreation movement has helped to bring together all of the elements in American life which are so vitally concerned with recreation. Through the years the recreation profession has grown into a separate, independent profession. As the recreation profession has developed it has provided more and more of the skilled leadership in the movement. At the same time, the civic, business, industrial and social leaders of local communities and the nation have come to participate through their work as sponsors, supporters, and members of the board of directors of the National Recreation Association. In a very real sense they are the trustees of the movement. And the professional staff of the Association serves as the secretariat for the movement.

America faces even more profound social and economic challenges today than it ever has in the past. The problems of American cities which loomed so large during the beginning of the twentieth century, the troubles of war and depression, were major obstacles on the road to progress.

But today's cold war, the new leisure resulting from the extensive use of electronics, the development of atomic energy and the concept of automation are challenges which stagger the imagination.

In fact, the economic and social changes evolving today are completely fabulous. It is almost breathtaking to realize that since 1906 the average workweek has decreased from sixty hours to less than forty and that, in just the past few years, automation has developed to a point where predictions of the thirty-hour- and even the twenty-four-hour-week are becoming commonplace.

Think of the challenges that this brings to all of us in recreation! No longer will people's thinking be centered largely around their working time; by the very nature of the technology, working time will be a very minor part of living.

Non-working activities—recreation activities, if you will—must give the opportunities to make life an exciting, creative, adventurous experience.

Back in 1906 the factory worker produced goods valued at eighty-four cents per hour in terms of our present dollar. Last year, by the same dollar measurement, this productivity had increased to $2.41 per man-hour, and it is estimated that it will reach $3.90 by 1975. this increased productivity is used one-third in more leisure time and two-thirds in a higher standard of living. George Soule, the noted economist, in a recent book, *Time For Living*, predicts that within three generations the average American family will have an income in terms of today's purchasing power of $25,000.

Now, for the first time, the great bulk of American people are able to enjoy vast numbers of different kinds of recreation activities which a few years ago were restricted to only the few who were well-to-do.

Since 1906 the population of the United States has doubled. By 1960 it will probably reach 177 million and by 1975, it is expected to increase some thirty-five per cent to 221 million. There are now more children in school than there were people in the United States in 1860. The year of 1954 was the eighth consecutive year that the birth rate had run over three and a half million. Owing to increased longevity since 1906, the number of people over sixty-five has more than quadrupled. In 1906 one out of every twenty-five persons was over sixty-five years of age. In 1950 it was one in every twelve and in 1980 it will be one in every seven.

These are just a few of the astounding figures which help to describe the nature of the new social conditions which challenge society and especially those in a position of civic or professional leadership in the recreation movement.

It has been wisely said by President–Emeritus William Russell of Columbia University, "Too much leisure with too much money has been the dread of societies across the ages. That is when nations cave in from within. That is when they fail."

During the past fifty years, the National Recreation Association joins with everyone in the recreation movement in meeting eagerly the new challenges. This is a time of great hope for all mankind. It is a time when the recreation forces the nation and the world are destined to play an ever greater role in man's continuing search for peace and happiness.[1]

(Signed) Joseph Prendergast
Executive Director,
National Recreation Association

Consultng Service for the Ill and Handicapped

In 1953 the Hospital Recreation Consultant Service was created. Through this service, known as Consulting Service on Recreation for the Ill and the Handicapped, efforts were made to help hospitals develop effective recreation programs for the benefit of their patients and the help them understand the importance of fully qualified professional recreation leadership in conducting such programs. Under the suspices of this service a nation-wide study of hospital recreation was made.

(1) R.M. January 1956

Key Long–Term NRA Staff

George D. Butler,
Director of Research

Charles E. Reed,
*Director of
Field Service*

Thomas E. Rivers,
*Director of
International Recreation*

Abbie Condit,
Director of Publications

Arthur M. Williams,
Administration

Virginia Musselman,
Director of Program Services

Willard C. Sutherland,
*Director of Personnel
Services*

George A. Nesbitt,
*Director of
Technical Assistance*

Editor's note: Arthur M. Williams was employed by the Playground Association of America in 1910 and worked
until his retirement in 1963, giving him the longest tenure (53 years) of any employee in the Association's history.

New Membership Plan

In 1951, Prendergast established a non-voting membership based on "service associates" (individuals) and "service affiliates" (agencies). This membership concept is explained in the magazine notice. By the end of 1951 there were 1,035 individual non-voting members in 627 communities and 620 agencies in 529 communities affiliated for service.

National Recreation Association

The *National Recreation Association* is a nationwide, nonprofit, nonpolitical and nonsectarian civic organization, established in 1906 and supported by voluntary contributions, and dedicated to the service of all recreation executives, leaders and agencies, public and private, to the end that every child in America shall have a place to play in safety and that every person in America, young and old, shall have an opportunity for the best and most satisfying use of his expanding leisure time.

Service Affiliates

A service affiliation with the National Recreation Association is open to all nonprofit private and public organizations whose function is wholly or primarily provision of recreation services, and which include recreation as an important part of their total programs, and whose cooperation in the Association's work would, in the opinion of the Association's Board of Directors, further the ends of the national recreation movement.

Service Associates

Service association with the National Recreation Association is open to all individuals who are actively engaged on a full-time or part-time employed basis, or as volunteers, in a nonprofit private or public recreation organization, and whose cooperation in the work of the Association would, in the opinion of the Association's Board of Directors, further the national recreation movement. Student Association is a special category for those enrolled full-time in colleges and universities, or taking recreation courses.

Contributors

The continuation of the work of the National Recreation Association from year to year is made possible by the splendid cooperation and support of several hundred volunteer sponsors, community chests and united funds, foundations, corporations, and individual contributors throughout the country, to help provide healthy, happy creative living for Americans of all ages.[2]

For further information regarding the Association and its specialized services, please write: Executive Director, National Recreation Association, 8 West Eighth Street, New York 11, New York.

---

(2) Hartsoe & Knapp. pp. 159, 1970

National Advisory Committees

**NATIONAL RECREATION ASSOCIATION
ADVISORY COUNCIL AND COMMITTEES**

BOARD OF DIRECTORS of the
NATIONAL RECREATION ASSOCIATION

National Advisory Council
Composed of
Chairmen of National and District Committees

District Advisory Committees   National Advisory Committees

District Advisory Committees	National Advisory Committees
New England	Administration
Middle Atlantic	Program
Southern	Research
Great Lakes	Personnel
Midwest	Defense
Southwest State	Recreation Publication
Pacific Northwest	Federal Recreation
Pacific Southwest	International

*National Advisory Committee
on Recreation Research*

The National Advisory Committee on Recreation Research, composed of outstanding leaders in the recreation and park fields, the field of recreation education and training, and related fields has been established to afford a liaison between the many agencies conduction research related to recreation, focus attention upon fundamental and realistic recreation needs, encourage and assist recreation research projects, and help the recreation movement and individual recreation agencies and leaders benefit from the results of research in recreation and in related fields.

*National Advisory Committee on Recreation
Programs and Activities*

The National Recreation Association, realizing that the backbone of the recreation movement is the provision of programs and activities that meet the needs and interests of all people, has established a National Advisory Committee on Recreation Programs and Activities. Subcommittees on Drama, Arts and Crafts, and Dance have been formed, and others are in the making. It is our hope that through these committees increased interest can be stimulated, new techniques developed, standards raised, trained leadership developed, and new material prepared and distributed.

National Advisory Committee
on Defense Related Services

The National Advisory Committee on Defense Related Services, composed of outstanding leaders in defense and recreation was appointed to help the National Recreation Association to develop special defense recreation services designed bring our country's local, state and national resources to bear on the recreation needs created by the impact of the national defense program.

National Advisory Committee on State Recreation

The National Advisory Committee on State Recreation is composed of state officials concerned with recreation services and programs. The Committee functions in the following ways: to help the National Recreation Association to be a clearing house on the subject of state sponsored recreation services; as a study group to help the Association determine problems and to help in the solution of these problems; to assist the Association in the dissemination of information on state recreation matters; to help coordinate the work of the Association in this phase of the recreation field with the activities of other national, professional and service organizations concerned with this aspect of recreation.

The Committee projects at present include work on the State Section of the Recreation and Park Yearbook for 1955 to be published this fall, identifying problems common to the administration of state recreation services and recommending principles relating to the solution of these problems, formulating and recommending to the national Recreation Association a policy statement on the role of state government in organized recreation.

National Advisory Committee
on Recreation Administration

The National Advisory Committee on Recreation Administration, composed of administrators of public recreation and park services in communities both large and small throughout the country, has been appointed to study a variety of important and currently difficult administrative problems, and to make available to the Association and to the national recreation movement the best information and experience obtainable for meeting these challenging questions.

National Advisory Committee on Recruitment,
Training and Placement of Recreation Personnel

This national advisory committee of the National Recreation Association has been set up to strengthen personnel work in the recreation field through the cooperation of the Association and recreation executives and leaders throughout the country, bringing about an alertness not only to local needs but to the needs of the recreation profession and to the best use of the Association's resources and services.

National Advisory Committee for
The International Recreation Service
of The National Recreation Association

The horizon shows much of international import for recreation in the 50th Anniversary year of the National Recreation Association.

The International Recreation Congress, in Philadelphia, is anticipated eagerly by recreation leaders in all parts of the world. The Cooperative Community Recreation Project, with assistance by the State Department's International Educational

Exchange Service and with hospitality promised by scores of American cities, is another of the many projects involving the International Recreation Service and its National Advisory Committee.

Through the activities of this service and its advisory committee the recreation knowledge and experience of many countries are being exchanged for the benefit of all.

National Advisory Committee
on The Publishing of Recreation Materials

The National Advisory Committee on the Publishing of Recreation Materials, composed of representatives of a variety of recreation publications-national, state, and local-has been established for the purpose of: a) building a closer working relationship between the national Recreation Association and leaders in the recreation field on matters pertaining to publishing activities; b) strengthening the network of recreation publications across the country generally, thus contributing to the stature of the recreation profession. This purpose will be accomplished through advisory functions which also are twofold; one, advisory to the Association; two, advisory to the field. The committee will also act as a clearing house for an exchange of recreation and publishing information.

NRA Headquarters, 8th Street, New York City

In 1955 the Association purchased the building in which the Whitney Museum of Modern Art had been located for many years at 8 West 8th Street, New York City, and reconditioned it for office use. This attractive headquarters building is owned and occupied by the National Recreation Association.

The First Half Century

Otto T. Mallery

A short lifetime ago—fifty years—the National Recreation Association was born, welcomed by President Theodore Roosevelt at a White House meeting of the Association's board of directors. Twenty-five years later President Herbert Hoover again made the White House a sounding board for the recreation needs of the American people by holding a meeting of the board of directors.

For fifty years the NRA has been a part of the persistent conscience of the American people, whispering what ought to be. When the whispers went unheeded a little shouting cleared the lungs.

Joseph Prendergast

The idea that play was a part of normal growth was then a novel idea. The NRA asserted that city life was ill-suited for children. In the planning of our cities the children had been left out. I was one of those children who tried to play football on an alley paved with cobblestones. I also tried to roller skate on brick sidewalks. Then only a handful of cities provided playgrounds of any sort; now there are few that do not. Then there were no trained play leaders; now the play leader is a member of a respected profession taught by many colleges whose graduates make the playgrounds hum.

Among NRA's honored presidents was Joseph Lee, philosopher of play, who wrote Play and Education, John H. Finley, college president and editor of The New York Times, and Howard Braucher, idealist turned executive, statesman in social work.

Joseph Lee, John Finley, and Howard Braucher left indelible impressions, not only on the NRA but on their times. They, and many unknown soldiers in the ranks, have made it possible for the NRA in its fiftieth year to strive with increasing success to make the profession of recreation leadership one of the most outstanding influences in the American way of life. By games sports, and carry-over skills in arts and crafts and other cultural interests, recreation leaders are equal partners with school teachers in molding incentive and character. The NRA will always be fighting the battles of the recreation leader against political pressure and for the highest professional standards.

The ultimate strength of the National Recreation Association lies in the devotion and civic spirit of thousands of laymen and women on boards, committees, and foundations who steadily hold the line and keep advancing it.

NRA's Fiftieth Anniversary is marked by three outstanding events: our new home headquarters, a building of charm and adequacy—the reconditioned former Whitney Art Museum—is in full swing. The first nation-wide drive for resources to permit the NRA to meet ever-increasing demands upon its staff, publications, and services is being planned. The final great event will be the International Recreation Congress in Philadelphia, September 30 to October 5, the first in twenty years and the most far-reaching ever attempted, with participants from many lands.

The NRA persuaded the International Educational Exchange Service of the State Department to invite a number of recreation leaders from different countries. Fifty or more American communities have been organized to receive these overseas leaders into their recreation and civic lives for varying periods—weeks or months.

The International Recreation Congress has grown out of two missions undertaken by the International Recreation Service of the NRA when Mr. and Mrs. Thomas E. Rivers visited thirteen countries in 1952, and twenty-two countries on a second trip in 1955.

We are fortunate to have Joseph Prendergast as executive director. His Zeal, devotion, and ability find a keen response in the enthusiastic cooperation of a staff second to that of no other civic organization.

The workers of fifty years ago, including myself, did not foresee the scope, the widening horizons of activities, or the potent influence NRA and recreation would come to wield. May the next fifty years be even more fruitful in the pursuit of happiness, through a sound mind in a sound body, both mind and body more and more engaged in creative leisure-time activities satisfying to the deepest needs of men.

(Signed) Otto T. Mallery
Chairman, National Recreation Association
Board of Directors

SUSAN M. LEE
Second Vice-President
New York, N. Y.

PAUL MOORE, JR.
First Vice-President
Jersey City, N. J.

OTTO T. MALLERY
Chairman of the Board
Philadelphia, Pa.

Meet Today's Officers and Board Members

GRANT TITSWORTH
Third Vice-President
Noroton, Conn.

The National Recreation Association is happy to introduce the members of its board, that group of outstanding citizens which carries the responsibility for the policy making and interpretation of the Association and its services, and for building financial support for the Association. Its members give and raise a substantial percentage of the NRA's contribution income.

F. W.H.
ADAMS
New York, N. Y.

F. GREGG
BEMIS
Boston, Mass.

MRS. ROBERT WOODS
BLISS
Washington, D. C.

MRS. ROLLIN
BROWN
Los Angeles, Calif.

HOWARD H.
CALLAWAY
Hamilton, Ga.

HODDING
CARTER
Greenville, Miss.

MRS. ARTHUR G.
CUMMER
Jacksonville, Fla.

ADRIAN M. MASSIE
Treasurer
New York, N. Y.

HARRY P.
DAVISON
New York, N. Y.

GAYLORD
DONNELLEY
Chicago, Ill.

ANTHONY DREXEL
DUKE
Locust Valley, N.Y.

RICHARD A.
FARNSWORTH
Houston, Tex.

MRS. HOWARD A.
FRAME
Los Altos, Calif.

MRS. PAUL
GALLAGHER
Omaha, Neb.

ROBERT
GARRETT
Baltimore, Md.

MRS. NORMAN
HARROWER
Fitchburgh, Mass.

MRS. CHARLES V.
HICKOX
Michigan City, Ind.

FREDRIC R.
MANN
Philadelphia, Pa.

HENRY W.
MEERS
Chicago, Ill.

WILLIAM C.
MENNINGER
Topeka, Kan.

JOSEPH PRENDERGAST
Secretary
New York, N. Y.

CARL E.
MILLIKEN
Augusta, Me.

MRS. RUTH E.
PEELER
Seattle, Wash.

MRS. RICHARD E.
RIEGEL
Montchanin, Del.

WILLIAM S.
SIMPSON
Bridgeport, Conn.

MRS. WM. L.
VAN ALEN
Edgemont, Pa.

FREDERICK M.
WARBURG
New York, N. Y.

National Recreation Association Serves the World

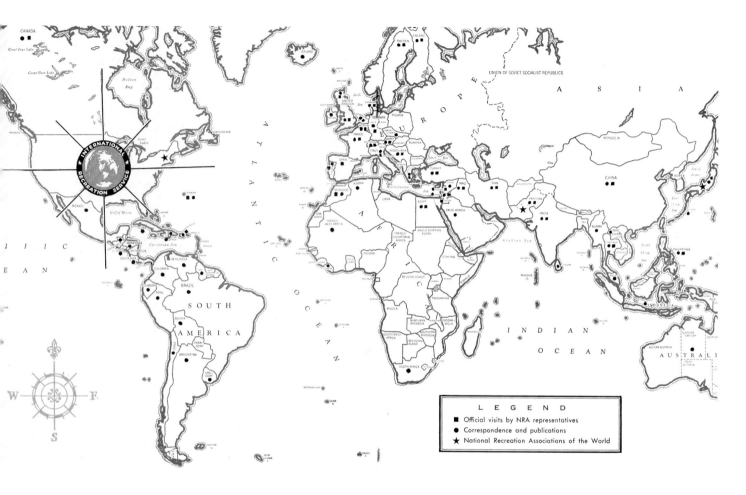

In The United States–1955:

    3,837 communities registered for service

    1,082 field visits

    3,769 professional and lay leaders at nine district conferences and one Congress

    10,000 employed and volunteer leaders in 140 cities received leadership training

    23,449 organizations and individuals in 5,389 communities used
    correspondence and consultation services

Other Countries–1955:

    22 countries visited by official representatives of NRA

    91 NRA memberships for organizations and individuals in 14 countries

    41 countries have subscribers to *Recreation* magazine

    19 countries are represented on International Congress Advisory Committee

    300 communities in 54 countries received correspondence and publications in answer to inquiries.

NATIONAL RECREATION ASSOCIATION

A Service Organization Supported by Voluntary Contributions

JOSEPH PRENDERGAST, *Executive Director*

HONOR ROLL OF SPONSORS

The National Recreation Association is proud to publish the names of present sponsors who have served the field through the Association for ten years of more. Those listed below constitute an honor roll. They have made a notable contribution to the development of recreation in America.

We take this opportunity to express our deep appreciation.

SPONSORS WHO HAVE SERVED FOR TWENTY OR MORE YEARS

F. GREGG BEMIS
Boston, Massachusetts

MRS. PAUL L. BORDEN
Goldsboro, North Carolina

WARD M. CANADAY
Toledo, Ohio

C. SEWALL CLARK
Philadelphia, Pennsylvania

MRS. G. H. A. CLOWES
Woods Holes, Massachusetts

MRS. F. F. COUCH
Bethlehem, Pennsylvania

F. TRUBEE DAVISON

Locust Valley, New York

*Deceased

MRS. WILLIAM G. DWIGHT*
Holyoke, Massachusetts

BLAIR J. FISHBURN
Roanoke, Virginia

EDGAR FRIEDLANDER
Cincinnati, Ohio

ROBERT GARRETT
Baltimore, Maryland

MAX GUGGENHEIMER
Lynchburg, Virginia

MRS. NORMAN HARROWER
Fitchburg, Massachusetts

MRS. WALTER C. JANNEY*
Bryn Mawr, Pennsylvania

DR. TULLY C. KNOLES
Stockton, California

MRS. H. DUTTON NOBLE
Auburn, New York

MRS. BRACE W. PADDOCK
Pittsfield, Massachusetts

MRS. BERT PRINTZ
Youngstown, Ohio

WILLIAM H. PUTNAM*
Hartford, Connecticut

REV. CHARLES A. ROSS
Elizabeth, New Jersey

MRS. ALGER SHELDEN
Detroit, Michigan

BEN F. TUCKER
Long Beach, California

SPONSORS WHO HAVE SERVED TEN YEARS OR MORE

Mrs. Copley Amory, Jr., *Cambridge, Mass.*
Dr.Roy H. Baribeau, *Battle Creek, Mich.*
Hon. Willard M. Benton, *Kansas City, Kan.*
Mrs. Frances W. Bird, *Wianno, Mass.*
Hon. James M. Corcoran, *Evanston, Ill.*
Mrs. J. Gerry Dobbins, *Litchfield, Conn.*
Gaylord Donnelley, *Chicago, Ill.*
Richard Farnsworth, *Houston, Tex.*
L. Harris French, *Waterbury, Conn.*
C. R. Frye, *Shreveport, La.*
Mrs. Clarence J. Gamble, *Milton, Mass.*
Colin Gardner, III, *Middletown, Ohio*
Mrs. John Grew, *Dover, Mass.*
William L. Hinds, *Syracuse, N.Y.*
Mrs. William C. Huntoon, Jr., *Providence, R.I.*
Mrs. Siegel Judd, *Grand Rapids, Mich.*
Thomas V. Kenney, *Troy, N.Y.*
Arthur W. King, *Duluth, Minn.*
Mrs. Ledlie I. Laughlin, *Princeton, N.J.*
Robert H. Loomis, *Newton, Mass.*
Mrs. John R. McLane, *Manchester, N.H.*

Johnson D. McMahon, *Rome, N.Y.*
Mrs. Noel Miller, *Racine, Wis.*
Welles V. Moot, *Buffalo, N.Y.*
Mrs. Julian Pease, *New Britain, N.Y.*
Mrs. Samuel F. Pryor, Jr., *Greenwich, Conn.*
Mrs. Richard E. Riegel, *Wilmington, Del.*
Carl T. Schuneman, *St. Paul, Minn.*
Raymond D. Shepard, *Montclair, N.J.*
Arthur B. Shepley, Jr., *St. Louis, Mo.*
Fred B. Shoaf, *Fort Wayne, Ind.*
Mrs. Albert Spalding, *Great Barrington, Mass.*
Arthur Stangel, *Manitowoc, Wis.*
Harry C. Stine, *Kenosha, Wis.*
H. J. Stocksick, *Pasadena, Calif.*
Fred R. Stofft, *Tucson, Ariz.*
Mrs. Herbert J. Sturberg, *Norwalk, Conn.*
George C. Thompson, *Grand Rapids, Mich.*
Evans Ward, *Port Chester, N.Y.*
Mrs. Frederic Winthrop, *Hamilton, Mass.*

(3)

(3) R. M. April 1958, pp. 98

100 Days

T. R. Rivers

There isn't time to prepare a full report for this issue of *Recreation* on the one hundred packed, inspiring, and I hope helpful, days which Mrs. Rivers and I spent as ambassadors of recreation, in the name of all recreation workers and friends in the United States, to the leaders and peoples of twenty-two European and Middle East countries. A brief report must serve for the time being.

The purposes of the trip were, I believe, generally accomplished: interchange of recreation information, promotion of the International Recreation Congress, helping to implement the Cooperative Community Exchange Project, urging formation of national recreation associations in the several countries, and the possible federation of these national units into an International Recreation Association. From ragged children in Arab refugee camps to royalty we proclaimed the "chance to play" as the right of a child and a source of enduring satisfaction for youths and adults. The response and cooperation which we received in carrying out specific objectives were beyond our expectations.

Scandinavia's interest in and provision for certain aspects of recreation are phenomenal. Sven Salén, Sweden's great industrialist, will be on our International Advisory Committee. In Finland, land of sports and weekend gardeners, Urho Saariaho, member of Parliament, came to our plane and thanked us again for coming to his country.

In Germany, from 10:00 a.m. to 4:00 p.m., some sixty leaders brought together by the Ministry of Education from all over West Germany faced frankly how our ideas and plans might help in the rebuilding of Germany. George von Opel, German industrialist and sportsman, is to be our committeeman from Germany.

In England, where we had a glorious week as guests of the National Playing Fields Association, the climax was our reception at Buckingham Palace. Accompanied by Admiral Norman, we were received by His Royal Highness, the Duke of Edinburgh, who has given active leadership to the recreation movement in England.

Shah of Iran receives gold medal and certificate from T.E. Rivers, executive secretary, International Recreation Service.

The chairman of our dinner meeting in Holland said: "You have given us a different picture of America than we often get. We like this one. You can count on our cooperation."

In Yugoslavia—a new nation struggling with many problems, economic, political and social, wavering between the East and the West—we found a real hunger for international contacts and a deep desire to learn all that would help in their work for children.

In France, in accord with the historic pattern, the recreation program follows many lines, political, religious, economic and ideological; but the volume of recreation is tremendous—fifteen thousand amateur groups, for instance, performing fifty thousand plays a year. At a memorable luncheon in the shadow of Sacre Coeur on Montmartre, we recognized the contribution of the National Council of Youth, the League of French Teaching, and the work of the French Government. Deep appreciation was expressed for our presence and for bringing together these great forces for recreation France.

In little Belgium we were told that when two Belgians meet they form an organization. We saw files of twenty-two thousand private associations of all kinds of purposes but all more or less recreational.

On the Balcony of the Capitol in Rome, Mayor Rebechini pointed out the historic spots of ancient Rome below, told of his plans for recreation in modern Rome, and expressed the hope that his reelection might make it possible for him to attend the Philadelphia Congress.

General Katsotas, mayor of Athens, speaking earnestly said: "People who spend their time and energy and technical knowledge getting the people of the world working together on this problem make me closer to them. I know your work is important. I will back your ideas in Greece."

At an audience in Istanbul with His All Holiness Athenagoras, Patriarch of the Greek Orthodox Church, we presented a copy of Howard Braucher's *Treasury of Living*.

He opened it, read aloud a few lines from "America Has a Song," then said, "That is beautiful. This is the real America. She does have a head and abundant resources, but oh, her real greatness is her heart and her song. God bless you and God bless America. I shall treasure this book. It will continually remind me of the soul of the American people. May your leadership continue to bring the nations of the world closer together. I know recreation will help."

Refik Koralton, chairman of the National Assembly in Turkey, said, as we parted: "We will ponder what you have told us. Thank you for coming to Turkey."

In Teheran, our farthest point east, as guests of Iran we were privileged to share in the forwarding of a national recreation movement under the chairmanship of Prime Minister Hussein Ala. In an audience with His Majesty the Shah in the Jade Marble Palace, that perfect example of Persian art and architecture, he thanked us for our help to Iran and spoke with personal knowledge of the developments under way and with conviction of what recreation could do for the youth of Iran. Later that same afternoon, Mr. Ala barely escaped an assassin's bullet.

Fired by the hot stream of liquid gold that flows from newly discovered oil, Bagdad in Iraq is a cauldron in which ancient cultures are being streamlined for twentieth century living. The youthful eyes of His Majesty the King gleamed as we outlined our hopes for recreation in Iraq. He expressed his hearty approval of what we were doing and gave his assurance of Iraq's cooperation in the international recreation movement.

For five days in Jordan we experienced superb Arab hospitality on all social levels from villages to the royal palace. We had our eyes opened to one of the most valiant struggles for social welfare we have ever seen. His Majesty King Hussein Ibn Talal greeted us with outstretched hand. "You are welcome. Jordan is your country while you are here. I have heard about your mission. Let me know if there is anything we can do. Our resources are small but we have an asset in our people, and we want to be counted among the nations working for the people's welfare."

I still glow when I think of what we saw and felt in Egypt. In that ancient land of the Pharaohs a revolution is in progress which is kin to a religious revival. It was a stirring experience to work with those young men and women so conscious of their role as nation builders and so clear that, this time, the people's welfare is the goal and that recreation is one of the essentials.

To our friends here and there and everywhere our heartfelt thanks! Your support, your cooperation, your readiness to look ahead and work in unity give promise of building another great instrument for enriching the human spirit.

Make a Wise Investment

In times like these, invest in boys and girls. Men talk about buying stock at the bottom. When you invest in a boy or girl, you are always buying at the bottom. You are sure that the youngster is growing up, and there is no telling how far.

I invite every man and woman in the world to take a flyer in Childhood Preferred. I predict a great future for this security. It has investment merit combined with the most exciting speculative possibilities.

You are sure to get a man or woman; you may get a great man or a great woman,—Bruce Barton in *The Jungle Weekly*, Berkeley Lions Club, Berkeley, California.[4]

HERBERT HOOVER

The Waldorf–Astoria Towers
New York 22, New York
September 21, 1956

The International Advisory Committee greets and welcomes you with hope and confidence.

The store of knowledge and techniques available for improving human life is tremendous. Here is a superb opportunity for the dissemination and exchange on one important aspect of life–recreation.

Mutual understanding, respect and admiration are attitudes that can be best developed by people to people contact such as we are to have here. Only on such a foundation can the human family flourish or even survive.

Few fields offer greater promise in bridging the barriers of language and culture than that of recreation. Let us make the most of it here and in the years to follow.

(Signed) Herbert Hoover
Honorary Chairman
International
Recreation Congress

With former President of the United States Herbert Hoover as honorary chairman, an outstanding International Advisory Committee is being formed for the International Recreation Congress which will meet in Philadelphia September 30-October 5. Distinguished leaders in government, industry, and in youth and recreation movements of fifteen countries have already accepted membership on the committee. Mr. Hoover served as honorary president at the First International Recreation Congress in 1932 at Los Angeles.

4) R.M. February 1956
Editors note: International Recreation Association changed its name to World Lwisure and Recreation association in 1967.

Field Services 1956

Field Services

Upon request, NRA field representatives go into the offices and meeting rooms, and to the playgrounds, recreation centers, hospitals and institutions, churches, military installations, and other places where people are other places where people are making plans, training leaders or conducting recreation programs. They work with professional and volunteer leaders, executives, boards, and citizens groups in public and private recreation agencies on local, state, and national levels. This on-the-spot service takes NRA to the people.

In 1963, members of the NRA field staff made 1,211 visits to 620 communities and 100 military installations. They participated in 128 meetings of state recreation societies and 73 meeting of other organizations. They visited 50 colleges and universities; they planned and participated in 23 meetings of their district advisory committees and conducted nine district conferences. They conducted 42 leadership training institutes which reached more than 2,000 people. They made 56 surveys, plans, and special evaluations of recreation areas and facilities and programs. These services were performed by NRA district representatives, training consultants, and planners. Field service was also given by other NRA staff members—specialists in program, cultural arts, and the ill and handicapped.

Service to State Agencies. Field Service representatives work with state park and recreation agencies, conservation, health, welfare, institutions, planning, extension, economic development, commissions on aging fitness, and children and youth. Common types of services include technical assistance, information, personnel training, resource development, promotion of legislation, and assistance to state recreation societies and associations.

Service to Federal Agencies

As new federal agencies and programs get under way , the field staff of NRA gets acquainted with government representatives in their districts. NRA's representative have worked closely with public housing authorities, the U.S. Forest Service, Housing and Home Finance Agency, Bureau of Outdoor Recreation, Department of Health, Education and Welfare, Department of Labor, Youth Division, and the Bureau of Land Management.

Service to the Armed Forces. An important phase of NRA's field service is work with Armed Forces installations. In 1963, an NRA national training specialist conducted workshops and made field visits to twenty-eight Air Force bases in twenty-five states. The director of NRA Field Services spent two months in Europe making a appraisal of the Air Force recreation center program, visiting fifteen bases in Germany, France and England; district representatives visited bases and adjacent communities giving technical help; conducting workshops, making surveys, recruiting civilian recreation leaders, and encouraging cooperative base-community relationships. One hundred military installations were visited by NRA representatives. The National Advisory Committee on Defense Related Services gathered material for a booklet on *Military—Community Cooperation Through Recreation*, published early in 1964.

Visits to Colleges and Universities.

The Field Service maintains a close relationship with the colleges and universities which offer a major in recreation. NRA representatives visit the schools as often as possible, speak to classes, and interview students.

Services to Voluntary Agencies.

Extensive field service is given to non-government voluntary agencies of all kinds. Leading the list are community councils operating under various local names. In 1963, over fifty of these councils, community, county, regional, and a few state-wide in scope, were serviced by NRA's district representatives.

Service to community councils cover a wide range, including technical assistance on specific problems, planning facilities and camp sites, program aids, training, help in improving coordination, surveys, and speaking at meetings.

New National Internship Program

For several years the National Recreation Association conducted an internship program. A small fund made available to the Association just prior to World War II was used to pay a very modest stipend to a few interns each year. The depletion of this resource and interruption by the war resulted in termination of this program.

As is so often the case, the greatest source of help had been overlooked—the recreation executives and agencies themselves. Personal discussion with a number of these executives encouraged the Association to believe that there were enough American cities with sufficient funds and concern to support such a program. Dr. Paul F. Douglas, chairman of the NRA's National Advisory Committee on Recruitment, Training and Placement of Recreation Personnel, was especially intrigued with the unique idea of anchoring the financing in the local departments themselves. If this could be accomplished, it would assure a permanent nationwide internship program not dependent upon funds from foundations and other outside sources here today and gone tomorrow.

Its purpose was to provide intensive postgraduate education in recreation leadership and administration through a cooperative program of work and study, pooling resources of the National Recreation Association, community recreation agencies, the recreation profession, colleges and universities.

This plan called for the selection a group of outstanding graduates each year in a coordinated work-study program.

Interns were placed in selected communities under a program coordinated by the National Recreation Association and under its general supervision. Each intern received special training under the direction of the agency executive and his supervisors. This involved rotated tasks and on-the-job experience in all phases of administration and supervision of recreation. A continuing study program with directed reading was part of the year's work.

Upon satisfactory completion of the training period a special certificate of achievement was awarded the intern, to become part of his professional credentials. Also, he was given special assistance in placement in the type of position, department, or specialization of his choice.

The National Recreation Association as the national service agency, was responsible for recruiting, preliminary screening, and placement of interns with the agencies. Appropriate recreation agencies for placement of individual interns were selected. Progress reports were received, analyzed, and evaluated.

First In The Nation

Charles Hartsoe, at left, is the first man in the nation to complete the internship program of the National Recreation Association in Philadelphia, Pa. Hartsoe took his internship with the Philadelphia Department of Recreation, one of the most progressive systems in the nation. He received the award designating the completion of the program from Mrs. William L. Van Alen, Vice president of the NRA, and from Robert W. Crawford, commissioner of recreation in this city. Hartsoe spent the year learning all the fundamentals of recreation after attending Springfield College and the University of Illinois. He learned programming, maintenance, administration, and all the other phases of recreation work.

Robert Toalson of Dodge City, Kansas, is seen receiving his certificate of achievement, certifying completion of his National Recreation Association internship with the Philadelphia Department of Recreation from Recreation commissioner Robert Crawford. Mr. Toalson is now assistant recreation superintendent in Oak Park, Illinois. He is accompanied by his wife, Deanne.

Editors note: Bob Toalson later served as the long time director of the Champaign, IL Park and Recreation District. He also served as president of both the National Recreation Park Association and American Academy for Parks and Recreation Administration.

International Advisory Committee
for the International Recreation Congress

Herbert Hoover

Members Who Have Accepted

BRAZIL—Mrs. Ethel Bauzer Madeiros

CEYLON—W. J. A. van Langenberg

EGYPT—His Excellency Staff Major Kamal El–Din Hussein

ENGLAND—The Right Honorable The Lord Luke of Pavenham

FRANCE—Raymond Cortat, Director of the Bureau of Education and Director General of Youth and Sports*

GERMANY—Dr. H. C. Georg von Opel

INDIA—G.D. Sondhi

IRAN—Abolfazl Sadry, General Director of Iranian Physical Education Department, Ministry of Education

Members Who Have Accepted

IRAQ—His Excellency Arkan Abadi

ISRAEL—Norman Lourie, Chairman Israel Playing Fields Association*

ITALY—Dr. Guido Vianello, National Commissioner, National Association for the Welfare of Workers*

JAPAN—Soichi Saito

NORWAY—Rolf Hofmo

THE PHILIPPINES—General Carlos P. Romulo

SWEDEN—Sven Salen

VENEZUELA—Lieutenant Colonel Frank Risquez, National Sports Institute*

Other countries will be represented on the committee. Invitations have been extended to leaders in Australia, Belgium, Canada, Colombia, Denmark, Pakistan, Syria, and Uruguay.

The following is a short biography on the four committee members: Madeiros, Langenberg Excellency Hussein, Lord Luke Pavenham.

Mrs. Ethel Bauzer Madeiros has been working in the field of recreation for the last ten years. She is in charge of the preparation of a manual on recreation for the elementary school teacher which will be printed and distributed by the Government of Brazil. She is a graduate of the University of Brazil and received her M.A. from Northwestern University in the United States. At present she is technical advisor for the Ministry of Education and Culture and is in charge of extension courses and post-graduate lectures in Rio de Janeiro.

W.J.A. van Langenberg is a member of the committee recently appointed by the Prime Minister of Ceylon to report on the encouragement of sport and recreation in that country. He is a graduate of the University of London and a member of the Order of the British Empire. He has always been interested in sports and has held many executive offices in sports organizations. He is permanent secretary to the Ministry of Posts and Broadcasting in Ceylon.

His Excellency Staff Major Kamal El-Din Hussein is Minister of Education in Egypt, head of the Supreme Council for Youth Service, and member of the Permanent Council for Public Welfare Services. He is a graduate of the Military College and of the Staff College where he served as a lecturer. He is one of the outstanding young leaders in the new government of Egypt.

The Right Honorable The Lord Luke of Pavenham is one of the leading industrialists of England, and his list of directorships is long. He was educated at Eton and Trinity.[5]

(5) R.M. May 1956

The Launching of The International Recreation Association

Thomas River, IRA's director general, left, and his board chairman, Lord Luke.

The long dreamed of International Recreation Association is now a reality:

After extensive conferences and correspondence with leaders of youth and other recreation agencies, government and non-government, in all parts of the world;

And in response to a resolution form a group of nineteen foreign authorities responsible for recreation and youth services in thirteen countries, brought to America by the United States Department of State to study the recreation movement of America;

And after formal request by the International Advisory Committee of the International Recreation Congress organized to aid in conducting this world gathering of recreation leaders;

And after the approval of the National Advisory Committee on International Recreation Service, NRA, a group of forty-six professional recreation authorities representing the professional recreation movement in America;

And with the active leadership and support of the National Recreation Association (U.S.A.), a national citizen agency which for fitly years has served the recreation forces of America;

The International Recreation Association-incorporated under the laws of the State of New York-was established in Philadelphia, Pennsylvania, October 3, 1956.

Services

The new Association will:

Maintain a central office to service the world's recreation agencies.

Provide correspondence and consultation services on specific problems.

Provide field service to countries desiring help with central recreation agencies.

Encourage the exchange of recreation leaders among nations.

Cooperate with the United Nations and its affiliated agencies.

Publish a bulletin for recreation.

Arrange for international and regional conferences.

Encourage the contribution of funds-public and private-to the development of recreation services for all mankind.

The International Recreation Association Board approved a budget of $201,266 for the year 1957, to provide for a headquarters staff, field service to countries, world recreation service bulletin, and regional conferences. Services are to be provided in accord with the approved budget only if and when funds are secured.

Board Of Directors

Arkan Abadi — Iraq
Former Minister of Social Welfare

Dr. Panoyioties Bratzoities — Greece
President of the University of Athens

Mrs. Howard Braucher — United States
Wife and co-worker of the late president of the NRA, one of the organizers and leaders of the movement

Raymond Cortat — France
Director General of Youth and Sports

Dr. Norman Cousins — United States
Editor of the Saturday Review

Dr. J. A. DeKoning — Holland
President of the Council on Cultural Contacts

Howard Henderson — United States
Vice-President of J. Walter Thompson Company

Staff Major Kamal El-Din Hussein — Egypt
Minister of Education

Yukio Kagayama — Japan
President of the Japan National Recreation Association

Thabet Nazif Khalidi — Jordan
Deputy Representative to the United Nations

Dr. C. T. O. King — Liberia
Ambassador and Permanent Representative to the United Nations

T. Y. Lee — China
Manager of New York Office of Bank of China

Norman Lourie — Israel
President of National Playing Fields Association of Israel

Lord Luke of Pavenham — England
President of National Playing Fields Association of England

Otto T. Mallery — United States
Chairman of the NRA Board of Directors

Mrs. William L. Matheson — United States
Social and civic leader

Mrs. Ethel Bauzer Medeiros — Brazil
Social and civic leader

Prof. Miro Mihovilovic — Yugoslovia
Distinguished Educator

Dr. Doris W. Plewes — Canada
(Temporary Liaison)Consultant on Recreation for Ministry of Welfare

Joseph Prendergast — United States
Executive Director of NRA

Lt. Col. Frank Risquez — Venezuela
Director of National Sports Institute

T. E. Rivers — United States
Executive Secretary of NRA International Recreation Service

Julio J. Rodriguez — Uruguay
Leader of recreation for forty years

General Carlos Romulo — Philippines
World-known and respected statesman

Dr. Abolfazl Sadry — Iran
Leader of recreation and physical education

Sven Salen — Sweden
Industrialist and President of Outdoor Recreation Association of Sweden

G. D. Sondhi — India
Leader in sports and recreation for thirty years

Sir Percy Spender — Australia
Ambassador to the United States

Dr. Armando Uribe — Columbia
Department of Social Action

Dr. Giovanni Valente — Italy
President of ENAL (National Association for the Welfare of Workers)

Mrs. William L. Van Alen — United States
Social and civic leader and member of NRA Board of Directors

H. S. van der Walt — Union of South Africa
Secretary for Recreation, Arts and Science

W. J. A. Van Langenberg — Ceylon
Minister of Communications

Dr. H. C. Georg Von Opel — Germany
Industrialist and leader in recreation

Robert Wilder — United States
Executive Vice-President of National Forge and Ordnance Company

Many Years of Service by NRA Staff Members

RETIRED . . . . These people served the Association for many years and until their retirement . . . .

James Edward Rogers
Field Service
1911-1949

E. Beatrice Stearns
Work with Volunteers
1921-1954

John W. Faust
Field Service
1923-1955

George W. Braden
Field Service
1921-1948

ACTIVE . . . . These people have served on the staff of the Association for twenty-five years or more . . . .

Mae Blaesser—*General Files*
Benjamin Burk—*Printing*
George D. Butler—*Director of Research*
Elizabeth Clifton—*Secretary to the Executive Director*
Vera Dahlin—*Accounting*
George Dickie—*Executive Secretary of Federal Inter-Agency Committee*
Miriam Dochtermann—*Survey and Planning Service*
Mary B. Gubernat—*Recreation Personnel Service*
Lulu M. Lydell—*Los Angeles Office*

George A. Nesbitt—*Director of Correspondence and Consultation Service*
Charles E. Reed—*Director of Field Service*
Thomas E. Rivers—*Assistant Executive Director*
Rose J. Schwartz—*Director of Special Publications*
Emily H. Stark—*Accounting*
Willard C. Sutherland—*Director of Recreation Personnel Service*
Arthur Williams—*Assistant Executive Director*
Louise Winch—*Mailroom*

Mary Buchannan Gubernat accepted employment with the National Recreation Association over forty-six years ago, and upon her retirement, on January 1, 1956, she will have set a record for continuous uninterrupted service of any employee in the history of the Association.

During her long and faithful service with the Association she has registered hundreds of leaders for recreation as a career field, interviewed many hundreds of persons, and handled a large volume of jobs in both public and private agencies. To many in the field, she is a warm and trusted friend, whose interest in their problems extended far beyond the duties of her job. In some cases, she has counseled two generations, as sons have followed fathers into the recreation field.

Mary Gubernat (right) counsels a job applicant.

At the age of eighteen, Mary started catching the 6:25 a.m. train in Plainfield, New Jersey, for work in New York City. Now, after over eight thousand round trips and over a half million miles later, she has truly earned her retirement. Turning down an offer to continue, she states, "The work, I like it, but the trip I can't take it longer." Actually she has spent approximately three years of her life on the road, traveling to and from work.

Five examples of playground equipment in Philadelphia designed to exercise
children's creativity as well as their muscles.

Selected Publications on Recreation Programming.

New Helps for
Your Summer Playground Program

(Available through the National Recreation Association)

Summer Playground Notebook $1.00

The 12 illustrated bulletins on playground activities sent last summer to cities conducting summer playgrounds only are now available bound in an attractive cover.

Arts and Crafts for the Recreation Leader, by FRANK A. STAPLES 1.50

An illustrated guide for beginners as well as more experienced leaders in craft groups. Information is given on types of projects suited to different age levels, together with directions for a number of projects such as finger painting, candlemaking, tie dyeing, spatter printing, woodworking, and many others.

Training Your Playground Leaders, by GEORGE D. BUTLER .... .35

An institute syllabus designed to help communities faced with the problem of using play leaders with little experience. Suggestions are offered for organizing and conducting recreation institutes.

Training Volunteers for Recreation Service, by GEORGE D. BUTLER .... .50

Eight typical training course outlines, with suggestions for organizing and conducting institutes.

Some Leadership "Do's," by ETHEL BOWERS .... .10

A reprint from RECREATION, February 1944, this pamphlet, addressed primarily to the play leader in the field of social recreation, discusses concisely some of the things the leader should be and know.

Know Your Community .... .25

Suggestions for making a recreation survey.

Standards for Neighborhood Recreation Areas and Facilities .... .15

Essential standards for playgrounds, playfields, and indoor recreation centers are outlined and suggestions offered for local cooperation.

Standards—Playgrounds, Playfields, Recreation Buildings, Indoor Recreation Centers .10

The main features of *Standards for Neighborhood Recreation Areas and Facilities* are presented in briefer and more popular form.

Standards for a Neighborhood Playground .... .15

A model plan showing how a 5-acre site may be effectively utilized as a playground.

Nature in Recreation, by MARGUERITE ICKIS 1.00

How to inject fun into the program by introducing nature in camping, handcraft, games, dramatics, music, and dancing.

"Service to Servicemen" .... .25

A series of bulletins telling how to make *Buddy Boxes* for servicemen—a game kit for the serviceman's pocket; a *Picture Pac,* an album that fits in a watch pocket; a *Home Town Newspaper.*

AND KEEP IN MIND —

Some of the older but always practical books and booklets:

The Picnic Book, $1.25; *Parties Plus—Stunts and Entertainments; Let's Plan a Party; Fun for Threesomes,* each $.50; *Games for Children,* $.50; *Leader's Nature Guide,* $.35; *Victory Gardens—Harvesting and Drying,* $.25; *Your Victory Garden,* $.15; *Teen Trouble,* $.10; *Day Camping,* $.25; *88 Successful Play Activities,* $.60; and many other publications. Send for complete lists.

And there's always RECREATION, the monthly magazine. Price $2.00 a year. If you have not seen a sample copy of this magazine, send for one.

NATIONAL RECREATION ASSOCIATION
315 Fourth Avenue, New York 10, N. Y.

For the CHRISTMAS SEASON

Give a Play—or an evening of short plays each sponsored by a neighborhood group of a community organization. Don't forget the youngsters!

The St. George Play, MP 56..	.10
Festival of Light	.10
A Christmas Revel (in *The Christmas Book*).....................................	.50
Christmas Customs and Legends Around the World, MP 255	.10
The Seven Gifts, a Christmas Pantomime (Christmas Kit No. 2)**	.35
A Christmas Pageant—Dances, Drills, Dramatics, MP 378	.15

Make Christmas Music—Go carolling, not just once but every night for the week before Christmas. Put candles in the windows to welcome the singers, and don't forget the customary "bite and sup" for them.

Finish up the week with a community carol sing at the Community Center or Park or town square.

Christmas Carol Leaflets	.80 per 100

Have a Union Church Service—with massed choirs and instrumental groups from all the churches and synagogues as background for a dramatization of the Christmas story and the Jewish Hanukkah.

Joy to the World (See The Christmas Kit No. 1)*	.35

Plan a Party—or a series of parties so that the whole community can have a get-together for Christmas fun and frolics.

A Community Christmas Party, MP 295...	.15
A Polar Christmas Party	.10
The Christmas Kit No. 1*..	.35
Watch Night Party (New Year), MP 346......................................	.05
Crown Your Twelve Months Merrily (Twelfth Night) MP 265	.10
A "Turn Over a New Leaf Party" (New Year) MP 171	.10
Beginning-of-the-Year Games (See Christmas Kit No. 2)**	.35

Hold a Fair—and make it gay with Christmas entertainment and booths where Christmas goodies and gifts are on sale.

Christmas Fairs (See Christmas Kit No. 1)*	.35

Make Decorations—Get the whole community together to make decorations for the home or the community center. Have a tree-cutting expedition and a time when everybody can come together to make decorations and ornaments and novelties.

Make Your Own Christmas Tree Ornaments, MP 257	.10
Thanksgiving and Christmas Decorations from Garden and Woods, MP 284.......	.15
Christmas Novelties for Everyone	.10
Gifts and Gadgets Made of Paper, MP 297...................................	.15
Christmas Kit No. 1*	.35
Christmas Kit No. 2**	.35

Have a Christmas Storytelling Bee—with everybody in the community coming prepared to tell a Christmas tale, old or new, true or imagined.

Your foreign-born citizens and their children can add a lot to this with tales of Christmas customs in other lands.

Stories of Christmas Carols, MP 60...	.15

Use THE CHRISTMAS BOOK, a storehouse of ideas for planning your Christmas program whether it be musical, dramatic, traditional, or just plain social .... .50

*The Christmas Kit No. 1 contains—Joy to the World, a Christmas Pageant; Christmas Fairs; Cutting Christmas Greens; two Christmas parties; Christmas Suggestions for Children; Suggestions for Novel Christmas Cards.
**The Christmas Kit No. 2 contains—Some Christmas Quiz Suggestions; You Can Make Your Own Christmas Cards; Christmas Windows; Ways to Distribute Small Christmas Gifts; Ice-breakers and Games for Christmas; Mixers for Christmas Dances and Parties; Beginning-of-the-Year Games; The Seven Gifts.

All program materials mentioned may be ordered from

NATIONAL RECREATION ASSOCIATION

315 Fourth Avenue, New York 10, N. Y.

Spring—Easter—May Day

If you're in need of program material for Spring, Easter, and May Day (and who isn't?) let us solve your problems with these bulletin helps which were made to order for you

Easter and Spring

An April Shower .... $ .10
(Complete plan for a party in April, from preparty games to refreshments. Reprint from RECREATION, March 1941)

Easter Crafts and Games .... (MP 299)   .15
(Includes directions for making a number of favors, greeting cards and other craft projects. Also rules for a number of Easter party games)

Easter Egg Hunts .... (MB 694)   .05
(Suggestions and hints for egg hunts, adaptable for large and small gatherings)

An Easter Eggsibit .... (MB 861)   .05
(A complete party plan)

"Peep Show" Easter Eggs .... (MB 1164) .05
(Plaster craft for favors or decorations)

Program Suggestions for Easter .... (MP 244)   .05
(A bibliography listing plays, pageants, pantomimes, and services of worship)

Stories of the Easter Carols .... (MP 120)   .10
(Also includes plans for caroling groups)

May Day

Heigh-Ho for a Merry Spring, by Augustus Zanzig 15
(Suggestions for a simple festival. Reprint from RECREATION, April 1935)

May Day Echoes, by Marion Holbrook .... (MP 105)   .15
(A pageant-play for the grades and junior high school. Roman Floralea, Old English, and modern May Day episodes)

May Pole Dance .... (MB 491)   .05
(Directions for this traditional ceremony)

Pageants and Festivals Suitable for May Day Celebration ...... (MB 85) Free
(A bibliography)

Play Days .... (MB 796)   .05
(Organization, program, and procedure)

Traditions for May .... (MB 1179) .05
(Old English traditions adaptable to festivals)

Troubadours of Provence .... (MP 104)   .10
(A May Day fragment for high school or college use based on old Provencal custom of holding a tournament of song each May)

Youth Day Out of Doors .... (MP 199)   .05
(Suitable activities)

NATIONAL RECREATION ASSOCIATION

315 Fourth Avenue, New York City

YOUR ANNIVERSARY ALBUM

Pictures tell the story, or do-you-remember-when?

Dusting off the old recreation album, we find between its covers the reflections of a bygone era—of places, faces, events and years full of purpose and plans, learning-by-doing, fine people, teamwork, and fun. It has caught some few unforgettable moments in the thrilling story of the opening up of a new field in which man strives to be of service to man.

Many such useless lots are to be transformed into playgrounds.

Four minds with but a single thought. Where will they play? (Promotion picture).

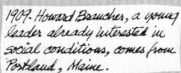

1909. Howard Braucher, a young leader already interested in social conditions, comes from Portland, Maine.

In Elmira, N.Y. spirited citizens wield pick and shovel; Mayor Peck is at the plow.

Action on Echo Playground, Los Angeles, about 1907.

Play in Seward Park, New York. This two and five-eighths acres of land cost the city $1,800,000 in 1897.

National staff at Recreation Congress Grand Rapids, Mich, 1916.

Offices move from apartment to Floors 30 to 41 in Metropolitan Life Insurance Tower, One Madison Ave, New York City.

Atlantic City, 1927. Dr John Finley, Mrs. Charles D. Lanier, Mayor Walsh of Yonkers, Joseph Lee.

Gustavus Kirby, Otto Mallery, Howard Braucher, Walter May, wreathed in Congress smiles.

The Maypole dance on Independence Day, 1912, in Madison, Wisconsin, was a gala affair.

Dorothy Enderis took recreation job in Milwaukee, 1912, guided recreation in that city for thirty-six years.

Do we need play in institutions?

E. T. Atwell joins staff in March, 1919.

The Association moves across the street to the 19th and 20th floors of 315 Fourth Avenue (about 1922).

1934 Congress in Washington: Dr. John H. Finley introduces the speaker, Mrs. Roosevelt. Left to right: Mrs. Henry Morgenthau, Dr. McCurdy, John Colt, Mrs. Roosevelt, Mrs. Thomas Edison, Mr. Butterworth, Dr. Daniel Poling, Hon. Austin E. Griffiths.

Playgrounds create an urgent need for leadership, a challenge for the Association.

Rose Schwartz surveys a few of the Association's publications for which she is responsible. She joined the staff in 1913.

New reception room at 8 West Eighth Street, 1956. Ronny (Ella Binger), the receptionist, has been with the Association twenty-seven years.

Chapter Eight

1960s

RECREATION

NATIONAL RECREATION ASSOCIATION   •   FEBRUARY 1965   •   60c

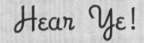

Hear Ye!

You are cordially invited to attend

The 44th
National Recreation Congress

with headquarters in the

New Sheraton Hotel

in the

City of Philadelphia

from September 30--October 5, 1962

under the sponsorship of

The American Recreation Society

and

The National Recreation Association

with the cooperation of

The Philadelphia Department of Recreation

The Pennsylvania Recreation Society

and

The Federation of National Professional
Organizations for Recreation

Mark the dates
and clear
your calendar now!

From 1960 Yearbook Published by National Recreation Association

RECREATION and PARK YEARBOOK 1961

A Nation-wide Inventory of the Public Recreation and Park Services of Local, County, State and Federal Agencies for the Year Ending December 31, 1960

George D. Butler, *Editor*

Muriel E. McGann, *Associate Editor*

Copyright 1961 by the

NATIONAL RECREATION ASSOCIATION

8 W. Eighth Street, New York 11, N. Y.

Price $5.50   Printed in U.S.A.

The table below lists, by state and city: Population, Managing Authority, Parks (Total Number and Acreage; Acquired 1956–1960 Number and Acreage), School Recreation Areas (Number and Acreage), Regulation Baseball Diamonds, Bathing Beaches, Golf Courses (9-hole, 18-hole), Softball Diamonds, Swimming Pools Indoor, Swimming Pools Outdoor (Shallow, Deep), Tennis Courts, and Paid Workers [All Paid Workers Total and Full-time Year-round; Paid Leadership Total (Men, Women) and Full-time Year-round (Men, Women)].

No.	State and City	Population	Managing Authority	All Paid Total	FT Yr-round	Ldr Men	Ldr Women	FT Men	FT Women
	Alabama								
1	Anniston	33,320	Parks & Recreation Dept.	80	15	10	11	5	2
2	Atmore	8,221	City Recreation Committee	7		6	1		
3	Bessemer	32,681	Park & Recreation Board	22	7	15	5	5	2
4	Birmingham	339,211	Park & Recreation Board	272	229	23	51	13	15
5	Brewton	6,209	Board of Education	10		8	2		
6	Chickasaw	9,283	Council Park & Recreation Committee						
7	Childersburg	4,865	Park & Recreation Board						
8	Decatur	28,765	Park & Recreation Board	33	3	5	8	1	1
9	Dothan	31,237	Recreation Dept.	40	8	25	4	7	1
10	Enterprise	11,358	Community Center Board	9	2	7	2	2	
11	Fairfax	6,000	West Point Manufacturing Co.	7		4	5	2	3
12	Florence	31,518	Park & Recreation Dept.	40	9	19	7	4	1
13	Fort Payne	7,029	Recreation Board	7		4	3		
14	Gadsden	54,440	Recreation Board	74	4	8	31	1	1
15	Homewood	20,287	Park & Recreation Board	33	8	11	8	2	2
16	Huntsville	71,880	Parks & Playgrounds Dept.	85	37	24	29	4	1
17	Lanett	7,619	West Point Manufacturing Co.	7		5	2	3	1
18	Langdale	5,000	West Point Manufacturing Co.			4	2	2	1
19	Mobile	191,393	City Recreation Dept.	111	34	64	37	5	19
20	Montgomery	133,546	Parks & Recreation Dept.	79	36	24	14	6	7
21	Mountain Brook	12,492	Public Works Dept.	4		1	1		
22	Opelika	14,174	Board of Parks & Recreation	30	4	16	5	1	
23	Phenix City	27,402	Park & Recreation Dept.	38	23	6	11	2	2
24	Prichard	47,241	Recreation Dept.	38	1	10	9	1	
25	River View	2,500	West Point Manufacturing Co.	5	3	2			
26	Selma	28,273	Park & Recreation Dept.	31	7	8	5	2	1
27	Shawmut	4,500	West Point Manufacturing Co.	9	4	6	2	2	2
28	Sheffield	13,472	Recreation Dept.	47	17	11	5	3	1
29	Sylacauga	12,691	City Recreation Dept.	47	6	13	22		4
30	Talladega	17,593	City Recreation Board	17	3	10	2	2	1
31	Tarrant	7,174	Parks & Recreation Dept.	15	4	9	6	2	2
32	Troy	10,149	Recreation Dept.	28	2	11	6	1	1
	Alaska								
1	Anchorage	43,753	Parks & Recreation Dept.	24	1	2	4		1
	Arizona								
1	Bisbee	9,850	School District & City Council	7	1	3	4	1	
2	Flagstaff	18,162	City Park Dept.	16	1	6	2		
3	Glendale	15,659	City Recreation Board	28		2	10		
4	Globe	6,141	City & Schools						
5	Kingman	4,512	Parks & Recreation, & Health & missions	3					
6	Mesa	33,547	Parks & Playgrounds Dept.	100	20	38	48	3	3
7	Phoenix	434,277	Park & Recreation Dept.	447	167	217	77	17	9
8	Prescott	12,560	Park & Recreation Dept.	21	5	10	5	2	1
9	Scottsdale	9,924	Parks & Recreation Dept.	17	1	8	7	1	
10	Tempe	24,236	Parks & Recreation Dept.	72	21	14	23	2	
11	Tolleson	3,864	Elementary School District	7		5	2		
12	Tucson	209,305	Parks & Recreation Dept.	538	148	175	92	15	5
13	Yuma	23,811	Recreation & Park Dept.	120	21	70	32	2	
	Arkansas								
1	De Queen	2,853	Herman Dierks Park Commission	1					
2	Hope	8,380	Parks & Recreation Dept.	16	3	7	1	1	
3	Little Rock	105,7?7	Parks & Recreation Dept.	153	42	23	17	11	2
4	Marianna	5,105	Lions Club	2		1	1		
5	Morrilton	6,005	City Park Commission	5					
6	North Little Rock	57,211	Parks & Recreation Commission	18	10				
7	Pine Bluff	43,586	Park Commission	34	14				
	California								
1	Alameda	53,606	Recreation & Park Dept.	138	48	48	39	3	4
2	Albany	14,749	Park & Recreation Dept.	23	8	10	7		
3	Alhambra	54,464	Park & Recreation Dept.	108	38	21	21	1	
4	Anaheim	103,405	Park & Recreation Dept.	260	40	148	49	4	1
5	Arbuckle	327	Union Elementary School	5		5			
6	Arcadia	41,044	Recreation Dept.	49	3	26	22	2	
7	Arden Park	8,500	Recreation & Park District	11	3	3	2		
8	Artesia City	10,013	City Council	4	1	1	2		
9	Azusa	20,361	Recreation Dept. & Park Dept.; City School District	60	10	16	10	1	
10	Bakersfield	56,143	Dept. of Public Works—Park Div.; Recreation Dept.	191	5	58	53	2	2
11	Bell	19,371	Recreation Dept.	29	4	15	10		
12	Bellflower	45,600	Dept. of Parks & Recreation	35		10			
13	Belmont	15,906	Recreation Dept.	13					
14	Berkeley	108,539	Recreation & Parks Dept.	139	82	45	32	14	7
15	Beverly Hills	30,563	Recreation Dept.	49	13	22	16	6	2
16	Big Bear Lake	4,000	Park District	10	6	2			
17	Big Creek	670	Elementary School District	7	1	2	1	1	
18	Bloomington	12,000	Recreation & Park District	12	1	7	2	1	
19	Blythe	16,000	Palo Verde Unified School District	13	1	4	2	1	
20	Brawley	12,546	Recreation Dept. & Park Dept.	36	5	15	10		

Foreword

The 1961 Recreation and Park Yearbook presents a picture of the public recreation and park movement in the United States in the year 1960. For the second time in its long history the Yearbook includes reports of Federal and state agencies as well as information about the services rendered by local and county authorities. The comprehensive scope of the 1961 Yearbook in contrast with the limited coverage of the first issue that appeared in 1907, illustrates the remarkable growth of the movement and the increasingly close relationships between park and recreation authorities at different levels of government.

The Yearbook contains a section describing the work of thirteen Federal agencies and data concerning the services of 350 state agencies. It consists primarily, however, of information submitted by 2,762 municipal or county authorities that operate parks and other recreation areas or that provide recreation programs under leadership. Reports from 206 private agencies that render similar services to the public are also included. Because of the increasing number county park and recreation agencies, a separate section is devoted to their services.

The major section of the 1961 Yearbook, describing the work of local and county authorities, is comparable to those in the issues for 1950 and 1955. it contains reports from more agencies in a larger number of localities than the earlier Yearbooks. Most of the larger cities are included and a considerable percentage of the smaller cities and counties providing recreation or park service. Nevertheless, like its prediceasrs, the picture it presents is far from complete, because several hundred agencies known to have parks or to conduct community recreation programs under leadership failed to respond to repeated requests for a report.

Every effort is made to assure accuracy in the figures submitted by the various agencies and published in the Yearbook. The attainment of this objective necessitates a huge volume of correspondence with the reporting agencies in order to eliminate apparent inaccuracies and inconsistencies in the reports. The promptness with which most park and recreation officials responded to inquiries about their reports is sincerely appreciated.

This volume, like previous Yearbooks, has been made possible through the cooperation of a large number of individuals and agencies. The types of data gathered in the study reflect the expressed desires of many park and recreation leaders as well as the need to assure a degree of community in order that the Yearbook may provide data which record trends in the movement. It is impossible to mention all who had a part in the preparation of the Yearbook, but the National Recreation Association wishes to make special acknowledgement of the following:

Local, county, state and Federal officials who submitted detailed reports

Members of the Association's District Advisory Committees who helped in the preparation of mailing lists and encouraged authorities in the District in submit their report

The National Park Service for granting permission to reproduce figures from its publication, "State Park Statistics, 1960"

The state recreation associations that submitted lists of recreation and park authorities and assisted in the collection of reports

The American Institute of Park Executives for its advice and cooperation with reference to the study

The Federated Department Stores of Cincinnati, Ohio, for their contribution toward the cost of this publication.

The National Recreation Association believes that widespread and effective use of the 1961 Recreation and Park Yearbook will justify the time and effort so generously contributed by many individuals and agencies.

(Signed) Joseph Prendergast
Executive Director

In High Gear

—your 43rd National Recreation Congress

The camera focuses on interesting people and events during the busy and colorful 43rd National Recreation Congress in beautiful Cobo Hall, Detroit, October 1-6, 1961.

Above. The crowds wait impatiently while the Honorable Louis C. Mariani, mayor of Detroit (left), cuts the ribbon and officially opens the enormous 43rd National Recreation Congress exhibit area. Host Edward T. McGowan, first deputy superintendent of parks and recreation, shares his electric cart. Standing, left to right, are Ray Butler, new executive secretary, American Recreation Society, and Joseph Prendergast, executive director, National Recreation Association (the two agencies cosponsored the Congress).

Above. The concrete floors of the exhibit hall were made to bloom with grass, trees, and flowers by the creative staff of the Detroit Parks and Recreation Department. In this oasis delegates gratefully sat and chatted on the benches.

Right. A panorama of one the most spacious exhibits area Congress delegates have ever had. Over one hundred exhibitors took advantage of the plenty of elbowroom to show their products to best advantage. There was room for program demonstrations, games of all kinds, conference areas and a Cracker Barrel Corner for impromptu meetings.

Left. Charles Hartsoe (seated), secretary of the Congress, and Ed McGowan take time out from a social evening for some further checking of Congress arrangements and business. The big meeting kept them on the go all the time.

Right. William Frederickson, Jr. (left), new president of the American Recreation Society, and Dr. Dan Dodson, keynote speaker on "the Dynamics of Recreation Programming"

Right. At the annual National Recreation Association Luncheon, special citations were given to Secretary of the Interior Stewart L. Udall, for his untiring efforts to preserve the nation's natural resources for recreation, and to Nathan L. Mallison, superintendent of recreation in Jacksonville, Florida, for his many years of service "to the cause of better recreation for all people."

Below. A serious interlude at the reception: Paul Lohner (with briefcase) of Brick Township, New Jersey, shows a map of his area to (left to right) NRA District Representative Temple Jarrell, Mrs. E. M. Silva of the Orange State Recreation Association, Robert H. Huey and Marion Wood Huey of Miami Beach.

A helping hand. Jack Woody, superintendent of recreation in Miami Beach, explains program to delegate Carolyn Harvie, recreation worker at the Illinois State Psychiatric Institute.

Mrs. Eunice Kennedy Shriver arrives at the Congress accompanied by Miami Beach Vice-Mayor, Barnard Frank. As executive vice-president of the Kennedy Foundation, which is particularly concerned with the problem of mental retardation, Mrs. Shriver addressed a luncheon session on the recreation problems of retardates and research being done in the area.

Facts and resources. The ever-popular Congress Resource and Consultation Center included the National Recreation Association Recreation Book Center, the NRA Job Mart, NRA insurance desk, and the Recreation Magazine exhibit. Here, delegates browsed through the latest books and other materials in the field.

The National Recreation Association In 1964

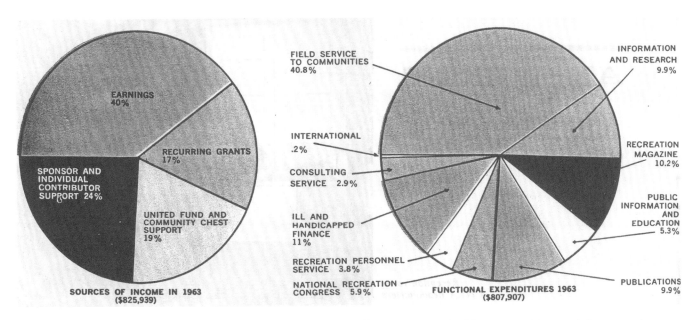

SOURCES OF INCOME IN 1963
($825,939)

EARNINGS 40%

RECURRING GRANTS 17%

SPONSOR AND INDIVIDUAL CONTRIBUTOR SUPPORT 24%

UNITED FUND AND COMMUNITY CHEST SUPPORT 19%

FUNCTIONAL EXPENDITURES 1963
($807,907)

FIELD SERVICE TO COMMUNITIES 40.8%

INTERNATIONAL .2%

CONSULTING SERVICE 2.9%

ILL AND HANDICAPPED FINANCE 11%

RECREATION PERSONNEL SERVICE 3.8%

NATIONAL RECREATION CONGRESS 5.9%

INFORMATION AND RESEARCH 9.9%

RECREATION MAGAZINE 10.2%

PUBLIC INFORMATION AND EDUCATION 5.3%

PUBLICATIONS 9.9%

What Is the National Recreation Association?

It is a national, voluntary, non-profit, nonpartisan and nonsectarian organization through which professional and lay recreation leadership can unite to provide the many nationwide services in the recreation field essential to the sound growth of the recreation profession and the recreation movement.

What Is its Purpose?

It is dedicated to serving all recreation executives, leaders, volunteers and agencies, public and private, to the end that every child in America shall have a place to play in safety and that every person in America, young and old, shall have an opportunity for the best and most satisfying use of his expanding leisure time.

Who Are its Constituents?

In 1964, the Association's constituents are the 2,071 recreation agencies in 1,480 communities affiliated with the Association for service, the 4,536 recreation leaders in 2,237 communities associated with the Association for service, the 13,950 financial contributors in over 2,700 communities, and the general public to which its services are ultimately directed.

How is the Work of the Association Financed?

NRA's 1964 budget of $997,000 has received the approval of the National Budget and Consultation committee sponsored by the United Community Funds and Councils of America and the National Social Welfare Assembly. Approximately a third of NRA's support comes from it's own earnings, including general service fees and reimbursement for special services, sales of publications, and interest on endowments. The remaining two-thirds of its support comes from several hundred volunteer sponsors, community Chest and United Funds, foundations, corporations and individual contributors throughout the country.

How Is It Governed?

By a sixty-member Board of Trustees, composed of lay and professional recreation leaders and other outstanding representatives of the citizen and professional resources available to help meet the expanding recreation needs of the American people.

THE WASHINGTON LETTER
of the National Recreation Association

1750 PENNSYLVANIA AVENUE, N.W., WASHINGTON, D.C. 20006

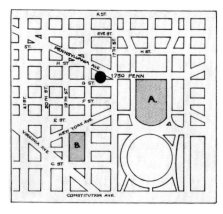

NRA's Washington office (black dot) is strategically located just one block from the White House (A), two blocks from the Department of the Interior (B), and other federal offices.

NRA ADDS NEW OFFICE IN WASHINGTON, D.C.

As a part of its expansion program, the National Recreation Association has re-established an office in Washington, D.C. to give special attention to federal and state recreation matters. With the greatly increased activity of the federal government in recreation and the growing amount of federal funds available to state and local governments for recreation, the NRA recognizes that the communities and recreation agencies it serves need more help than ever before in their relationships with federal agencies. Federal agencies also need the help and services which NRA can provide through its long and deep experience in community recreation matters.

The new NRA Washington staff will analyze, interpret, and report all pending federal and state recreation legislation, and actively involve the NRA and its Service Associates and affiliates in the development of federal recreation related activities. A part of the new Washington service will be the periodic publication of *The Washington Letter*, published in November, dealt with "Federal Assistance Programs Available to States, Local Government, and Non-Profit Agencies for Resources."

The relationships NRA has established with key federal agencies over the years will be particularly helpful in increasing the effectiveness of the Washington office. From 1946 to 1963, the Association had an office in the U.S. Department of Interior and provided a staff person who served as executive secretary of the Federal Inter-Agency committee on Recreation. This committee was disbanded in 1963 after the establishment of the Recreation Advisory Council by Executive Order of the President and the establishment of the Bureau of Outdoor Recreation by the Secretary of the Interior.

The new office will be strategically located just one block from the White House and two blocks from the Department of Interior. We extend an invitation to our friends to make it a point to visit NRA's new office when in Washington.

Acting in an advisory capacity to the Board of Trustees are the National Advisory Commission and National Advisory Council. The commission, a twenty-member lay group, is composed of officially appointed representatives of national voluntary agencies, plus distinguished citizens who are active in the field of recreation, and representative board members of local recreation agencies. The council is made up of the chairmen of the National and the District Advisory Committees of the Association and the president of the Federation of National Professional Organization for Recreation. This council represents more than seven hundred professional recreation leaders serving on NRA's National and District Advisory Committees. In addition, 130 state and community lay leaders served on the Association's four state and eleven local advisory committees in 1963.

Between 1906 and 1964, the Association raised and expended a total of $45,083,561.48 for the advancement of the recreation profession and the national recreation movement. On December 31, 1963 its assets totaled over $1,000,000.

Washington Representatives

Kenneth J. Smithee

Newest addition to the National Recreation Association staff is **Kenneth J. Smithee,** former parks and recreation director in Maricopa County, Arizona, who is credited with developing the nation's largest locally operated regional parks system. Mr. Smithee plans to report to NRA's Washington headquarters on February 10th to begin his newly created job. He will serve as special consultant on parks and recreation to counties throughout the fifty states.

As director of the Maricopa County department, Mr. Smithee developed the county regional parks system from a tiny operation into a 93,000-acre regional and sub-regional program comprising eleven parks, He also developed and was instrumental in the transfer to various cities in the county of seventeen urban parks containing a total of 750 acres, and with improvements valued at $1,300,000. His successor in Maricopa County is Eddie Brown, superintendent of parks for the county since 1962.

Focus on Sports and Fitness

Verna Rensvold, NRA Midwest Rep, Bud Wilkinson, Former Oklahoma University Coach and President of Lifetime Sports Foundation, planning for a Lifetime Sports program in Topeka, Kansas. Joe Bannon, Director of Recreation and Parks, Topeka

Confering at President Eisenhower's conference on Fitness of American Youth are (left to right) Joseph Prendergast, NRA; Ted Banks, The Athletic Institute Vice President Richard M. Nixon and George Hjelte, Los Angeles Department of Recreation and Parks; George Sargisson, Recreation Promotion and Service, Wilmington, Delaware.

The White House
Washington, D.C.

The use of free time in our free society has deeper significance to Americans today than at any other time in our history. As the Outdoor Recreation Resources Review Commission has made clear, rising population, increased urbanization, more leisure time, higher incomes, and greater mobility have combined to pose an unprecedented challenge for effective use of our free time.

It is appropriate, therefore, that the theme of National Recreation Month is "Free Time—A Challenge to Free Men."

In discovering new and creative uses for our leisure, we shall be demonstrating to the world how free men—through their freely chosen pursuits—may serve themselves and the common good. This new, dynamic concept of recreation can be a meaningful expression of our physical fitness, our mental alertness, and our cultural development.

In observing June as National Recreation Month, I urge all citizens to discover the new potentials of their leisure—new opportunities and meaning in their free time.

(Signed) John F. Kennedy

Chapter Nine

THIS IS YOUR NRA

AN INTRODUCTION

In April 1964, the National Recreation Association completed fifty-eight years of service directed toward the provision of adequate and satisfying recreation opportunities for the people of America. The Association, founded in 1906, is a national, voluntary, civic organization through which professional and lay citizenship participation can unite to provide the many nationwide services in the field of recreation which are essential to the sound growth of the recreation profession and the recreation movement.

This Is Your NRA is a report on the work and services of the Association typical of any current year, based on the figures of 1963. It is addressed to all Service Affiliates and Service Associates of the Association and to all other persons who are concerned with the provision of adequate and satisfying recreation opportunities for the people of America.

It is significant that this report confines itself to the work of the previous year, for the Association fully realizes that we are on the threshold of a new era for recreation and if the challenges of the future are to be met successfully, the Association must act with vision and boldness in planning for the years ahead. One of the characteristics of the Association over the years has been its ability and willingness to adjust its activities and services to economic and social changes and needs as they occur.

Discussions by the Association, the American Institute of Park Executives, the American Recreation Society and other recreation and park agencies may lead to mobilizing and structuring the resources of the various service and professional organizations into a bold new co-operative approach directed toward helping the nation achieve the best possible use of a growing leisure time.

This Is Your NRA presents a proud record; it provides a prelude of things to come. Your comments and suggestions in developing a design for the future are most welcome.

James H. Evans

Chairman of the NRA Board of Trustees

HEADQUARTERS
8 WEST EIGHTH STREET
NEW YORK, N. Y. 10011

CORRESPONDENCE AND CONSULTATION

THIS might be called the "grass-roots" of NRA service. It covers the entire field of recreation, reaches individuals and organizations from every state in the Union and in at least ninety other countries throughout the world. It is a service to which anyone can turn for a prompt, friendly, and interested reply to any question or problem in the recreation field.

This kind of free service has been an important function of the Association since the day the organization was founded. The ability of CCS to answer thousands of inquiries each year is not based on the knowledge and education of any one person, but upon the accumulated information and experience of the whole recreation movement, kept current by close correlation of the Association's library and information files, recreation records, new publications, field reports, reports of conferences, studies and research from many sources, and by cooperation of all the NRA staff and the magazine RECREATION.

The numbers and diversity of the letters answered enables CCS to constantly feel the pulse of the recreation movement. It quickly becomes aware of special needs, interests and trends, and discovers areas of information needing more study and development of within-the-department information sheets to be used with replies to various inquiries.

The director of CCS is also responsible for meeting, in person, inquirers who choose to visit the office instead of sending a letter, and for talking with persons who choose to telephone instead of sending a letter or visiting the office.

International Recreation Service. From the standpoint of correspondence, the International Recreation Service is an extension of CCS's regular domestic correspondence service mentioned above. The cases originating outside the United States and its territorial possessions are handled in much the same manner but on the let-terhead of the NRA International Recreation Service. In 1963, the International Recreation Service load included 180 requests from forty-three countries.

The consultation service of the International Recreation Service includes conferences with individuals from other countries who are visiting the United States, under various auspices, and for varying lengths of time. Most of these visitors from abroad are especially interested in learning about the history and services of the National Recreation Association and about the way in which public recreation is conducted in American communities.

The third work aspect of the International Recreation Service is the responsibility of the director to serve as the secretary of the National Advisory Committee for the International Recreation Service. This is a committee of fifteen, representing each of the eight NRA field districts, Canada, and Europe. An annual meeting is held at the National Recreation Congress.

Stockroom holds hundreds of publications handy for shipment.

One of the many busy offices that make NRA service possible.

PUBLIC INFORMATION AND EDUCATION

As PART of its service, the department gives advice and help on the techniques of communication to NRA Service Affiliates and Service Associates. Information and publicity help is available to any recreation and park leader, individual citizen or group interested in bettering recreation in their area. To reach "average readers," PIE works with national and local media—writers and researchers —as they tell the recreation story through books, including textbooks, leading magazines, newspapers, radio and television.

National Recreation Month. Recognition of the importance of recreation at the highest national level is given through the annual June Recreation Month message from the President of the United States, arranged for by PIE. A comprehensive kit with suggested organization, program, and publicity ideas for June is sent as an annual service to all NRA Affiliates. While the supply lasts, kits are also available to representatives of other interested organizations. This material is designed to help local and national groups highlight their own recreation services. Special display material, a brochure on National Recreation Month, and suggested sports for local radio and TV stations and a suggested proclamation for mayors are provided. Arrangements are made in cooperation with state recreation societies to obtain statewide proclamations from state governors.

Honors. PIE administers another special service to NRA Affiliates: the citations program honoring laymen who have given outstanding service to the cause of better recreation. The more than three hundred citations awarded annually provide an opportunity for NRA Affiliates to strengthen relations with community leaders

and highlight the importance of recreation.

Help With Local Bond Issues. The department helps local and state groups interpret the need for legislation or special bond issues for open space or recreation facilities. Special material, brochures, kits, and other publicity which can be adapted to educational campaigns are provided.

Work With Councils of Social Agencies and Other Related Groups. PIE initiates and helps carry through programs for other national groups to interpret the need for adequate recreation facilities and wise planning of free time. In communities where NRA is a member of the United Fund or Community Chest, kits of information, not only about NRA but also stressing the importance of all phases of recreation, are provided each year to support the local fund-raising campaign—contributions which enable local agencies and councils of social agencies to continue their vital services.

PIE also works actively to develop relationships with other national groups, such as the National Council of Churches, the National Jewish Welfare Board, the National Catholic Welfare Conference, the National Federation of Settlements and American Association of Retired Persons, providing them with information about the numerous services available to them through the Association.

Newsletters. PIE prepares ten monthly issues of two different *Newsletters,* one to NRA Affiliates (agencies) and one to NRA Associates (individuals.) Releases on appointments or changes of recreation personnel with national significance are regularly sent to specialized publications and the general press.

*The executive office
with the executive
and personnel directors
in conference.*

PERSONNEL

THE NRA Personnel Service provides the professional workers of the country with the opportunity to have their personnel credentials maintained at a central place. Some thirteen thousand personnel records are in its combined active and inactive files. Five hundred and fifty-six new registrations were added in 1963, and 889 men and women were on its active personnel list at the close of the year.

In 1963, the Personnel Service received over nine thousand communications related to personnel subjects which resulted in over seventeen thousand outgoing communications. This included over six thousand notices to candidates about position vacancies which numbered over four hundred. It also included 964 sets of formal confidential personnel records sent to employers on request.

Request for information. Both employers and professional leaders request personnel services other than those pertaining to employment. Employers need information on many subjects, such as personnel policies and practices, salaries, standards, and in-service training. For the workers, guidance, counseling and information on various professional matters are supplementary services. Over three hundred individual interviews were conducted in 1963.

Recruitment. Six universities were visited by the director of the Association's Personnel Service in 1963, re-

sulting in thirty faculty and 163 individual student interviews in addition to student group meetings. Many other visits were made by field representatives of NRA.

With the help of the National Advisory Committee on Recruitment, several important recent developments have occurred, such as the preparation of a script and set of recruiting slides and launching of a bulletin.

Recruitment and News. The Ralph Van Fleet Scholarship program; the inclusion of recreation as a career field in the *College Placement Annual* (240,000 distribution); the Peace Corps' occupational manual, and the *Dictionary of Occupational Titles*—these and other special activities, together with the continuous distribution of recruiting materials and the interpretation of recreation at career conferences and special meetings, help to round out the total recruiting effort.

Internship. Six interns were enrolled in a National Internship program in 1963, replacing those who had completed the training the preceding year. Since the program started in 1958, forty-three interns have been enrolled, receiving over $172,000 from cities in stipends.

Publications and Studies. The department carries on various studies and prepares needed publications. It recently revised and reprinted a "standard," *Playground Leaders — Their Selection and Training*. Another major publication *Forceful Commu-*

nication Through Visual Resources was published in 1963.

The 1963 student inventory and curriculum study made by the Undergraduate Education Committee brought up to date the list of universities conducting major recreation curriculum and produced current information on the status of professional preparation and on the supply and demand of recreation personnel. The Placement Committee conducted a salary and wage administration study completed in 1963. Also, a small piece was prepared, helpful for recruiting, entitled *Are You Proud of Your Profession, Mr. Recreation Executive?* The committee is now revising the publication *Personnel Standards in Community Recreation Leadership.* Twenty-eight positions will be added as a result of new developments and trends affecting recreation personnel.

Institute for Administration. The Personnel Service is also responsible for the annual National Institute for Recreation and Park Administrators. The Institute quota of one hundred executives is always oversubscribed.

In addition to general recruiting and selection services, the director of the Association's Personnel Service has served on examining boards for top executive positions. He also participates in district conferences, national conferences, meetings of the National Social Welfare Assembly and the National Committee on Accreditation.

PROGRAM SERVICE

THE NRA Program Service is highly visible and widely used. Much of it is direct service through correspondence, consultations, telephone inquiries, attendance and participation in conferences, workshops, and meetings. Some is indirect through preparation of special resource lists, program material, book reviews, magazine articles, books, and booklets.

It is a perfect example of how one NRA service dovetails neatly with other NRA services and, in so doing, adds strength to the total service. For example, the over two thousand inquiries about activities that come to the Program Department extend NRA's Correspondence and Consultation Service.

Activities and Correspondence. The wide range of inquiries is fascinating. Questions about programs for all age groups come from government agencies and leaders, churches, youth-serving agencies, PTA's, business and professional clubs, educators at all levels, men and women from all walks of life. The Program Service also helps answer inquiries related to program activity received by other NRA departments, such as the NRA International Service, Defense-Related Services, and the Consulting Service on the Ill and Handicapped.

Publications. When a gap is evident in current program literature, efforts are made to fill it. For example, the

Day Camp Program Book, written for NRA and published by Association Press in 1963, answered a real need in existing literature. Each year, some four thousand copies of the Program Service's ever-popular *Playground Summer Notebook* are snapped up by recreation departments, youth-serving agencies, and recreation leaders. In 1963, the service prepared an article on games for Grolier's revised *Child's Book of Knowledge.*

Additional factual information and data have been made available to and published by the *Music Educators Journal, Back Stage,* and *Arts Management.*

Work with Other Organizations. The director of Program Service represents the NRA on the executive committee of the National Committee On Children and Youth, on the Education Recreation Committee of the National Social Welfare Assembly and on the Film Committee of the Thomas A. Edison Foundation. The Association's special consultant on the performing arts works with other organizations involved specifically with cultural-arts services.

Recreation and the Cultural Arts. Ever since the NRA added a consultant on the performing arts to its staff, interest in and development of cultural recreation has increased steadily. *The Performing Arts as Recreation* series of pamphlets published as supplements to RECREATION Magazine, have been prepared by the service. They include *Dance Is Recreation, Music Is Recreation, Drama Is Recreation, Poetry Is Recreation.*

NRA's National Advisory Committee on Programs and Activities, recognizing the progress in cultural recreation programing, has worked on prep-

aration of a *Guide to the Organization and Administration of Cultural Recreation Programs,* with data from ninety-six public recreation agencies.

Special field services on the performing arts have included consultation on cultural programs for the U.S. First Army, the North Carolina State Recreation Commission, the West Orange, New Jersey, Creative Arts Program, and city and county recreation agencies.

Other special program services have included leadership training for Red Cross volunteers in Nassau County, New York, help in planning and conducting sessions on cultural recreation at the North Carolina State Recreation Society Conference and the Connecticut Governor's State Recreation Conference, and a music workshop for Oglebay Institute, Wheeling, West Virginia.

Services to special organizations have been given by the consultant as a member of the Board of the American Educational Theatre Association and the U.S. Institute of Theater Technology, as regional governor of Region #14 (New York, New Jersey, Eastern Pennsylvania) of Children's Theatre Conference (CTC); vice-chairman of the Advisory Council for Children's Theatre (ACCT); and as a member of the board of trustees for the Masterworks Foundation, Morristown, New Jersey, and Creative Arts, Inc., West Orange, New Jersey.

Specific plans are in the offing for joint undertakings by the John F. Kennedy Center for the Performing Arts and the National Recreation Association, which is an affiliate of the center, with a view toward assisting in the implementation of the recreational aspects of the National Cultural Center Act of 1958.

FIELD SERVICE

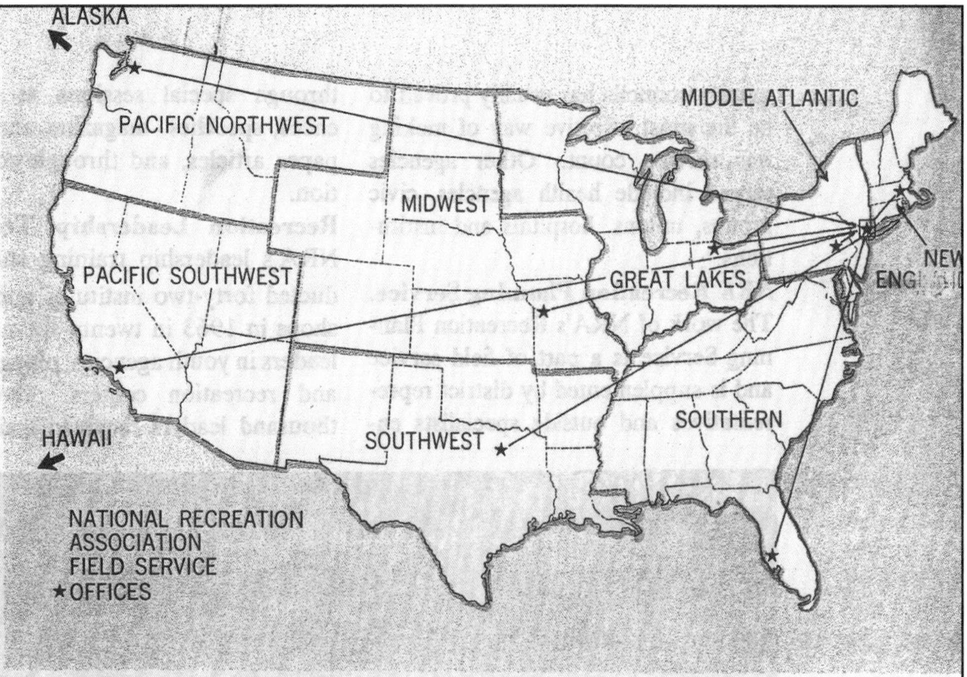
ALASKA
PACIFIC NORTHWEST
MIDDLE ATLANTIC
MIDWEST
PACIFIC SOUTHWEST
GREAT LAKES
NEW ENGL
HAWAII
SOUTHWEST
SOUTHERN
NATIONAL RECREATION
ASSOCIATION
FIELD SERVICE
★OFFICES

NRA Takes Its Services to the People.

UPON REQUEST, NRA field representatives go into the offices and meeting rooms, and to the playgrounds, recreation centers, hospitals and institutions, churches, military installations, and other places where people are making plans, training leaders or conducting recreation programs. They work with professional and volunteer leaders, executives, boards, and citizens groups in public and private recreation agencies on local, state, and national levels. This on-the-spot service takes NRA to the people.

In 1963, members of the NRA field staff made 1,211 visits to 620 communities and 100 military installations. They participated in 128 meetings of state recreation societies and 73 meetings of other organizations. They visited 50 colleges and universities; they planned and participated in 23 meetings of their district advisory committees and conducted nine district conferences. They conducted 42 leadership training institutes which reached more than 2,000 people. They made 56 surveys, plans, and special evaluations of recreation areas and facilities and programs. These services were performed by NRA district representatives, training consultants, and planners. Field service was also given by other NRA staff members—specialists in program, cultural arts, and the ill and handicapped.

Service to State Agencies. Field Service representatives work with state park and recreation agencies, conservation, health, welfare, institutions, planning, extension, economic development, commissions on aging, fitness, and children and youth. Common types of services include technical assistance, information, personnel training, resource development, promotion of legislation, and assistance to state recreation societies and associations.

Service to Federal Agencies. As new federal agencies and programs get under way, the field staff of NRA gets acquainted with government representatives in their districts. NRA's representatives have worked closely with public housing authorities, the U.S. Extension Service, Veterans Administration, National Park Service, U.S. Forest Service, Housing and Home Finance Agency, Bureau of Outdoor Recreation, Department of Health, Education and Welfare, Department of Labor, Youth Division, and the Bureau of Land Management.

Service to the Armed Forces. An important phase of NRA's field service is work with Armed Forces installations. In 1963, an NRA national training specialist conducted workshops and made field visits to twenty-eight Air Force bases in twenty-five states. The director of NRA Field Services spent two months in Europe making an appraisal of the Air Force recreation center program, visiting fifteen bases in Germany, France and England; district representatives visited bases and adjacent communities giving technical help, conducting workshops, making surveys, recruiting civilian recreation leaders, and encouraging cooperative base-community relationships. One hundred military installations were visited by NRA representatives. The National Advisory Committee on Defense Related Services gathered material for a booklet on *Military-Community Cooperation Through Recreation*, published early in 1964.

Visits to Colleges and Universities. The Field Service maintains a close relationship with the colleges and universities which offer a major in recreation. NRA representatives visit the schools as often as possible, speak to classes, and interview students.

Services to Voluntary Agencies. Extenive field service is given to non-government voluntary agencies of all kinds. Leading the list are community councils operating under various local names. In 1963, over fifty of these councils, community, county, regional, and a few state-wide in scope, were serviced by NRA's district representatives.

Services to community councils cover a wide range, including technical assistance on specific problems, planning facilities and camp sites, program aids, training, help in improving coordination, surveys, and speaking at meetings. Working through the community councils has usually proved to be the most effective way of making this service count. Other agencies served include health agencies, civic groups, unions, hospitals and institutions.

NRA Recreation Planning Service. The work of NRA's Recreation Planning Service is a part of field service and is supplemented by district representatives and outside specialists engaged to serve on the team of consultants to make recreation studies of various types. These include comprehensive long-range plans of area and facilities, program, personnel, budget and administration, as well as site plans and limited studies and evaluations. In 1963, studies of fifty-six communities were completed or in process. Sound recreation planning is promoted by NRA's Planning Service

through special sessions at conferences, speeches, magazine and newspaper articles, and through consultation.

Recreation Leadership Training. NRA's leadership training staff conducted forty-two institutes and workshops in 1963 in twenty-six states for leaders in youth agencies, playgrounds, and recreation centers. Over two thousand leaders received training in

Field representatives give on-the-spot park and recreation service.

social recreation activities, games, rhythmics, and creative dramatics. Many of these workshops were conducted at Air Force bases with leaders from adjacent communities participating. Three recreation training courses were given to fifty Peace Corps volunteers in training at Columbia University. Nine recreation workshops were given by NRA for rural leaders in New Hampshire.

District Recreation Conference. NRA's nine district conferences held in 1963 attracted a total attendance of 3,584. Paid registrations accounted for 2,587. Guests, speakers and exhibitors 1,314. There were 185 commercial exhibits and 71 educational exhibits. Seventy-one agencies cooperated in sponsoring the conferences.

District Advisory Committees. Each NRA district has a committee to advise the district representatives, help plan the district conference, improve communication between recreators, recruit recreation personnel, and carry on special projects to strengthen recreation in the district. Members are appointed by state recreation societies and by NRA. Examples of specific projects include the sponsorship and staffing of a booth at the two-day annual career exposition at Pennsylvania State College; establishment of a variety of scholarship funds, a program standards and evaluation procedures project in the Great Lakes area; an inventory of all full-time and part-time recreation personnel in the Midwest and an annual Recreation Executives School co-sponsored with the University of Kansas; a board and commission handbook in the Pacific Southwest in cooperation with the Sacramento County Department of Parks and Recreation; a directory of all parks and recreation conferences in the Pacific Northwest and a program to encourage cooperation and coordination between agencies in the field.

NATIONAL RECREATION CONGRESS

THE National Recreation Congress is sponsored by the National Recreation Association and the American Recreation Society. In 1963, 2204 delegates from the fifty states and fifteen foreign countries attended the 45th National Recreation Congress in St. Louis. Forty-five different sessions were held, ranging from an all-Congress "day-in-depth" dealing with the subject of leisure to small special-interest sessions, such as the one on ice-rink maintenance. The 46th National Recreation Congress will be held in Miami Beach, October 4-9.

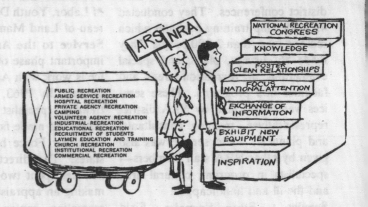

ANSWERING YOUR QUESTIONS

Reception room at NRA headquarters.

What Is the National Recreation Association?

It is a national, voluntary, non-profit, nonpartisan and nonsectarian organization through which professional and lay recreation leadership can unite to provide the many nationwide services in the recreation field essential to the sound growth of the recreation profession and the recreation movement.

What Is its Purpose?

It is dedicated to serving all recreation executives, leaders, volunteers and agencies, public and private, to the end that every child in America shall have a place to play in safety and that every person in America, young and old, shall have an opportunity for the best and most satisfying use of his expanding leisure time. Its specific services are described in the pages that follow.

Who Are its Constituents?

In 1964, the Association's constituents are the 2,071 recreation agencies in 1,480 communities affiliated with the Association for service, the 4,536 recreation leaders in 2,137 communities associated with the Association for service, the 13,950 financial contributors in over 2,700 communities, and the general public to which its services are ultimately directed.

How Is the Work of the Association Financed?

NRA's 1964 budget of $997,000 has received the approval of the National Budget and Consultation Committee sponsored by the United Community Funds and Councils of America and the National Social Welfare Assembly. Approximately a third of NRA's support comes from its own earnings, including general service fees and reimbursement for special services, sales of publications, and interest on endowments. The remaining two-thirds of its support comes from several hundred volunteer sponsors, Community Chest and United Funds, foundations, corporations and individual contributors throughout the country. Between 1906 and 1964, the Association raised and expended a total of $45,083,561.48 for the advancement of the recreation profession and the national recreation movement. On December 31, 1963 its assets totaled over $1,000,000.

How Is It Governed?

By a sixty-member Board of Trustees, composed of lay and professional recreation leaders and other outstanding representatives of the citizen and professional resources available to help meet the expanding recreation needs of the American people. They are listed on Page 4.

Acting in an advisory capacity to the Board of Trustees are the National Advisory Commission and National Advisory Council. The commission, a twenty-member lay group, is composed of officially appointed representatives of national voluntary agencies, plus distinguished citizens who are active in the field of recreation, and representative board members of local recreation agencies. The council is made up of the chairmen of the National and the District Advisory Committees of the Association and the president of the Federation of National Professional Organization for Recreation. This council represents more than seven hundred professional recreation leaders serving on NRA's National and District Advisory Committees. In addition, 130 state and community lay leaders served on the Association's four state and eleven local advisory committees in 1963.

Why Is Lay Involvement So Important in the Work of the Association?

• To represent the citizen at large for whom recreation services are provided.

• To increase the objectivity and the broader acceptance of services and leadership provided by the Association.

• To provide an effective liaison between recreation and the various social and economic segments of society.

• To effectively interpret and promote recreation to the

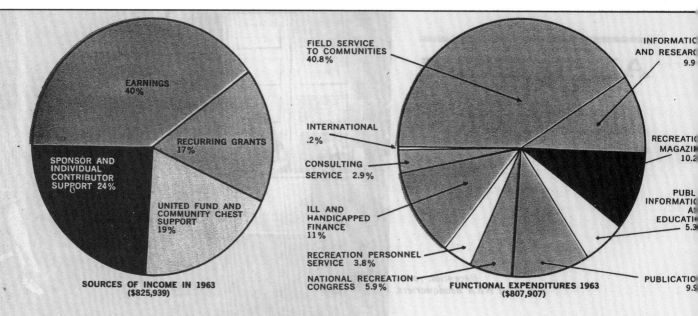

EARNINGS
40%

RECURRING GRANTS
17%

SPONSOR AND
INDIVIDUAL
CONTRIBUTOR
SUPPORT 24%

UNITED FUND AND
COMMUNITY CHEST
SUPPORT
19%

SOURCES OF INCOME IN 1963
($825,939)

FIELD SERVICE
TO COMMUNITIES
40.8%

INFORMATIC
AND RESEARC
9.9

INTERNATIONAL
.2%

CONSULTING
SERVICE 2.9%

ILL AND
HANDICAPPED
FINANCE
11%

RECREATION PERSONNEL
SERVICE 3.8%

NATIONAL RECREATION
CONGRESS 5.9%

FUNCTIONAL EXPENDITURES 1963
($807,907)

RECREATIC
MAGAZIN
10.2

PUBL
INFORMATIC
AI
EDUCATI
5.3

PUBLICATIO
9.9

public at large and to secure adequate backing and support from both the public and private sectors of the nation.

Why Is Professional Involvement So Important in the Work of the Association?

- To provide the best technical counsel and advice available on the recreation problems and service needs of the nation.
- To strengthen and expand the body of technical knowledge in the field of recreation.
- To relate the standards and practices of the profession to the overall recreation movement.

Why Does the Combined Lay and Professional Approach Provide Better Recreation Service to the Nation?

The strength of the national recreation movement lies both in the diversity and in the wide range of the combined experience and viewpoints of the professional and lay leadership of America. The layman's special contribution lies in the areas of broad public policy, support, interpretation, and public education. The professional contributes his technical knowledge, skills, and experiences, with each contributing to the other's special competency. The National Recreation Association is a joint enterprise whose aim is to serve the people and communities of the country.

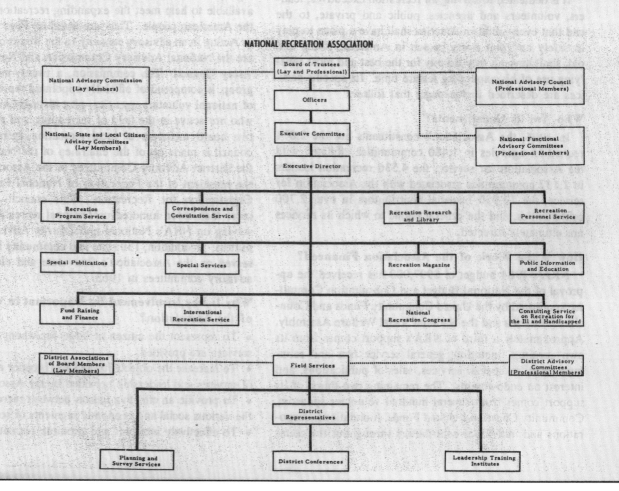

ILL
AND
HANDICAPPED

The NRA Consulting Service on Recreation for the Ill and Handicapped is dedicated to assisting the ill, the handicapped, and the aged, whether institutionalized or in the community, to achieve their maximum potential for socialization.

The basic services of the Consulting Service include personal consultation, correspondence, development of books and literature on recreation for all disabilities, training workshops, lectures and research. The department answers over two hundred inquiries every month. These include requests for literature, problem solving, program planning, activity ideas, and research data.

One of the basic tasks of the department has been to develop a continuous up-to-date flow of diversified materials and literature kits covering all disabilities and all age levels. The Consulting Service also prepares the "Rx for the Ill and Handicapped" column appearing regularly in RECREATION Magazine. This carries news of interesting developments on programs, research, and personnel concerned with recreation for the ill and handicapped.

The Consulting Service participates in national and regional conferences, provides speakers and offers workshops, demonstrations, and training programs. It works with health agencies through the National Interhealth Agency Committee on Recreation which it organized. This committee, representing nine national health agencies and the National Recreation Association, works on common interests and problems. Two new manuals have resulted as part of the work of this committee. The Consulting Service prepared *A Program of Recreation for the Homebound Person with Cerebral Palsy* and *Modified Sports and Games for the Retarded*. The first printing of the cerebral palsy pamphlet has already been distributed by United Cerebral Palsy, Inc.

Work with the aging, especially the institutionalized, is an important phase of this department's work. Specialized literature, workshops, and training programs on recreation are provided for our senior citizens.

Research. The Consulting Service conducts surveys for hospitals, schools, health agencies, camps and communities, churches, with recommendations on personnel, program, equipment, and facilities. The Service developed a project for the Arthritis and Rheumatism Foundation, and a federal Public Health Service study, "A Community Recreation Referral Project," is now under way in Philadelphia.

Another ongoing project is "A Recreation Service for the Homebound" now being carried on in Chicago with the participation of multiple-sclerosis, arthritis, and rheumatism agencies of Chicago, the Chicago Park District, and the Chicago Welfare Council. The project has trained and equipped volunteers visiting the homebound weekly. Plans include bringing many of these people out into an activity center for social recreation outside of their homes.

The director of the Consulting Service works closely with national organizations for the handicapped on programs, surveys, and publications. He has helped develop a series of manuals on recreation for the retarded for the National Recreation Committee of the National Association for Retarded Children. He is also NRA representative on the Arthritis Committee of the International Society for the Rehabilitation of the Disabled.

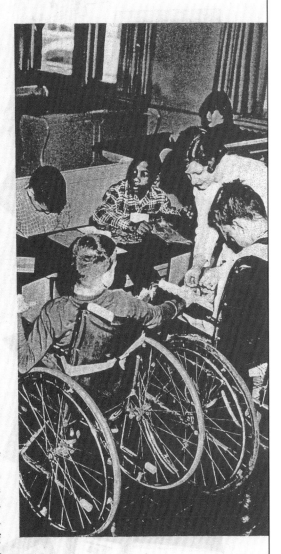

The Recreation Book Center. More than seven hundred publications on leadership, arts and crafts, physical fitness, hobbies, public relations, and all other phases of recreation administration and service are available for inspection and purchase in the Recreation Book Center located in NRA headquarters. Professional or volunteer recreation and park workers, and all others interested in recreation in any setting will find, in this carefully screened collection, basic and supplementary books for any type of recreation library. The Recreation Book Center offers recreation leaders the opportunity to select, from the lists of ninety-eight commercial publishers, the resource material they need. The center's list is revised annually and new publications added.

More than ninety percent of the twenty-two thousand volumes sold annually are ordered by mail. For the benefit of those who cannot visit NRA headquarters to make their selections in person, the Association publishes AGBOR (*A Guide to Books on Recreation*), a thirty-two page annotated list of the center's books. A new edition of this catalogue is sent to all NRA Service Associates, Affiliates, and subscribers to RECREATION Magazine each September.

Throughout the year, flyers listing all the publications in special-interest categories are sent to individuals and groups and are widely used at conferences. All the books available through the center are on display at the National Recreation Congress. Many Congress delegates have expressed the feeling that this is one of the most valuable features of the Congress.

Special Publications. In subject areas not covered adequately through other sources, members of NRA's own staff have been called upon to provide the needed material. These books usually are published for the Association by commercial houses, as in the case of *The Camp Program Book* and *The Day Camp Program Book*. Smaller manuals, such as *Standards for Municipal Recreation Areas, The Conduct of Playgrounds,* and *Outdoor Skating Rinks with Natural Ice,* are produced on NRA's own press and distributed through the Book Center.

The Special Publications Service also is responsible, annually, for the editing and production of *Selected Papers Presented at the National Recreation Congress* and the papers presented at the annual National Institute in Recreation Administration. *The Playground Summer Notebook,* eagerly awaited each spring by playground leaders all over the country, is published by the Association through its Publications Service.

The annual *NRA Directory* of Advisory Groups, Service Affiliates, Service Associates, and Professional Societies and Associations is sent each spring to all those listed in its pages. The directory is the most nearly complete "Who's Where" available for the recreation field.

Through Service Association or Affiliation with NRA, individuals and groups can serve the cause of recreation and, in turn, receive the services of the oldest and largest lay-professional recreation organization in the world.

Recreation Exhibits. Manufacturers of all types of recreation supplies and equipment exhibit their products annually at the National Recreation Congress and the eight NRA District Conferences. The opportunity to examine a wide variety of manufactured items, attractively displayed in one place, is another special service of the National Recreation Association. NRA also creates and provides displays and exhibits for meetings and conferences of other groups—local, state, and national—interpreting the values of recreation and the services of the Association.

RESEARCH AND LIBRARY

GATHERING and disseminating information on all phases of recreation was one of the most important services undertaken by the Playground Association of America (as NRA then was known) immediately after its organization in 1906. Its operation as clearing house continues in importance to this day. It is basic to NRA services and enables the Association to act as a research and publication center.

The Association's *Recreation and Park Yearbook,* published at five-year intervals, is a unique record of the growth of recreation leadership, expenditures, and services in the United States. Government and other agencies, as well as individuals, turn to the Association as the only source of such facts and figures as these:

Information gathered through surveys and by other means has aided the recreation field to gauge its progress and establish standards. Four of the Association's publications, *Introduction to Community Recreation, Playgrounds: Their Administration and Operation, Recreation Areas — Their Design and Equipment,* and *Community Sports and Athletics,* have become standard texts in recreation courses.

An important part of the Association research is its recreation library. Here some five thousand bound volumes, two hundred periodicals and forty-four vertical files provide NRA Service Associates and students with an incomparable collection of current and historical material on all phases of recreation.

Recognizing the need for increasing basic knowledge in the whole field of recreation, and for developing evaluative scales and techniques, the Association now is establishing a National Institute for Recreation Research. This will review and analyze existing research material, determine the areas of greatest need, initiate and carry out research projects in these areas, cooperate with universities and other agencies in the conduct of research, and disseminate information.

The work of the Institute will provide the recreation movement with the instrument of accountability which it has lacked and will enable the professional to demonstrate the actual relationship between service and results. The Institute will be an appropriate recipient of grants from government agencies and private foundations. The National Recreation Association anticipates that the National Institute for Recreation Research will prove to be one of its most important contributions to recreation, in this country and around the world.

	PLAYGROUNDS AND RECREATION CENTERS	LEADERS	EXPENDITURES
1920	4,293	10,218	$ 7,199,430
1930	10,385	24,949	38,518,195
1940	15,657	38,926	57,538,111
1950	24,367	58,029	268,911,957*
1960	37,077	99,696	567,171,765*

*Includes expenditures for parks

Largest recreation library in the world.

RECREATION
A MONTHLY SERVICE

PUBLISHED by the National Recreation Association since 1907, RECREATION Magazine has for many years been accepted as a standard resource on current recreation and parks affairs, trends, problems. It is used by boards and commissions, local superintendents, directors and other professional leaders, and by citizen leaders and groups — in interpreting recreation aims and values to the public, in speeches, in planning local areas and facilities, and in providing recreation and park services. It acts as a help in fund raising, bond-issue promotion, recruiting, orientation and training of staff and volunteers. It is a text or reference for recreation majors in colleges and universities. A bound volume of one year's issue forms an up-to-the-minute recreation textbook, rounds out the professional's library.

Distribution. The total distribution of the magazine, as of December 31, 1963 *(ABC Report)*, is 13,400, of which 10,885 are paid subscriptions.

Its circulation covers every state in the union and its possessions, varying per state from New York's 1,051 paid subscriptions to Nevada's fourteen paid subscriptions. Canadian subscriptions total 328, while 247 go to foreign countries, 187 to military or civilian personnel overseas. Additional, uncounted, unlisted circulation where one copy receives group use covers individuals in college classes and on large recreation department staffs. The ABC audit covers 1,090 libraries where one copy is used by many.

Content. The magazine's total number of pages in 1963 was 494. Its five sections—General Features, Administration, Program, Recreation Digest, Regular Departments—covered forty-five broad categories of subject matter, while eighty pages were given to advertising.

Advertising. RECREATION is a basic medium for advertisers who want to develop or promote equipment and

services for the recreation market and, increasingly, as recreation and park departments merge and the magazine's park content grows accordingly, it is becoming the same for the park market. In 1963, 92 advertisers expanded the advertising pages to a total of 80 as against 26 advertisers and 29 pages in 1943, and 59 advertisers and 46 pages in 1953.

The National Advisory Committee on the Publishing of Recreation Materials. This NRA committee, founded in 1958, serves a twofold purpose: advisory to the NRA and advisory to the field in raising the standard of recreation publications. The editor of RECREATION serves as the committee's secretary and liaison person with the Association. This year, the committee is being expanded into the National Advisory Committee on Communications, with subcommittees on a variety of media and techniques of communication.

Editorial Coverage by NRA Districts				
District	Articles	Short Items	Mention	Total
New England	5	10	3	18
Middle Atlantic	15	10	7	32
Southern	13	6	5	24
Great Lakes	15	16	7	38
Midwest	8	5	4	17
South West	5	6	3	14
Pacific Northwest	6	10	5	21
Pacific Southwest	8	17	6	31

1963 Text Allocation (Ten Issues)			
Section	No. of Pages	No. of Articles	Short Items
General Features	135	73	5
Administration	61	29	2
Program	60½	27	8
Recreation Digest	16½	9	1
Regular Departments	146	79	3
Total Text	417	217	19

Chapter Ten

Merger

COMBINING
•
RECREATION MAGAZINE
•
AMERICAN RECREATION JOURNAL
•
PARKS AND RECREATION MAGAZINE
•
PLANNING AND CIVIC COMMENT

PARKS & RECREATION

OFFICIAL PUBLICATION OF THE NATIONAL RECREATION AND PARK ASSOCIATION • JUNE 1966

After agreement was finally reached by the various boards of directors of the merging bodies, their elected heads conferred with Laurance S. Rockefeller, who was to become the first president of the National Recreation and Park Association. Left to right: Frank McInnis, American Association of Zoological parks and Aquariums; Frank Vaydik, American Institute of Park Executives; Stuart G. Case, American Recreation Society; Laurance S. Rockefeller; James H. Evans, National Recreation Association; Conrad L. Wirth, National Conference on State Parks.

The Merger of National Recreation and Park Organizations

The decade of the 1960s marked a new era for the NRA, especially in its views regarding the role of the professional recreation leader in the governance of the Association and perhaps more importantly in the relationship the NRA was to develop with professional organizations in the recreation and park field. The election of two prominent practitioners, **George Hjelte** and **Robert W. Crawford**, to the board in 1960 marked the increasing recognition by Prendergast and the directors of the growing importance of the professional administrator in the direction of policy in the Association.

By this time the board was undergoing another change in its citizen leadership. With the sudden death of industrialist Grant Titsworth in 1960, the directors elected lawyer-banker **James H. Evans** as their new chairman. Evans had become interested in the NRA while serving on the NRA citizens committee in Chicago. He assumed a more active role in the affairs of the Association upon his transfer to New

Robert W. Crawford
Commissioner of Recreation
Philadelphia, Pennsylvania

George Hjelte
General Manager of the
Recreation and Park Department
Los Angeles, California

James H. Evans
Chairman, Board of Trustees
National Recreation Association

York City as vice-president of the Reuben H. Donnelley Corporation. Evans had been an active member of the executive committee, and his leadership and public relations skills had gained the attention and respect of his fellow directors. It was these same abilities in human relations that would make Evans a central figure in the creation of the National Recreation and Park Association. While serving on the NRA Board of Trustees, Jim Evans became president of Seaman's Bank for Savings and later chairman and CEO of the Union Pacific Corporation.

An important national development taking place at this time, and one which was to indirectly influence the future of the NRA, was the work of the **Outdoor Recreation Resources Review Commission** (ORRRC). This bipartisan congressional study panel had been established in 1958 and charged with the responsibility of determining the outdoor recreation needs of the American people for the next forty years. The work of the Commission, chaired by wealthy

conservationist Laurance S. Rockefeller, was focusing national attention upon the increasing demand for outdoor recreation opportunities by the American public. While the NRA's executive director, Joseph Prendergast, and board member **Luther Gulick** served on the advisory council to ORRRC, much of the impetus for and direction of the study came not from recreation and park organizations but rather from conservation groups such as the Isaac Walton league.

The ORRRC report served as an important stimulant in encouraging the NRA and related organizations to explore ways in which they might cooperate and utilize their resources more effectively. For the NRA it reinforced the fact that the recreation field was growing so rapidly that the Association itself could no longer exercise the leadership it once did. NRA vice-president Luther Gulick, nephew of the founder of the Playground Association of America and a member of the ORRRC advisory council, summed up the changing situation for his fellow directors by stating, "the nation stands on the threshold of tremendous developments in recreation and parks, greater than for two generations; it is important to develop a whole new general strategy, to take a broad look and start anew, concentrating on positive moves." Gulick, who headed the Institute for Public Administration, was becoming an increasingly active and influential member of the NRA board. He along with board chairman Evans and professional administrator Crawford infused a new vitality and leadership into the board.

Luther Gulick

Resources of the Merging organizations

Financial Position

NRA	95%	$1,018,933
AIPE	3%	$27,947
ARS	1%	$7,582
NCSP	1%	$11,805

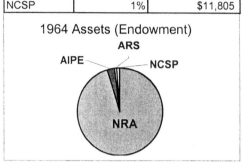

NRA	77%	$872,230
AIPE	16%	$191,341
ARS	4%	$47,638
NCSP	3%	$43,722

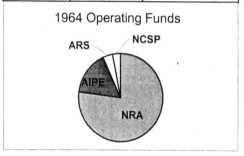

Staff

NRA	84%	34
AIPE	12%	5
ARS	2%	1
NCSP	2%	1

NRA	81%	60
AIPE	13%	10
ARS	3%	2
NCSP	3%	2

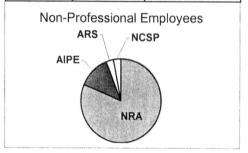

Constituents

NRA	71%	20693*
AIPE	10%	2,917
ARS	16%	4,527
NCSP	3%	800

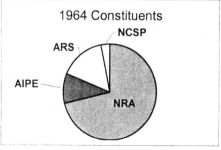

*includes 14,213 citizen contributors

Editor's note: the year 2005 value of the NRA assets adjusted for inflation would be $6,328,776.

By the time of the ORRRC study there was a clear national trend in support of the unified administration of recreation and parks at the local level. As a natural outgrowth of this movement, the National Recreation Association and the American Recreation Society, the recreation-oriented national organizations, became more concerned with park issues, and the American Institute of Park Executives (AIPE), a major advocate for the municipal park movement, became involved to a greater degree with recreation matters. As a result of these overlapping interests, organizational philosophies and goals became somewhat similar, while competition for members and revenue became more intense. Duplicate institutional services, such as national conferences, magazines, and membership promotion, became a matter of consideration not only by members but for exhibitors and advertisers as well. Many professional leaders in the filed alluded to the increasing confusion between recreation and park groups and openly spoke out in favor of combining organizations.

Among organizations likely to consolidate, the NRA was by far the largest in the terms of financial resources and staff. Its budget for 1963 was $924,000. the NRA staff was made up of approximately one hundred full-time members of which some thirty were professional. The Association had an endowment fund just short of one million dollars and owned a headquarters building in New York City valued at approximately a half-million dollars. Its members and individual contributors numbered eighteen thousand, most of the NRA's financial support was from philanthropic sources with only three percent of its budget coming from membership fees. In addition to its New York headquarters, the Association maintained staff in Washington, D.C. and in eight regional offices throughout the country.

The American Recreation Society, celebrating its twenty-fifth anniversary in 1963, had by that time increased its membership to 4,200 which continued to approximate the number of recreation leaders who belonged to the NRA. The ARS was organized into special interest sections which included armed forces recreation; hospital recreation; public and park recreation; professional education; county, state, and federal recreation; private and voluntary agencies; and religious organizations. An executive director, an administrative assistant, and a secretary made up the ARS staff. The annual operating budget was approximately $50,000, of which 70 percent came from membership dues and the remainder from the sale of advertising and publications. The ARS published its own magazine, *The American Recreation Journal*, and jointly sponsored an annual national convention with the NRA.

The American Institute of Park Executives had been established in 1898 primarily to gather and disseminate information on public parks and recreation areas. By 1963 AIPE's membership included some two thousand park and recreation administrators who constituted the voting membership of the organization. In addition there were about a thousand local park and recreation board members affiliated in a non-voting capacity. The AIPE's operating budget was just under $190,000, of which approximately 22 percent was derived from membership dues. Much of AIPE's income was generated from a strong commercial exhibit component of their national conference and from an especially successful publication program. While AIPE was regarded essentially as a park-oriented organization, it had attracted a sizable group of recreation administrators to the point where its membership was almost evenly divided between park and recreation practitioners. The AIPE headquarters was located at Oglebay Park in Wheeling, West Virginia.

Closely affiliated with the park executives was the American Association of Zoological Parks and

Aquariums, an autonomous organization created in 1924 and dedicated to wildlife conservation. Many of the general services of AAZPA were jointly operated for purposes of economy with AIPE out of Oglebay Park. The zoological group was not particularly active in the merger negotiations but merely followed the leadership of the AIPE.

By way of comparison, the total yearly expenditures of both the ARS and the AIPE amounted to just over one-quarter of the existing budget of the NRA. There was the same magnitude of difference on financial resources between the AIPE and ARS. The American Institute of Park Executives had four times the annual budget of the American Recreation Society.

Through Conrad Wirth's efforts the **National Conference on State Parks** (NCSP) became an active participant in merger discussions. The NCSP had been formed in 1921 by Stephen Mather and other leading conservationists for the purpose of encouraging the states to acquire and preserve scenic areas of importance. Its membership included professional resource managers and citizens concerned with the development of state parks.

One of the most technical aspects of the lay-professional issue was its perceived relationship to the tax status of any new organization created through the merger. One of the prerequisites for the NRA's involvement in negotiations was preservation of the full tax-exempt status of the Association, the most favored tax status among the organizations discussing merger. The Association was tax-exempt under Section 501(C)(3) of the Internal Revenue Code. The major benefit of this particular tax classification was that contributions to such designated organizations were deductible for federal income, estate, and gift tax purposes. The AIPE and ARS, on the other hand, were both classified for tax purposes as trade or profes-

sional associations under a different section of the Internal Revenue Code, which prohibited donors from deducting contributions as tax-deductible gifts. Under federal regulations, the NRA thus was characterized as a charitable, educational, and scientific organization operating exclusively in the public interest while the ARS and AIPE were interpreted to be professional associations operating to promote the specific interests of their own members.

One of the early obstacles encountered in the formulation of a plan for merger was the question of how to reconcile the unique differences that existed between the organizations. The ARS and AIPE were both professional membership societies with voting members who elected their officers and board members, who in turn staffed their committees. On the other hand, the National Recreation Association was a national voluntary service organization with no voting members but rather service associates (individuals) and service affiliates (agencies). Committee members were appointed on the recommendations of staff. Professionals who joined the NRA had no voting powers over its board of trustees or its budget. Basic organizational differences were a problem during earlier NRA-ARS discussions, but the issue of professional rights and governing power gained new momentum with the combined support of the AIPE and the ARS.

Over the years the Association had been built upon the concept of serving the public interest. Thus the NRA board maintained a strong stance that any unified organization must direct its broad programs to the recreation interests of the nation through public education and service to both lay and professional interests, communities throughout the county, and public and private recreation agencies.

Thus with a seeming stalemate in the negotiations between AIPE and ARS on the one hand and NRA on the other, the potential for organizational conflict and competition grew stronger. Out of this environment

James H. Evans

Luther Gulick

Susan M. Lee

Robert W. Crawford

Key leadership for the NRA's involvement in merger negotiations was provided by board
chairman James H. Evans and vice-presidents Luther Gulick,
Susan M. Lee, and Robert W. Crawford.

of confusion and concern emerged the unsolicited counsel of some elder statesmen in the park and recreation field.

An important option to end the deadlock in negotiations came from Charles K. Brightbill, head of the Department of Recreation and Park Administration at the University of Illinois. Brightbill, a former NRA staff member and a past president of the American Recreation Society, had not been involved in formal negotiations up to this point. He earlier had advocated total organizational unification, fearing that a merger of only two of the groups would create further dissension in the recreation and park field.

Brightbill's proposal, along with others resulted in a special meeting of key board leaders of NRA, ARS, AIPE and NCSP without staff present.

The meeting, held in Chicago on December 5, 1964, was hosted and chaired upon mutual consent by Robert W. Ruhe, a respected and well-informed recreation and park administrator in Skokie, Illinois, who had not been active in previous merger negotiations. The meeting, during a major midwestern snowstorm, produced a proposal for merger that was unanimously endorsed by all of the board representatives in attendance. The principles agreed to constituted the basis for the formation of the National Recreation and Parks Association.

The proposal for merger which was to change the future destiny of the NRA expressed these beliefs and conditions:

Proposal for Merger

It is the expressed belief of the officers of the American Institute of Park Executives, American Recreation Society, National Conference on State Parks, and National Recreation Association that each organization reaffirm its strong conviction that the ever-increasing needs and demands for recreation and park facilities and services can best be served through the collective and unified strengths of lay and professional persons.

It is further recognized and reiterated that a unified and concerted effort on the part of all aforementioned organizations shall result in more effective services. To this end, it is believed that these organizations should collectively utilize their respective talents and resources by joining into one service and professional association dedicated to the task of unification of effort in the recreation and park field.

The implementation of such beliefs can best be accomplished by a merger of all lay and professional societies and organizations dedicated to this common purpose in the following manner:

1. The establishment of an association by amending the present charter of the National Recreation Association so as to include the principles and objectives of the new organization, while at the same time preserving the benefits derived from the existing charter which has been tested and proven over the last half century.

2. The name of the new organization shall be National Recreation and Park Association.

3. There shall be established a policy-making body called the Board of Trustees to govern the National Recreation and Park Association consisting of 60 members, twenty of whom shall be laymen, twenty professional persons and twenty laymen nominated by the professional group.

4. There shall be established an Administrative Board consisting of twenty members from the Board of Trustees, ten of whom shall be professionals and ten of whom shall be laymen. These members shall be chosen by the Board of Trustees. This Administrative Board shall be responsible for supervising the carrying out of the directions and policies of the Board of Trustees and employ the staff as authorized by the Board of Trustees.

5. There shall be established a professional division of the National Recreation and Park Association governed by a Board of Governors and representing the various professional interests and sections. The professional groups shall initiate their own form of organization and determine the best methods of the organization, geographic representation, and selection on the Board of Governors.

6. There shall be established a lay division of the National Recreation and Park Association governed by a Board of Directors and representing the various lay and civic interests in the recreation and park field. This lay group shall initiate their own form of organization and determine the best methods of organization, geographic representation and selection on the Board of Directors.

Apparently the success in reaching an agreement was in large part a result of the able and determined elected leadership of the negotiation organizations. NRA representatives Evans and Crawford were effective in helping to achieve a consensus on the issue of a predominantly lay board. The board structure agreed upon was similar to the formula suggested earlier by former ARS president Charles Brightbill.

Once the proposal for merger was agreed upon, Evans, along with Luther Gulick and Conrad Wirth, persuaded Laurance S. Rockefeller, who had headed the Outdoor Recreation Resources Review Commission, to accept the role of president of the new organization.

In accepting the presidency of the newly-formed Association, Laurance S. Rockefeller stated: "We have entered a new era in the country…an era where parks, recreation and the quality of the environment have become a major item of public concern. With these developments come heavy responsibilities. So it is timely, fitting and important that we strengthen our ties of organization and mutual cooperation. Our combined strength will be far greater than the sum of the individual components. The stakes are great for our organizations, for our professions and for the public good."

New NRPA Board President, Laurance S. Rockefeller and new Chairman, James H. Evans.

Merger Passed by Board

At a special meeting of the National Recreation Association Board of Trustees chaired by James H. Evans, on January 22, 1965, the thirty board members attending unanimously passed the following resolution for merger of the National Recreation Association, American Recreation Society, American Institute of Park Executives and the National Conference of State Parks:

THAT the Proposal for Merger dated December 5, 1964, be approved and that the Special Committee of the Board (consisting of James H. Evans, Susan M. Lee, Luther Gullick, and Robert W. Crawford) be authorized and directed to work out with the Board representatives of the other organizations the details of the merger to be submitted for the consideration of the Board at its next meeting on May 26, 1965.

James H. Evans, new Chairman of the NRPA Board stated, "For all of us in the recreation and park movement in this country, January 1966 marked the dawn of a new day. Each leading organization in our field, with years of tradition and experience behind it, has officially joined the others to form one association, the National Recreation and Park Association, devoted to a common cause. In forming this Association we do service to the American people. We not only increase our reach and effectiveness and open new possibilities previously impossible to us, but we set an example for other groups in other fields where disunity has flourished."[1]

Founding meeting of the NRPA Board of Trustees, August 13-14, 1965, at the American Hotel, New York City.

Members of the NRPA Administrative Board (left to right): First Row–Frank Vaydik, Mrs. Richard M. Colgate, Susan M. Lee, Mrs. Virginia Wiltbank, Endicott P. Davison, Sal J. Prezioso; Second Row–James S. Stevens, Jr., Stewart G. Case, Conrad L. Wirth, William Penn Mott, Jr., William Frederickson, Jr., Dr. Garrett G. Eppley. Chairman, Conrad L.Wirth. Not shown is Luther Gulick.

For the National Recreation Association January 1966 indeed marked the dawn of a new era, albeit an age which had been arising within the field of parks and recreation for at least a generation. How the ideas, people, and services of the Association; its followers; its colleagues; and its related organizations were to fare after the rendezvous is another tale.[2]

Editor's note: following the merger the American Association of Zoological Parks and Aquariums withdrew and reverted back to the original state of an independent autonomous organization.
(1) Parks and Recreation Magazine. February 1966. pp. 137
(2) Knapp & Hartsoe. pp. 199 1970

EPILOGUE
A Look Ahead

The story of the National Recreation Association is the story of me and lots of career-driven folks like me. My life is a living testimony of the National Recreation Association's purpose and legacy in America. When I was all of six years old, the NRA celebrated its 50th anniversary. As a young child my parents took me to our town's park, let me play, encouraged me to take music lessons, taught me board games, played low organized games, taught me how to hunt and fish, allowed me to play with my friends after school—at school, before anyone referred to it as "after school" activities, and helped me to form my own creative expression.

Millions of children like me growing up then did not realize that a national recreation organization had been looking out for us. We did not know that such an organization was developing standards and training programs for leaders to make sure we were safe and having fun. We did not know that a national organization was influencing us to stay in school, graduate and serve others in this movement we call parks and recreation.

Established in 1906, the NRA evolved during decades of massive social change. Its mission rallied and brought together teachers, community leaders, and social workers. Its legacy was to ensure the health and happiness of America's families and children.

Today America celebrates the 100th Anniversary of the NRA. Its legacy of watching over our nation's children has been passed on to the National Recreation and Parks Association and from our shared view, the American Academy for Parks and Recreation Administration.

As a college student in the late 1960s, I was introduced to the historical patriarchs and matriarchs of parks, playground and recreation: Jane Addams, Luther Gulick, Joseph Lee, Henry S. Curtis, Joseph Prendergast, Lawrence S. Rockefeller, and from my home state and where I grew up— Dorothy Enderis. During my college years, America was embroiled in an unpopular war and the college scene was a hotbed of social debate, demonstration and action. How did we deal with the stress of social change? We played, we marched, we sang and we did many of the things I mentioned earlier. Our creative expression was formed after several years of participating in public recreation.

Our country is once again in a state of enormous change. Local and global issues affecting our livelihood are being debated, demonstrated and acted on. As parks and recreation practitioners and teachers, we are deeply involved in protecting youth and children, re-invigoration our neighborhoods, preserving our environment, fighting for equality and inclusion, celebrating our diversity, and demonstrating to the healing values of play and recreation. While a lot has changed since 1906, in many respects we are still the same; living in an ever-changing and increasing stressful time. We are still in need of the vision and values promoted with the origin of the NRA.

Written in 1956, then– Executive Director Joseph Prendergast wrote, "During the past fifty years the National Recreation Association has worked through many critical periods in American life. We are in the midst of an evolution in living far surpassing anything before. In the momentous days ahead, all of us in the recreation movement face challenges far beyond those before. It is a time when the recreation forces of the nation and the world are destined to play an ever greater role in man's continuing search for peace and happiness."

Our shared challenge is to preserve our history, celebrate its legacy and "Build Better Communities," I am proud to recognize the talents of this publication's editors and the work they have contributed to provide us with direction and hope. Now it's our turn.

Dale Larsen

President, American Academy for Parks and Recreation Administration

BIBLIOGRAPHY

Books

America Recreation Society, Its Early Years, 1937-1952, American Recreation Society, Washington, D.C. 1953.

The Atwell Story, National Recreation Association, New York, 1951.

Howard Braucher Memorial Booklet, National Recreaton Association, New York, 1949.

A Treasury of Living, (Selected writings of Howard Braucher), National Recreation Association, New York, 1949

Butler, George D. (1965) *Pioneers in Public Recreation*, Minneapolis: Burgess Publishing Company.

Crawford, Robert W., *Reflections of a Recreation Professional*, Arlington, VA: National Recreation and Park Association, 1993.

Ibrahim, Hilmi, *Pioneers in Leisure and Recreation*, Reston, VA: American Alliance for Health Physical Education, Recreation, and Dance, 1989.

Knapp, Richard E. and Charles E. Hartsoe, (1970), *Play for America*, Alexandria, VA: National Recreation and Park Association.

Kozar, Andrew J., *The Sport Sculpture of R. Tait McKensie*. Champaing, IL: Human Kenetics Books.

Rivers, Thomas E., *My Sixty Years in Recreation Working for Life Enrichment*, Alexandria, VA:

National Recreation Resources Review Commission. *Outdoor Recreation for America*, Washington, D.C., 1962

Periodicals

Playground Magazine
Playground and Recreation magazine
Recreation Magazine
Parks and Recreation Magazine

The National Scene
1 9 0 6

★ The American flag had only forty-five stars in 1906. Probably the greatest news story of that year was the San Francisco earthquake at 5:13 A.M. on April 18. Only a week after the calamity the *Boston Transcript* could print these lines:

> "Some San Francisco folks intend
> This summer to foresake her;
> Because the earth is not a Friend
> Although it is a Quaker."

Two days after the earthquake, bread sold for a dollar a loaf in San Francisco—and wealthy citizens whose money had been in banks were borrowing from those whose bank was a pocket.

In New York, at the other end of the country and under more normal conditions, strictly fresh eggs were seventeen for a quarter and butter was twenty-three cents a pound. The classified advertisements listed a six-room housekeeping apartment on West 69th Street, furnished and with bath, at ten dollars a week; or a nine-room steam-heated apartment, also with bath, in a two-family house in Brookline, Massachusetts, could be rented for thirty-five dollars a month.

Grade school teachers in Boston received increases in salaries that year by vote of the Peabody School Committee; thereafter they were to receive up to a maximum of five-hundred dollars a year. Neat "cash girls" were wanted in New York department stores for three dollars a week with one day off.

Four-cylinder Pope-Hartfords cost twenty-five hundred dollars. This automobile "takes all the hills on the high gear" and runs "five to fifty miles an hour on the level without changing gears." One person in eight hundred owned a car—an Ardsley, Cadillac, Peerless, or Packard; a Studebaker, Oldsmobile or Pope-Hartford.

The Pennsylvania Railroad advertised "eighteen hours from New York to Chicago."

The "aeroplane" was three years old and already "the problem of the century, mechanical flight," was solved. The Wrights had made one hundred and sixty flights, averaging a mile each, and the machine had attained a speed of slightly more than thirty-eight miles per hour.

The *Literary Digest* had an article about the effect of the telephone on our American dialects. "The use of the telephone is bringing about greater similarity in different parts of the country," asserted the president of Southern Bell Telephone and Telegraph Company.

The *San Francisco Examiner* for April 16, 1906, in a front page story, reported telephone communication between that city and New York: "The long distance telephone would seem to have been perfected." Three days earlier the mayors of San Francisco and Oakland were reported as having exchanged wireless telegrams, the first such messages transmitted between those cities.

The *Ladies Home Journal* carried an article by Jane Addams, "The First Five Years at Hull House." *Munsey's Magazine* for September stated that "all told, New York City is spending three hundred thousand dollars a year for school playgrounds."

In 1906 people were singing "Waltz Me Around Again Willie," "Forty-five Minutes from Broadway," "The Good Old Summer Time," and "Everybody Works But Father."

All three Barrymores were appearing on Broadway in the same play, Sir James M. Barrie's latest, *Alice-Sit-by-the-Fire*. *Charley's Aunt*, the "greatest of comedy successes," was playing; and there were *The Girl of the Golden West* with Blanche Bates, *George Washington, Jr.* with George M. Cohan, and Maude Adams in *Peter Pan*. (Maude Adams was the favorite actress of Yale's class of 1906, Ethel Barrymore was second and Julia Marlowe was third.) Emma Eames, Geraldine Farrar, Madam Schumann-Heink, and Caruso were singing at the Metropolitan.

In Boston, *Mrs. Wiggs of the Cabbage Patch* was playing; and the great Sarah Bernhardt was promised "late in the season" for a single performance in one act from each of four plays.

Dancing schools taught the glide-waltz, two-step, schottische, polka, half-time, and lanciers. Fashions were affected by the automobile—tourist coats had the "auto-cut", were made of silk and mohair of "dust-shedding qualities." Bathing suits could be had of either mohair or serge with "high or open neck, sailor collar, and with bishop or short sleeves."

There was considerable speculation among editors in 1906 as to presidential candidates for 1908. "Who knows," asked the *Washington Post*, "that the exigency will not arise that shall make it imperative for Mr. Roosevelt to enter the lists? He was drafted in 1900. What has been, may be." Beginning in early 1906, George Harvey, editor of *Harpers Weekly*, carried on a vigorous campaign for Woodrow Wilson's nomination as the Democratic candidate for 1908.

President Theodore Roosevelt was awarded the Nobel Peace Prize in 1906 for his success in bringing about peace between Russia and Japan.

This was the general national scene when the *Boston Transcript* for April 13, 1906, reported the formation, in Washington, D.C., on April 12, of the Playground Association of America. ∎

FIRST BOARD OF DIRECTORS
(Playground Association of America)

H. B. F. Macfarland of Washington, D. C., President of the Board of Commissioners of the District of Columbia.

Seth T. Stewart of New York, N. Y., Associate Superintendent of Schools in charge of Vacation Schools and Playgrounds of the New York City Board of Education.

Dr. Henry S. Curtis of Washington, D. C., Supervisor of Playgrounds.

Dr. Luther H. Gulick of New York, N. Y., Supervisor of Physical Education for the New York City Board of Education.

Myron T. Scudder of New Paltz, N.Y., Principal of the New Paltz Normal School.

Archibald Hill of New York, N. Y., Metropolitan Parks Association.

Miss Sadie American of New York, N. Y., President of the New York Section of the Council of Jewish Women.

Miss Mary E. McDowell of Chicago, Illinois, Social Workers, University Settlement.

Miss Marie Ruef Hofer of New York, N. Y., Lecturer at Teachers College, Columbia University.

Miss Amalie Hofer of Chicago, Illinois, Principal of the Pestalozzi-Froebel Kindergarten Training School, Chicago Commons.

Miss Beulah Kennard of Pittsburgh, Pennsylvania, President of the Pittsburgh Playground Association.

Mrs. Samuel Ammon of Pittsburgh, Pennsylvania, Pittsburgh Playground Association.

Dr. George M. Kober of Washington, D. C.

William H. Baldwin of Chicago, Illinois.

Mrs. Ellen Spenser Mussey of Washington, D.C.

Charles F. Weller of Washington, D. C., General Secretary of Associated Charties.

Dr. Rebecca Stoneroad of Washington, D. C.

Wallace Hatch of Washington, D. C., Secretary of the Playground Association of Washington.

LIST OF NATIONAL RECREATION CONGRESSES FROM

1907-1966

National Recreation Congresses Held by the National Recreation Association

Place	Date
Washington, D.C.	April 12, 1906

The first organization meeting of the national recreation movement was held at the White House. This was not, however, a Congress

Place	Date
Chicago, Ill.	June 20-22, 1907
New York, N.Y.	September 8-12,1908
Pittsburgh, Pa.	May 11-14, 1909
Rochester, N.Y.	June 7-11, 1910
Washington, D.C.	May 10-12, 1911
Cleveland, Ohio	June 5-8, 1912
Richmond, Va.	May 6-10, 1913
Grand Rapids, Mich.	October 2-6, 1916
Atlantic City, N.J.	October 9-12, 1922
Springfield, Ill.	October 8-10, 1923
Atlantic City, N.J.	October 16-21, 1924
Asheville, N.C.	October 5-10, 1925
Atlantic City, N.J.	October 18-22, 1926
Memphis, Tenn.	October 3-8, 1927
Atlantic City, N.J.	October 1-6, 1928
Louisville, Ky.	October 14-19, 1929
Atlantic City, N.J.	October 6-11, 1930
Washington, D.C.	April 13, 1931

The twenty-fifth anniversary meeting of the Board of Director of the National Recreation Association was held at the White House. Though not a Congress, this meeting marked an important milestone in the history of the movement.

Place	Date
Toronto, Canada	October 5-9, 1931
Los Angeles, Calif.	July 23-29, 1932
Washington, D.C.	October 1-5, 1934
Chicago, Ill.	September 30 – October 4, 1935
Atlantic City, N.J.	May 17-21, 1937
Pittsburgh, Pa.	October 3-7, 1938
Boston, Mass.	October 9-13, 1939
Cleveland, Ohio	September 30- October 4, 1940
Baltimore, Md.	August 4-8 1941
Cincinnati, Ohio	September 28- October 2, 1942
No congress—War Years	1943-1945

Atlantic City, N.J.	January 28-February 1, 1946
New York, N.Y.	October 13-17 1947
Omaha, Nebraska	September 26-30, 1948
New Orleans, La.	September 12-16, 1949
Cleveland, Ohio	October 2-6, 1950
Boston, Mass.	October 1-5, 1951
Seattle, Wa.	September 29- October 3, 1952
Philadelphia, Pa.	September 28-October 2, 1953
St. Louis, Mo.	September 27- October 1, 1954
Denver, Colorado	September 27-October 1, 1955
Philadelphia, Pa.	September 30- October 4, 1956
Long Beach, Ca.	September 30- October 4, 1957
Atlantic City, N.J.	September 22-25, 1958
Chicago, Ill.	September 28-October 2, 1959
Washington, D.C.	September 25-29, 1960
Detroit, Mich.	October 1-6, 1961
Philadelphia, Pa	Septmeber 30-October 5, 1962
St. Louis, Mo.	September 24-October 4, 1963
Miami Beach, Fl.	october 4-9, 1964
Minneapolis, MN	October 3-8, 1965
Washington, D.C.	October 9-13, 1966

Editor's note: Beginning in 1957, the American Recreation Society became a
Co-sponsor of the national Recreation Congress.

SELECTED PUBLICATIONS OF THE NRA

By 1965 the NRA had published over 2,000 books, pamphlets, reprints, and bulletins as well as the periodical *Recreation*. Several hundred of these items are listed in the printed catalogs of the library of Congress. The list that follows contains representative publications authored by staff and officers of the Association.

Books

Buther, George

Play AreasTheir Design and Equipment. (1928).

Playgrounds: Their Administration and Operation. (1936). New York: A. S. Barnes and Company, Inc.

New Play AreasTheir Design and Equipment (1938).

Recreation Areas: Their Design and Equipment. (1947). New York: A. S. Barnes and Company.

Pioneers in Public Recreation. (1965). Minneapolis: Burgess Publishing Company.

Introduction to Community Recreation. (1976). New York: McGraw-Hill. (Previous editions, 1949, 1959, 1967, 1968).

Curtis, Henry S.

Education Through Play, The Macmillan Co., New York, 1915.

Play and Recreation in the Open Country, Ginn & Co., New York, 1914.

The Playground Movement and Its Significance, The Macmillan Company, New York, 1917.

The Practical Conduct of Play, The Macmillan Company, New York, 1916.

Recreation for Teachers, The Macmillan Co., New York, 1918.

Gulick, Luther H.

A Philosophy of Play, Scribners, New York, 1920.

Lee, Joseph

Constructive and Preventive Philanthropy,The Macmillan Company, New York, 1902.

Play in Education, The Macmillan Company, New York, 1915.

(Reissued in 1942 by the National Recreation Association).

*Joseph Lee issue of *Recreation*, National Recreation Association, December, 1937.

Play and Playgrounds, Playground Association of America, New York, 1908.

How to Start a Playground, Playground Association of America, New York, 1910.

Play as an Antidote to Civilization, Playground and Recreation Association of America, New York, 1911.

Play for Home, Playground and Recreation Association, New York, 1912.

And many others.

Lies, Eugene T.

The New Leisure Challenges the Schools, National Recreation Association, New York, 1933.

Musselman, Virginia W.

The Day Camp Program Book, New York, 1963.(NRA)

NRA

Pangburn, Weaver W. *Adventures in Recreation*, New York, 1936

Rogers, James E.

The Child and Play, D. Appleton-Century Company, New York, 1932.

Sutherland, Willard C.

Recreation as a Profession in the Southern Region, National Recreation Association, New York, 1954.

Weir, Lebert H.

Camping Out: A Manual of Organized Camping, The Macmillan Company, New York, 1924.

Europe at Play, A. S. Barnes Company, New York, 1937.

Park Recreation Areas in the United States, Bulletin #462, U.S. Bureau of Labor Statistics, Washington, D.C., 1928

Parks: *A Manual of Municipal and County Parks*, A. S. Barnes & Company, New York, 1928.

William, Arthur

Recreation for the Aging, Association Press, New York, 1953.

Recreation for the Senior Years, Association Press, 1963.

Zanzig, Augustus D.

Music in American Life, New York, 1932 (NRA)

Selected Pamphlets

NRA. *Arts and Crafts for the Recreation Leader*…New York, 1943.

Charges and Fees for Community Recreation Facilities and Activities of Public Park, Recreation, and School Systems, New York, 1932.

Community Drama, New York, 1926.

Community Music, New York, 1926.

County Parks: A Report of a Study of County Parks in the United States, New York, 1930.

County Parks and Recreation, published jointly with the National Association of Counties, 1964.

Games for Children, New York, 1943.

Guidelines for the Organization and Administration of a Cultural Program in Community Recreation, New York, 1965.

Home Play, New York, 1945.

Howard Braucher Memorial Booklet, New York, 1949.

In-service Education for Community Center Leadership, New York, 1955.

Recreation and the Church: A Manual for Leaders, New York, 1946.

Recreation and Psychiatry, New York, 1960.

Recreation for Men: A Guide to the Planning and Conducting of Recreational Activities for Men's Groups, New York, 1944.

Recreation for Older People, New York, 1943.

Recreation for War Workers: A Guide for Workers in Charge of Recreation in War Plants, New York, New York, 1943.

Recreation Leadership Standards: Standards of Training, Experience, and Compensation for Positions in Community Recreation, New York, 1944.

Schedule for the Appraisal of Community Recreation, New York, 1951.

Standards for Neighborhood Recreation Areas and Facilities, New york, 1943.

Starting a Recreation Program in a Civilian Hospital, New York, 1952.

The Performing Arts as Recreation, pamphlet series, New York, 1962-65.

The Role of the Rederal Government in the Field of Public Recreation, New York, 1949.

Training Volunteers for Recreation Service…New York, 1946.

1964 BOARD OF TRUSTEES

From left to right, back (outside) row: Mrs. Rollin Brown, William Pond, Joshua Rose, Peter Ranich, Donald Jolley, Frederick Mandeville, Jr., Joseph Prendergast, Luther Gulick, James H. Evans, Endicott Davison, Susan M. Lee, John B. Tidwell, Jr., and George A. Lowrey, Jr.
In the front (inside) row, left to right: Neil Ofsthun, Mrs. Paul C. Gallagher, Lawrence Pierce, Robert Artz, Mrs. Richard Riegel, L. B. Houston, Mrs. George Francis, Thomas Lantz, Roscoe Ingalls Jr.

The National Recreation Association Board of Trustees luncheon in the Association headquarters in New York City, January 22, 1965. On that memorable date, they unanimously passed the proposal for the merger of the American Recreation Society, American Institute of Park Executives, National Conference of State Parks, and the National Recreation Association.

Introducing the 1964 NRA Board of Trustees

So that you may know them better, we take pleasure in introducing the full National Recreation Association Board:

F. W. H. Adams, New York City lawyer' former U.S. District Attorney and N.Y.C. Police Commissioner; was honorary president, Police Athletic League. **Alexander Aldrich**, lawyer; executive assistant to Governor of New York; past director, N.Y. State Division of Youth.

Robert M. Artz, superintendent, Willamalane Park and Recreation District, Springfield, Oregon; president-elect, Oregon Park and Recreation Society.

F. Gregg Bemis, businessman; chairman, Mayor's Advisory Recreation Committee, Boston; for many years, director, Community Recreation Services, Boston

Norborne Berkeley, Jr., NRA treatsurer; vice-president of the Chemical Bank New York Trust Company, New York City.

Edward L. Bernays, one of the country's leading publicists; trustee or director of many social-service organizations.

Mrs. Robert Woods Bliss, civic leader, Washington, D.C.; long active in National Trust for Historic Preservation.

Mrs. Rollin Brown, member, President's Committee for Employment of the Handicapped; director, public education and school relations, National Foundation.

Dr. Edwin S. Burdell, educator; dean, Rollins College; president-emeritus, Cooper Union, New York City; former UNESCO mission chief in Near East.

Howard H. Callaway, member of Congress; chairman of the board, Callaway Gardens, Georgia; trustee of the National Safety Council and Freedoms Foundation.

Mrs. Richard Morse Colgate, Oldwick, New Jersey; active in parks and recreation affairs in New Jersey and elsewhere.

Robert W. Crawford, NRA vice-president; commissioner of recreation, Philadelphia; board member, Citizens Committee, Outdoor Recreation Resources Review Commission; past-president, American Recreation Society.

Endicott P. Davison, NRA vice-president; lawyer; director, Union Theological Seminary; trustee, Groton School, Massachusetts.

Mrs. Fagan Dickson, vice-chairman, Parks and Recreation Board, Austin, Texas; active in many civic enterprises.

Charles E. Doell, superintendent-emeritus, Minneapolis Parks Department; author and co-author of park and recreation books; consultant.

James H. Evans, chairman, NRA Board; vice-president and director, Dun & Bradstreet, Inc.; director, The Reuben H. Donnelley Corporation.

Mrs. Howard A. Frame, civic leader, San Francisco Bay Area; member, Save San Francisco Bay Association; member Board of Governors, San Francisco Symphony; conservation leader.

Mrs. George T. Francis, Jr. vice-president, Educational TV Council; past chairman, Philadelphia Children's Theater.

S. Dale Furst, Jr., lawyer; president, the American Social Health Association; member of the Williamsport, Pennsylvania, Recreation Advisory Committee.

Mrs. Paul Gallagher, member and former chairman, Park and Recreation Commission Omaha, Nebraska; board member, Boys Town; campaigner for open space.

Dr. Luther Gulick, NRA vice-president; chairman. Institute of Public Administration; former New York City Administrator.

George Hjelte, general manager-emeritus, Los Angeles City Department of Recreation and Parks; a past-president of the American Recreation Society.

Louis B. Houston, director of parks and recreation, Houston; engineer; past-president, Texas

Recreation Society.

J.S. Hudnall, engineer concerned with use of land and water; has worked to strengthen recreation throughout Texas and the United States.

Roscoe C. Ingalls, Jr., New York investment banker; chairman, NRA's Investment Committee; active, hospital, community, and church financial activities.

Donald M. Jolley, superintendent of recreation and parks, Pittsburg, Kansas; past-president, Kansas Recreation Society.

Arthur H. Jones, North Carolina banker; active in community fundraising; and co-founder of Charlotte Nature Museum.

Augustus B. Kinzel, Jr., vice-president of research, Union Carbide Corp.; president, National Academy of Engineering.

Albert V. Labiche, New Orleans businessman and civic leader; treasurer of the Mississippi River Bridge Authority.

Thomas W. Lantz, superintendent-emeritus of public recreation in Tacoma; author; professor of political science.

Susan M. Lee, NRA vice-president. Daughter of Joseph Lee; engaged in camp administration; active on several boards and executive committees of national and N.Y.C. organizations.

Carvel C. Linden, Portland, Oregon, banker and civic leader; director of the Portland Chamber of Commerce.

George A. Lowrey, Jr., assistant professor, College of Health, Physical Education and Recreation at Texas Woman's University in Denton, Texas.

Frederick C. Mandeville, Jr., superintendent of recreation, Connecticut; former president of Jaycees and director of Meriden United Fund.

Mrs. P. P. Manion, Jr., civic leader; vice-chairman, Tulsa Park and Recreation Board; active in United Fund work.

Fredric R. Mann, Philadelphia businessman; chairman, Governor's Advisory Council of Recreation; active in many organizations.

Henry W. Meers, Chicago investment banker; member, Chicago Crime Commission; active, education and health fields.

Dr. William C. Menninger, famed Topeka psychiatrist; president, Menninger Foundation; active in social welfare.

Hamilton B. Mitchell, president, The Reuben H. Donnelley Corporation; past chairman, Recreation Commission, Pelham, New York; faculty associate, Graduate School of Business, Indiana University.

Rt. Rev. Paul Moore, Jr., Suffragan Bishop of Washington, D. C.; particular interest in inter-group relations.

Welles V. Moot, lawyer, corporation official and citizen planner; former chairman, Buffalo Planning Commission.

Neil A. Ofsthun, * director of Recreation Department, Rockville, Maryland.

Mrs. Conway H. Olmsted, Chicago civic leader; actively interested in the Rehabilitation Institute of Chicago.

Mrs. Roth A. O'Neil, member, Maricopa County Board of Supervisors, Phoenix; president, National Association of Parks and Recreation Officials.

Bernard L. Orell, vice-president, Weyerhaeuser Company; former director, Forest Products Division, U.S. Department of Commerce: interested in use of land for recreation.

Lawrence W. Pierce, lawyer; direc-tor, New York State Division for Youth; former deputy police commissioner of youth program in New York City.

William B. Pond, director, Department of Parks and Recreation, Sacramento County, California; past-president of the Washington Recreation Society.

Joseph Prendergast, NRA executive director since 1950; lawery with social work degree; honorary doctor of law.

Peter Ranich, technical assistant to recreation director, United Automobile Workers International Union, Detroit.

Mrs. Richard E. Riegel, civic leader, Wilmington, Delaware; member of the board, Delaware Hospital; especially concerned with parks and conservation.

Sanger P. Robinson, Chicago business-man; civic leader; active cultural activities; director, Chicago Boys Clubs.

Joshua R. Rose, member Recreation Commission, Oakland, California: assistant general secretary of the YMCA.

Fred R. Sammis, publisher, recreation and sports publications; member, Park and Recreation Commission, Darien, Connecticut.

Arthur B. Sheply, Jr., St. Louis lawyer; active on county Metropolitan Youth Commission in public-safety field.

William S. Simpson, vice-president-general manager, Raybestos; president, Museum of Art, Science and Industry, Bridgeport, Connecticut.

John Tidell, Jr., superintendent of the Parks and Recreation Commission, in Tupelo, Mississippi; past-president, Mississippi Recreation Association.

Gus Tyler, assistant president, International Ladies Garment Workers; pioneer of many union recreation projects.

Frederick M. Warburg, New York banker; former chief ofAthletics and Recreation Branch of Army Special Services.

Conrad L. Wirth, director-emeritus, National Park Service; consultant and advisor on conservation and parks, advisor to U.S. Secretary of the Interior.

National Recreation Association, Inc.
Endowment Fund Balance Sheet
As of December 31, 1963

Assets

Cash in banks	$1,182.53	
Real estate – 8 West 8th Street	300,000.00	
Marketable securities – bonds	199,584.08	
Marketable securities – preferred stock	30,796.19	
Marketable securities – common stock	340,996.89	
Bank for Savings	95,000.00	$967,559.69

Liabilities

Mortgage payable – 8 West 8th Street	112,258.00
	$855,309.69

Endowment Fund

Frances Ross Poley Memorial Fund	x	$ 5,214.41
Henry Strong Denison Fund	x	50,000.00
Grant Walker Fund	xx	125,721.00
Special Fund	xxx	213,052.66
Lucy Tudor Hillyer Fund		5,000.00
Emil C. Bondy Fund		1,000.00
"In Memory of J. I. Lamprecht"		3,000.00
George L. Sands Fund		12,990.11
"In Memory of Waldo E. Forbes"		1,403.02
Ellen Mills Borne Fund		3,000.00
C. H. T. Endowment Fund		500.00
Frances Mooney Fund		1,000.00
Sarah Newlin Fund		500.00
"In Memory of William Simes"		2,000.00
"In Memory of J. R. Jr."		250.00
Frances R. Morse Fund		2,000.00
Ella Van Peyma Fund		500.00
Nettie G. Naumburg Fund		2,000.00
"In Memory of William J. Matheson"		5,000.00
Alice B. P. Hannahs Fund		1,900.00
"In Memory of Alfred W. Heinsheimer"		5,000.00

"In Memory of Daniel Guggenheim"	1,000.00
Nellie L. Coleman Fund	100.00
Elizabeth B. Kelsey Fund	500.00
Sarah Fuller Smith Fund	3,000.00
Annie L. Sears Fund	2,000.00
John Markle Fund	50,000.00
Katherine C. Husband Fund	884.55
Ella Strong Denison Fund	200.00
Leilla A. Kilbourne Fund	7,020.50
Annie M. Lawrence Fund	961.38
Frederick Mc Owen Fund	1,000.00
Clarence M. Clark Fund	50,662.20
John G. Wartman Fund	500.00
"In Memory of Seaman F. Northrup"	1,000.00
"In Memory of Joseph Lee"	1,630.00
E M F Fund	500.00
Alexander Felman Fund	75.00
Wlliam Purcell Bickett Fund	17,208.52
"In Memory of Margaret Hazard Fisher"	1,100.00
Alice J. Shepley Fund	100.00
Ruel Crompton Tuttle Fund	1,007.52
Estate of Florence M. Bailey	250.00
Helen L. Jones Fund	504.00
Caroline B. Mc Geoch Fund	911.08
Caroline E. Reed Fund	2,685.19
B. May and Mr. & Mrs. Walter A. May Fund	7,861.50
The Valentine Perry Snyder Fund	50.00
Catherine W. Faucon Fund	1,000.00
Estate of Helen B. North	1,000.00
Mary F. Lanier Fund	100.00
Merry M.. Dennis Fund	195.52
Estate of Mrs. J. Warner Fobes	2,042.83
"In Memory of Mr. & Mrs. Adelbert Moot"	1,200.00
Estate Charles M. Cox	1,000.00
"In Memory of Jeanne H. Barnes"	15.00
Hugh Mc L. Landon Fund	5,000.00
"In Memory of C. Parker Levis"	500.00
"In Memory of Abbie Condit"	183.00

"In Memory of Isis Campbel McKinney"	230.00	
"In Memory of Edward L. Geary"	500.00	
Estate of Gertrude M. Kimball	1,000.00	
"In Memory of Howard Braucher"	13,719.38	
"In Memory of Mina M. Edison"	10,000.00	
"In Memory of E. T. Attwell"	2,758.01	
"In Memory of Lebert H. Weir"	35.00	
Estate of William Howell Reed	4,663.77	
Estate of Caroline G. Plant	1,000.00	
Estate of Corrine Fonde	97.09	
"In Memory of Elizabeth Hobart	8,051.35	
"In Memory of Mr. & Mrs. Edward W. Haskins"	500.00	
"In Memory of Irving H. Chase	500.00	
Estate of Austin E. Griffiths	3,000.00	
Estate of Ruth L.S. Childs	100.00	
E. Beatrice Stearns Fund	1,160.00	
"In Memory of Otto T. Mallery"	360.00	
Mrs. William G. Dwight Memorial Fund	100.00	
Myra T. Edgerton Memorial Fund	310.00	
Solon E. Summerfield Foundation, Inc.	1,000.00	
Estate of Julian Francis Detmer	1,000.00	
Alice B. Nichols Fund	166.91	
Frank C. Poucher Fund	11,838.25	
"In Memory of Grant Titsworth"	6,511.63	
"In Memory of C. Sewall Clark	2,000.00	
Mary F. Quirk Memorial Fund	1,399.00	
Walter M. Cabot Fund	175,450.00	
Special funds for Recreation Leadership Education:		
Howard Braucher Fund	1,000.00	
Joseph Lee Fund (Charlestown, W. Virginia Playgrounds)	379.81	
J. E. Rogers Fund	500.00	$855,309.69

x	Restricted		
xx	$50,000 of this fund is restricted		
xxx	Includes the following	– Action of 1910	25,000.00
		– Accumulation from capital transactions	302.66
		– Accumulated equity in building	187,750.00

Editor Note: The NRA Endowment Fund in 1963, adjusted for inflation, would have a value of $5,312,482 in 2005 dollars.